Youth Ministry and Theological Shorthand

*Living Amongst the Fragments
of a Coherent Theology*

Youth Ministry and Theological Shorthand

*Living Amongst the Fragments
of a Coherent Theology*

DAVID BAILEY

Foreword by Peter Ward

PICKWICK *Publications* · Eugene, Oregon

YOUTH MINISTRY AND THEOLOGICAL SHORTHAND
Living Amongst the Fragments of a Coherent Theology

Copyright © 2019 David Bailey. All rights reserved. Except for brief quotations in critical publications or reviews, no part of this book may be reproduced in any manner without prior written permission from the publisher. Write: Permissions, Wipf and Stock Publishers, 199 W. 8th Ave., Suite 3, Eugene, OR 97401.

Pickwick Publications
An Imprint of Wipf and Stock Publishers
199 W. 8th Ave., Suite 3
Eugene, OR 97401

www.wipfandstock.com

PAPERBACK ISBN: 978-1-4982-1941-9
HARDCOVER ISBN: 978-1-4982-1943-3
EBOOK ISBN: 978-1-4982-1942-6

Cataloguing-in-Publication data:

Names: Bailey, David, author. | Ward, Pete, 1959–, foreword.

Title: Youth ministry and theological shorthand : living amongst the fragments of a coherent theology / by David Bailey ; foreword by Peter Ward.

Description: Eugene, OR : Pickwick Publications, 2019 | Includes bibliographical referenc.

Identifiers: ISBN 978-1-4982-1941-9 (paperback) | ISBN 978-1-4982-1943-3 (hardcover) | ISBN 978-1-4982-1942-6 (ebook)

Subjects: LCSH: Church work with youth. | Church work. | Theology.

Classification: BV4447 .B30 2019 (print) | BV4447 .B30 (ebook)

Manufactured in the U.S.A.   JULY 26, 2019

Contents

Foreword by Peter Ward vii
Acknowledgments ix
Introduction 1

PART ONE. Scene Setting: Youth Ministry,
   Practical Theology, and the Evangelical Tradition

1. Living Amongst the Fragments of a Coherent Theology 17
2. Youth Ministry and Practical Theology 32
3. Christian Practices and the Mediation
   of the Evangelical Tradition 57

PART TWO. Echoes of a Coherent Theology:
   Theological Shorthand and Current Practice

4. The Youth Ministers 87
5. Narratives of Practice: Theological Shorthand
   and Relationships as Communicative Acts 97
6. Narratives of Practice and the Normative Voice
   within Youth Ministry 121
7. Youth Ministry, Living Amongst the Fragments? 147

PART THREE. Towards a Coherent Theology

8. Expanding the Fragments as Icons of Epistemology:
   Relationships and Trinitarian Theology 173
9. Expanding the Fragments as Icons of Epistemology:
   Participation, Relationships, and Trinitarian Theology 198
10. Towards a Coherent Theology:
    The Christian Story as Grand Narrative 221

Bibliography 243

Foreword

THERE IS AN INTRIGUING question in youth ministry that lies at the heart of this groundbreaking work. This question comes out of the immense effort that has been poured into theologically educating youth ministers. The question is, "What have we achieved?" Obviously there has been a growth in amazing and life-changing work with young people in churches and communities around the world but this is not quite what I mean by the question. Theological education is not simply about teaching people to be effective practitioners; it is fundamentally concerned with God. Teaching youth ministry then is about passing on a vision of the gospel of Jesus Christ and how this gospel can shape and reshape our lives and the lives of young people and the communities in which they live. If this is the root aim of all our educational efforts what have we achieved?

Dave Bailey has gone out there and talked with veteran youth ministers about their work and most crucially about the theology that underpins their work. His findings raise real questions about the task of theological education and also about the link between theology and practice more broadly. There is a key idea that offers what I think is the really eye catching and significant aspect of this book. Through his in-depth interviews Dave has identified what he calls "theological shorthand." This book fits within the growing field of theological ethnography. Within this area attention has been focused on what have been termed ordinary or operant theologies. In this context the notion of "theological shorthand" makes an original and I think desperately important contribution.

Without offering too much of a spoiler alert "theological shorthand" is the term that Dave Bailey came to use for the fragmented theological ideas that the youth ministers he interviewed seemed to make reference to as they talked about what motivated them in their work. In most cases these fragmented theological shorthand phrases seemed to be enough to generate sacrificial, long term and challenging ministries. When examined the fragmented theology represented what was taken away by these practitioners from their theological education. Maybe more to the point though these fragmented shorthand ways of speaking communicated something of the gospel and of the work of God for these people. Theological shorthand signals those aspects of theology that were portable. They were the useful elements that the youth ministers found they could live their lives out of because they spoke of God. Theological shorthand is a term for the theology that has actually been put to use in ministry.

As you will see Dave Bailey argues that perhaps this shorthand will need topping up and enriching. His suggestion is that it is the riches of theology of the Trinity that offers the most promising source for this task. I leave it to you to decide if you think he is right. For myself I am pretty sure that whatever we try and teach we will see our neatly honed theology turned into portable and useful shorthand by practitioners. Thinking about it I hear the theology of Trinity used in exactly that way when in some circles people talk reference the term *Missio Dei*. Theological shorthand is a great idea because it names what seems to be going on among practitioners as they assimilate theological education. The genius of this book is that Dave Bailey invented the phrase.

Peter Ward
Professor of Practical Theology, M. F. The Norwegian School of Theology and Professorial Fellow at Durham University.

Acknowledgments

IT IS THE SACRIFICIAL ministry of the youth ministers that form the heart of this book. For choosing to be there for young people when many are not, thank you.

My thanks to my former doctoral supervisor Professor Pete Ward for writing the foreword. Pete, as you will have seen, can succinctly sum up arguments, raise insightful questions and situate discussions within their broader contexts. Pete, thank you for the conversations over coffee during doctoral supervision—these discussions stimulated and gave birth to the notion of theological shorthand. Thank you for your wisdom, guidance, challenging questioning and constructive criticism.

I am especially appreciative and thankful to my friend and colleague Dr. Jeremy Thomson and for our far reaching theological discussions, over the years your friendship and our conversations have played an important part in my formation. Jeremy's comments on differing aspects of this work have helped sharpen and form some of the ideas below. I am indebted to my colleagues, students and former students at Oasis and Oasis College, for the chance to share ideas as the project progressed, their reflections helped shape my thoughts. I'm grateful for the inspiration provided through the International Association for the Study of Youth Ministry and Ecclesiology and Ethnography networks—for being able to discuss ideas from this work, the comments and conversations have been rich and helpful.

Abridged parts of this material were published in the book *Youth Work: Histories, Policy and Context* in a co-written chapter on *Youth Work and the Church* with Graham Bright.[1] A succinct description of

---

1. Bright and Bailey, "Youth Work and the Church," 145–56. Reproduced with permission of Macmillan Publishers Ltd.

theological shorthand and parts of chapter 7 were published by the *Journal of Youth and Theology*.[2] This previously published work is used with permission. Thank you to Integrity Music,[3] Song Solutions[4] and Hillsong[5] for permission to use the words of the worship songs in chapter 7. Thanks also to the staff of Wipf & Stock and Pickwick Publications; your help in bringing the manuscript to publication is very much appreciated.

Finally, I am grateful to my friends at Christ Church Orpington and for being part of a loving community. I am indebted to my family for their support, especially my Mum and Dad and Caroline, my wife. Daniel and Lydia, thank you for your patience!

---

2. Earlier versions of these ideas were published in Bailey, "Living Amongst the Fragments," and Bailey, "Enacted Faith."

3. Thankyou Music. Adm. by Capitol CMG Publishing worldwide excl. UK & Eurpoe, admin by Integrity Music, Part of the David C Cook family, songs@integritymusic.com.

4. Cristajoy Music/Bethel Music Publishing & Mercy Vineyard Publishing (adm Song Solutions www.songsolutions.org). All rights reserved.

5. Thankyou Music/Said And Done Music/ Kingswaysongs & Jonas Myrin/Capitol CMG Paragon (BMI) (Admin. SHOUT! Music Publishing (AUS/NZ)) & Omega Songs (BMI).

Introduction

Questions came in quick succession: "So how do you communicate your faith?" "How are you involved in mission amongst these young people?" Stumbling over my words and grasping after some attempt at theological expression, "incarnationally" and "through relationships" I replied hesitantly. This seemed to be enough to answer the questions from a well-meaning member of the congregation. I would now call this theological shorthand. This theological expression did not seem to fully articulate the nuances and complexities of my practice among young people, yet it evoked and had a connection with the deeper Christian tradition in which my practice took place. Since 1995 I have worked amongst young people on the fringes and margins of church life, as I sought to communicate the reality of Jesus amongst them. As a volunteer and then a full-time youth minister, working out of an Anglican church context, this practice was tempered with highs and lows, closeness and distance. These relationships felt like communicative orbits. Sometimes the relationships would be ones of encounter and connection, then, through a myriad of circumstances, young people would begin drifting away, become distant. In the following months, or in some cases years, a chance encounter would re-establish and re-connect the relationship. It was through these rich encounters with young people that I began to question my own theological understanding of practice. How did I communicate and live out my faith? How did these relationships function? Moreover, if the weakness of my own understanding of practice was limited, then this might point to a wider limitation amongst my fellow youth ministers and beyond into the related field of youth ministry.[1] The terms youth work and

---

1. Strauss and Corbin, *Basics of Qualitative Research*, 9–36, and Sheppard, *Being Christian*, 9.

youth ministry are debated, sometimes used interchangeable,[2] they can be seen as an unnecessary dualism.[3] It is Thomson[4] who offers the most robust critique of these, seeing that "youth ministry" does not discount the issue of providing welfare as in "youth work," but its prime focus is in the "building of the church." This is how the term is used in this study.

Being intrigued about how we talk about God and ministry, relationships, enacted mission and the complexities of situations and practice is the starting point for the research that gave rise to the book.[5] My experience led me to question how youth ministers worked amongst young people; how did they communicate and enact mission?

At art school and working as a graphic designer, I was intrigued by the values which lay behind the symbols that I was asked to design, why, what, and how did these communicate? As I trained as a youth minister through the Oasis Youth Ministry Course in 1997 I was introduced to the more formal aspects of theological training and the questions about my faith and practice became more theological. Now, as Senior Lecturer in Practical Theology at Oasis College, and involved in the theological education of practitioners, my interest in the enacting of faith is just as acute. Through my studies on the Doctorate in Theology and Ministry degree at King's College London, I have discovered the richness, beauty, and depth of Trinitarian theology. My experience and desire to explore the lived experience of enacted mission and the richness of Trinitarian theology are brought together through the discipline of practical theology.

This book combines my own experience of professional practice with my qualitative research into the lived experience of youth ministers engaged in mission[6] among young people who have no connection with the church. The original explorations, through my doctoral studies, showed that the youth ministers interviewed communicate in theological shorthand—they use straightforward language to describe the complex theology within practice. Following this original discovery, I augment the investigations by further interviews and analyzing other aspects of contemporary youth ministry in the UK, this includes a selection of Re-

2. Ward, *Youthwork*.
3. Brierley, *Joined Up*.
4. Thomson, *Telling the Difference*, 224–25.
5. Mason, *Researching Your Own Practice*, 178.
6. Here, mission is defined by the Triune communicative nature of God, the God we encounter in Jesus Christ and includes acts of proclamation, witness and service as is discussed below through the work of Vanhoozer.

source Guides from *Youthwork* magazine[7] and the examination of the words used within a number of current worship songs. Taken together, they highlight and provide a snap shot of theological shorthand in action. Therefore, this book and the research it conveys pivot around the question: How does theological shorthand operate within youth ministry?

Furthermore, the evangelical landscape under scrutiny is my tradition, so I very much look at this story from the inside. I am critical, but this is as a friend and participant within the theology that has shaped me. This has also been a little fragmented, I have been part of the Baptist tradition, the Methodist Church and attended and then employed by an Anglican Church. My reflections then, at least in part, are auto-biographical. The youth ministers interviewed, the Resource Guides and, worships songs under investigation all operate within this evangelical landscape. It is through my reflections that I have come to see the particular foibles of this specific tradition, I have moved from seeing a picture in grainy black and white, to viewing a picture in full color, a picture that dances with light and shade. Through my studies I have discovered the richness of the wider Christian story, the different perspectives and the depth of Biblical interpretation available. Growing up as evangelical I read the Bible and explored theology, but I can now see that I had the right musical notes, but I was not playing these in the right order! To change the metaphor again, my theology could be characterized as fragmented and thin.

Therefore, this book explores the notion of theological shorthand through the lens of youth ministry. Yet theological shorthand has a wider application within ministry more generally; and can be identified among many Christians' talk or singing about God, and their use of the Bible. If this can be identified as a problem, then it also operates as an opportunity, liminal spaces where God and the richness of the Christian story can be experienced and explored. It is a space were reality becomes altered, a place of transition, of waiting, the space between what was and what's next, a place of transformation.[8] This transformation is facilitated as key words function as icons of epistemology. What I mean by this is just as

---

7. *Youthwork* magazine is published monthly and exists to support Christian youth ministers working predominantly within a church context. It is published by Premier Christian Publications.

8. Hoey, *From Pi to Pie*, sees this as a term used to describe a state of between, liminality comes from the Latin limen for "boundary" or "threshold." As used by cultural anthropologists, it has generally referred to rites of initiation or "passage" that involve certain basic elements that include a transformative period.

icons in religious art are a way of facilitating reflection, then as key words are explored they act as icons, representing theological aspects of the story, it is representation with a meaning, they are symbols of the story. When these key words are used as icons they challenge us to explore the story, they witness to the deeper parts of the narrative we may not yet know, or have yet to see. Through reflection and thought they act as windows into a wider world, they become the keys that unlock the story, they are ways of developing theological literacy[9] and *phronesis*. Importantly, this gives youth ministers the language to articulate what participation in God's communicative action and the Christian story look like.

Influences

Theological shorthand is my term, but this work resonates with some aspects of Ward's[10] thinking. As Ward explores liquid ecclesiology, some of the ideas found within this book are foreshadowed in the communicative practices of the evangelical church that he explores, particularly in how the Gospel becomes marginalized and truncated This is hardly surprising, Pete was my doctoral supervisor and his influence can be seen in this study, furthermore, I am very grateful for his guidance through the doctoral process. The reach of King's College London can be noted in some of the authors drawn on below—including Luke Bretherton, Andrew Rogers, Nick Shepherd, Andrew Walker, and Andrew Wright. Some of Ward's work operates as a conversation partner, especially in chapters 3 and 5. Yet, if there are similarities there are also significant differences. This whole study is framed within the Trinitarian communicative action of God and has a particular focus on the embodied action and expression of youth ministry—rather than the more general expressions of the Gospel and ecclesiastical practice. My friend and colleague Jeremy Thomson has also influenced my thinking. I am immensely grateful for my conversations with Jeremy and for his time in reading a draft of the script, his input has helped sharpen some of the ideas below. Jeremy also

---

9. Wright, *Critical Realism*, also develops this notion as he explores critical realism and theology. Wright highlights the different debates within Trinitarian theology. He sees the divergent discussions around Trinitarian theology as part of the theological tradition that allows the evaluation of differing ideas. This resonates with chapters 8 and 9 of this book. The difference lies in that I approach the discussions through the lens of Canonical theology, whilst Wright adopts critical realism.

10. Ward, *Liquid Ecclesiology*.

introduced me to the work of Vanhoozer.[11] Vanhoozer is the substantial dialogue partner, it is his work that gives articulation to the relational aspects of the twelve youth ministers interviewed. Vanhoozer's thinking also enables us to see how the Resources Guides and worship songs under examination (however fragmented the theology is) take part in the process of divine communicative action. Additionally, this book, with all its limitations and flaws is also part of the same communicative process and this communicative action is part of the theodrama.

Theodramatic participation is faith seeking; through participation our actions of communication take part in God's Triune communicative work. Participation becomes an operative concept. Participation is when we come to know and love God as we participate in the communications of Word and Spirit.[12] Theology becomes a map for finding, locating and situating oneself in the Biblical mythos, the Bible's dramatic plot. Vanhoozer,[13] develops his idea of mythos from Ricoeur. Ricoeur focuses on the way in which mythos configures human action, but Vanhoozer expands the concept of mythos to understand divine action. This becomes communicative in the mythos of Christ, it is Christ who renders intelligible the arena of Triune communicative participation. This differs from Ward's[14] notion of abiding and also the participatory frameworks of Moltmann[15] and Fiddes.[16]

The present work develops my and Ward's[17] notion of expanding the fragments. Ward finishes his book with this idea—but this work takes this concept and through sustained dialogue with Trinitarian theology expands the fragments of how the youth ministers speak about their faith. Walker[18] notes, in talking about the postmodern world, that icons "proliferate but are profane," behind this sentiment is the idea of how reality has become fragmented. The notion of an icon is important. They can operate as windows into an alternative reality, particularly through the way the Christian tradition has used these to open up places of contemplation

---

11. Vanhoozer, *Remythologizing Theology*.
12. Ibid.
13. Ibid., 6.
14. Ward, *Liquid Ecclesiology*, 183–200.
15. Moltmann, *The Trinity and the Kingdom of God*.
16. Fiddes, *Participating in God*.
17. Ward, *Liquid Ecclesiology*, 208.
18. Walker, *Telling the Story*, 198.

and reflection. Expanding the fragments indicates that the words used can become icons of epistemology; they operate as ways of developing theological literacy, seeing, doing, seeking and deepening faith it is the practice of practical wisdom, *phronesis*. I set out how this process operates below through theodramatic dialogical reflection as these icons become virtues of epistemology, a way of grappling and wrestling with the complexity of theology expressed. Therefore, the fragmented and theological shorthand verbalized in words by the youth ministers, seen within the Resource Guides and articulated in the worship songs become windows that reveal the bigger story

The term fragment is important. I was alerted to the phrase as I read Hauerwas[19] and by his insights into Christian ethics in a fragmented and violent world. Hauerwas[20] via MacIntyre, sees that Christians live amongst the fragments of previous moral schemes and conceptual systems. Walker[21] also draws on MacIntyre and comes to a very similar conclusion to Hauerwas. The difference is that Hauerwas frames his discussion in terms of ethics and Walker in terms of seeking a return to a grand narrative as Christian retell the story in different places and contexts. Walker's thoughts are helpful and they resonate with both Hauerwas and Vanhoozer, However, they differ, for Walker the story is not historicist, in the sense that it does not hold the key to interpreting history (as the Christian narrative does in the work of Hauerwas and the theodrama does in Vanhoozer)—but it is teleological in the sense that the story, in the language of Tillich, is of ultimate concern.

It is from the reading of MacIntyre employed by Hauerwas and Walker that I construct the concept of theological shorthand, the notion that we speak in straight forward, foreshortened phrases and truncated words are used to describe complex theological practices. This is a simplification of theology. It is thin theology. In this process the depth of the story is short circuited, the beauty[22] of the story is lost. What happens is that we end up talking about God or ministry in platitudes and clichés, these may contain some fragmented aspects of the story, but the depth, complexity and mystery has vanished. Individual words are fragmented from the story and or from particular church traditions operating as

---

19. Hauerwas, *The Peaceable Kingdom*.
20. Ibid., 3–5.
21. Walker, *Telling the Story*, 3.
22. White, "Fire and Light."

theological shorthand, simple phrases that describe the complexity of lived practice. Within youth ministry these fragments circulate and it is at risk of becoming untethered from a coherent theology—the wider Christian story and its particular practices. Or to put this another way, it is at risk of becoming disconnected from the grand narrative.[23] Yet, at the heart of this is a paradox. The theological thought and language of the youth ministers interviewed is at risk from being disconnected from the wider Christian tradition, but at the same time, it fuels long term sacrificial ministry amongst young people. The language expressed is how youth ministers correlate and interpret their own theological education. This is theology put to use, it is transferrable and bite sized.

With this in mind, the book explores the notion of relationships as communicative action, through this, the language used by the youth ministers is seen as theological shorthand. In turn, this theological shorthand can be seen in the world the youth ministers inhabit, as demonstrated by the Resource Guides and worship songs that I will explore. This focus is important for as Hauerwas[24] sees via Wittgenstein, any attempt to anchor theology in some general account of human experience is mistaken—for the object of the theologian's work is seen and located in terms of the grammar and language used by believers. Of course, language and grammar do not operate in vacuum, they are also part of embodied practice and these three elements; language, grammar and enacted practice form the basis for the empirical work. Furthermore, through this work a deeper language and grammar is developed for youth ministry, facilitating a thicker description of practice that ties ministry into a Trinitarian frame work of theodramatic participation. The key aim is to help youth ministers articulate a theological literacy, to help them speak about God's divine presence and to be more faithful to the grand narrative[25] that they participate in.

Metaphors and Drama

I'll explore theological shorthand in more detail below, but it is important to see that shorthand is a metaphor—a rhetorical device for bringing

---

23. Walker, *Telling the Story*.
24. Hauerwas, *The Peaceable Kingdom*, xxi.
25. Walker, *Telling the Story*.

clarity and to make a point. As Vanhoozer[26] sees, the apostle Paul was adept at employing metaphors to communicate the significance of Jesus' death using imagery drawn from the battlefield (victory), commerce (redemption and slaves), temple (sacrifice) and law court (justification). As this book takes place within God's communicative action, God's theo-drama—then youth ministers are actors within this theological drama. For it moves people from being storytellers,[27] however important this is, to the stronger participatory language of story dwellers.[28] It is a reminder that theology is performed and embodied, but through the performance of this theology God is at work as we participate in God's communicative action, the theodramatic. Within my argument a further rhetorical and metaphoric device is utilized, Rublev's Icon of the Holy Trinity. At the beginning of each chapter this acts as a device to help facilitate thinking and reflection on divine theodramatic participation and helps us pay attention to how an icon may operate as a light that illuminates the story.

Why Read the Book? Distinct Contributions to the Knowledge of Youth Ministry

The book will appeal to youth ministers, clergy, academics, graduate and post-graduate students, but also informed volunteers involved in youth ministry. Through the discipline of practical theology, it correlates the voices of lived practice (the interviews with the youth ministers), a set of materials used to deepen faith (the Resource Guides) and contemporary expressions of sung worship (the songs). These are then brought into conversation and explored via different aspects of Trinitarian theology to deepen the grammar within contemporary youth ministry and develop theological literacy. It should be noted that it is not possible to generalize from the research undertaken, however, the ideas discussed should resonate with youth ministry practitioners. Consequently, the book seeks to make a distinctive contribution to the discussion and knowledge within youth ministry in the following ways:

The relationships that youth ministers establish with young people in the enacting of mission can be seen as communicative acts.

---

26. Vanhoozer, *Faith Speaking Understanding*, 28.
27. Walker, *Telling the Story*.
28. Vanhoozer, *Faith Speaking Understanding*, 29.

There is an emphasis on orthopraxis, the focus on relationships collapses the classic elements of the church's practices of *diakonia*, *kerygma* and *marturia* into the relational. This turns relationships as communicative acts into a contemporary practice, but this is not intentional and is not reflected upon theologically.

The expression of these relationships through the terms of like Jesus, being there, time and journey can be seen as fragments of a wider story and operate as theological shorthand. This is paradoxical, because this theological expression also fuels long term sacrificial service amongst young people.

Theological shorthand is a non-complex and straight forward way of talking about the complexity and nuances of lived practice. It means the opportunities to see God's Spirit at work, to articulate God's divine presence, to participate with God's communicative action are not given enough consideration or scope due to the fragmented and theological shorthand expression of the Christian tradition and the Biblical narrative.

As the work of the youth ministers is explored there is some theological misunderstanding and misrepresentation. This is especially seen in how they articulate being like Jesus, unintentionally playing down the wider work of God's Spirit and disconnecting youth ministry from the congregation and church. Ministry becomes, inadvertently, an individual pursuit. This creates a tension within practice, the boundaries between youth ministers and young people become blurred and this has an impact on the mental health of some practitioners.

The youth ministry literature can be seen as the normative voice of practice. This is a stronger voice than the Bible and the church traditions of which the youth ministers are a part. This is problematic as it risks untethering youth ministry from the wider ecclesial frameworks and the grand narrative. The emphasis of mission amongst young people is driven by individual youth ministers rather than located in and facilitated by congregations.

Theological shorthand and fragmented theology also operate in the wider arena of youth ministry, as seen in the Resource Guides and worship songs investigated, the notion of plastic hermeneutics is in play.

The words articulated as theological shorthand are fragments of a bigger story, but they can act as keys that have the potential to unlock the deeper story, to function as icons of epistemology. To facilitate this a more explicit and robust theological re-imagining of relationships as communicative acts has been advanced, locating this within a Trinitarian frame work of communication. Here, God's divine authorship is held within divine communicative action and through this theological re-imagination the practice of youth ministry is deepened and re-tethered into the richness of the Christian tradition.

This process develops intellectual virtue, theological literacy and *phronesis* amongst youth ministers. Providing a more extensive theological language and grammar that enables them to articulate their practice in deeper and richer terms. Youth ministers can develop as dialogical guides, giving them the tools to articulate God's divine presence, and their participation within the richness of the Christian story and grand narrative. This in turn facilitates them to act as dialogical guides amongst young people through the mutuality of purposeful presence and wise and contextual witness. It is a theology for youth ministry.

Chapter Outline

As these ideas of theological shorthand and the fragmentation of theology are explored, the first part of the book surveys the ground and lays out the methodological map behind the study. Chapter 1 outlines the limits of language and raises questions of epistemology. Here, C.S Lewis[29] helps us to see the difference between looking *at* and looking *along*. Looking *at* fragments, splinters and separates, whilst looking *along* seeks to take in the whole picture. As this is considered, the bigger picture of fragmentation is rendered via MacIntyre.[30] He helps to see how the fragmentations of moral schemes have taken place as humanity has moved into the modern world. The place of mystery is considered as theological shorthand is defined in more detail. The importance of the four voices of theology (operant, espoused, formal or normative)[31] for this particular study are highlighted.

Chapter 2 begins to chart the methodological journey, the relationship between youth ministry and practical theology is explored. The chapter raises important concerns and seeks to provide some answers by examining theology and its relation to practice. The dialogue between theology and epistemology is analyzed. The chapter defines the relevant discussions within practical theology and provides a theological

---

29. Vanhoozer, *First Theology*, 17.
30. MacIntyre, *After Virtue*.
31. Cameron et al., *Talking about God in Practice*, 54.

reflective framework through which Trinitarian theology can act as the normative voice for practice (however provisional this is). Importantly, the empirical work is situated within a theological hermeneutic provided by key methodological dialogue partners Swinton and Mowat.[32] In addition to this, the importance of a narrative approach for exploring practice and communicative action is outlined and defined.

Chapter 3 studies the relationship between youth ministry and Christian practice, the connection between doctrine and practice is considered and how theology acts as the normative voice in serving and critiquing practice is explored. Differing understandings of Christian practices are investigated. The second part of chapter 3 continues the analysis further as the mediation of the evangelical tradition is examined. Here, the pivotal place of relationships and the relational hermeneutic within evangelical thought is articulated and the influence and reach of Young Life on youth ministry in the UK is highlighted. Following this, the place of plastic hermeneutics and Biblical interpretation within the evangelical tradition is scrutinized. How ideas are passed on through a top down approach and the way the youth ministry literature becomes a normative voice for youth ministry practice is demonstrated.

Part two, examines current practice, this is the heart of the empirical enterprise. In chapter 4, the youth ministers whom I interviewed are introduced, this short, but pivotal chapter is a reminder that the youth ministers are real people, with real histories, in real situations as they seek to faithfully embody the Gospel. It is a reminder that the liminal spaces the youth ministers occupy is Holy Ground and that these people are actors and part of the theodramatic action. Chapter 5, summarizes the key research themes of how the youth ministers communicate their practice. This is primarily seen in the way the youth ministers enact and perform faith. The whole process can be seen as an embodied communicative act. It is a set of complex communicative practices, but is summed up through the simplified terms of relationships, like Jesus, being there, and time and journey. This is theological shorthand in action.

Chapter 6, then develops these themes in critical conversation with the selected literature on youth ministry[33] as missionary endeavor. The

---

32. Swinton and Mowat, *Practical Theology and Qualitative Research*.

33. Within the original research key literature was framed and chosen by drawing on the reading lists of the Oasis Youth Work and Ministry Course (1997–2009), Oasis College of Higher Education (2010–2016) and CYM, Midlands Centre of Youth Ministry (2006–2009).

relationship between embodied faith and the theological expression of youth ministry within the literature is considered and critiqued. Through this process, a problem with the theological expression of youth ministry is identified. Current youth ministry practice can be seen to be guided by the normative voice and expression of relationships that is articulated through the literature on youth ministry. Normative is not want is normal, but where the guiding theological frameworks come from that steer the practice of the youth ministers. This normative voice is louder than the ecclesial traditions of which the youth ministers are part. The emphasis on relationships as theological shorthand collapses the classic elements of the church's practices of *diakonia*, *kerygma* and *marturia* into the relational[34] short circuiting the Christian story. Although relationships as communicative acts can be understood as a contemporary practice, its practitioners do not intend it as such, nor do they undergird it by rigorous theological thought or reflection. This is theological shorthand as thin theology and the fragmentation of the wider Christian story and narrative.

In chapter 7, the songs and Biblical material investigated highlight the use of theological shorthand in the diet of worship and Biblical resources that youth ministers receive and consume. The Resource Guides operate primarily through the lens of observation, readers seem to view the story from the outside and they offer conceptualized understandings of church and the Bible outside of specific contexts and situations. This resonates with the mediation of the evangelical tradition from the top down as seen in chapter 3. Furthermore, the Resource Guides demonstrate the fragmentation of theology and the concept of plastic hermeneutics is prominent. Both the songs and the Resource Guides require the worshiper and reader to have a certain amount of theological and Biblical capital in order to piece the fragments, story and narrative together.

Part three, turns to construction. Chapter 8 returns to the theme of theological reflection, but this is reframed in the theodramatic. This is a development of the reflective conversations seen within chapter 2. Through this process the fragments and theological shorthand already

---

34. Dean, *Practicing Passion*, 158. Lays out a constellation of classical Christian Practices. In the data these are collapsed into relationships that function as communicative acts. As will be demonstrated, relationships include *marturia*, like Jesus includes *marturia* and *diakonia*, being there includes *diakonia* and time and journey includes *marturia* and *diakonia*. The practice of *kerygma* was very limited and almost nonexistent in the articulated practice of the youth ministers.

explored are expanded as key words are used as icons of epistemology, they are used to develop theological literacy. This is pursued through a critical conversation with Trinitarian theology via Moltmann, Fiddes, Kilby and Vanhoozer. Chapter 9 continues the investigation and exploration of the fragments and theological shorthand. Here, participation is offered as a key Trinitarian motif that seeks to reframe practice as the icons of epistemology, the key words, continue to be expanded and theological literacy deepened.

Chapter 10 draws the discussions to a conclusion. Here, the significance of the wider Christian story and narrative for understanding God and ourselves is expressed. This process facilitates a move from seeing the theological shorthand and fragments as icons of epistemology to developing the practice and skill of holding intellectual virtues. This means developing the capacity to reflect on and to trying to understand the Christian story and its differing theologies in as much depth as possible, whilst recognizing and navigating the tensions and contradictions within it—this is the process of theological literacy. Icons of epistemology operate as intellectual virtues, held within the theological virtues of faith, hope and love. This enables a critical dialogue and conversation on the depth and richness of theology that flows between doctrine and enacted practice and facilitates a range of canonical voices to inform, deepen and enrich the Christian story and grand narrative[35] as youth ministers act as dialogical guides. This presents opportunities to expand the grammar and language of how faith and practice are articulated.

---

35. Walker, *Telling the Story*.

PART ONE

Scene Setting:
Youth Ministry, Practical Theology, and the Evangelical Tradition

Chapter 1

Living Amongst the Fragments of a Coherent Theology

Rublev's icon depicts the mysterious story where Abraham receives three visitors as he camps by the oak of Mamre and a meal is served. Through the meal, the friendship and conversation continues, Abraham seems to be talking straight to God. It is a picture of Middle Eastern hospitality, both generous and spontaneous. On further inspection, at the outset of the story, the visitors are described as "three men" and as the conversation about Sarah begins it is no longer three men who speak, but "the LORD." The three have become singular, perhaps foreshadowing the Trinity.[1] In Rublev's imagination of the scene, set around a white table are seated three gold-winged figures. On this table lies a chalice-like bowl, shimmering gold and containing a roasted lamb. A house can be seen at the top left and a tree in the center, creating the backdrop. Less obvious is a rocky hill in the upper right corner. The composition is a great circle, echoing the conversation, the table becomes central with the focus on the chalice-bowl. Persson[2] continues that Rublev was the first iconographer to use a circle in his design, the symbol of perfection, unity and eternity having no beginning and no ending. The movement goes around and around, drawing us in, there is no place for our eyes to stop, we have the opportunity to take part in this picture, to reflect and discuss its meaning.

---

1. Persson, *The Circle of Love*, 37–38.
2. Ibid., 47.

The picture operates at a number of different levels, the three angels seated under Abraham's tree, yet it can be interpreted[3] as a visual expression of what the Trinity means, what is the nature of God, who is God and how do we approach God? What does it mean to be part of this story and conversation? Reading the picture from left to right, we see the Father, the Son, and the Holy Spirit, but there is space for us to be seated—to come in, to participate, to join in with the discussion, to access the meal, to be in communion. Persson sees that Rublev must have spent a long time in prayer and thought before painting the icon, because as he painted the icon he took some very bold steps. He made the conscious decision to eliminate the figures of Sarah and Abraham, leaving only the three figures to convey the idea of Trinity. Strictly speaking, icons are written, not painted, because iconography is not simply an art form. Rather, to construct and write an icon is to make the word of God present and Persson[4] sees that it is important that worshipers should learn to "read" them.

Early in 2017, I went to an evening at St Martins in the Fields in central London. The theme of the evening was: How does Academic theology serve the church? Leaving aside the fact that the title separates theology from the performed and lived, it was a fascinating and interesting evening of discussion by prominent theologians and practitioners. In some sense, the evening carried aspects of Rublev's icon, it was participative, discursive, and good natured and carried out in a tone reflective of the communion of Christians present. Nevertheless, the discussion was carried out in theological shorthand. Words and terms were used and tossed around freely. The term incarnation was one of these, and there was an assumption that we understood the language in the same way. Now, in many ways, a discussion of this sort cannot be had in any other manner, but quite quickly phrases or terms operate like fragments, like torn up pieces of paper blown about by the wind of conversation. These phrases are fragments of theology, fragments of the Christian tradition and story. These fragments or theological shorthand exist in our conversations, in our language about God.

---

3. Ibid., 42.
4. Ibid., 14.

Language and Epistemology

Vanhoozer[5] is critical about how language may limit reality. This is particularly shown in his critique of Derrida who sees that we have no non-linguistic access to the way things really are. For Derrida, we speak and think about things on the basis of certain language and the words and language used is largely a matter of arbitrary social convention. This is a system of difference, a pattern of distinctions and connections. Our words acquire meaning not by referring to actual things, but by differing from other words, what we know about things is culturally, which is to say linguistically constructed. Therefore, whatever we think is always/already shaped by the language system we employ. The tension here, is that within the notion of postmodernity the prism of language deconstructs everything and we are left with fragments, nothing is a given and everything is reduced to signs in an arbitrary system of signifiers. God can be seen only to exist within the realms of language and culturally bound expression—there is nothing outside the text. It is this that is problematic, and if this is the case, language becomes a labyrinth from which there is no exit to the real world, no exit to objective created realities. For if there is nothing in what we say—e.g. reality is just socially constructed through language, then ultimately what we say doesn't matter and we move towards the uncommitted life and "sickness unto death" as Kierkegaard might say.[6] Another way of thinking about language is required. Vanhoozer[7] via Wittgenstein draws an analogy between language and a toolbox. A toolbox may have a screwdriver, hammer, nails and some screws. For Wittgenstein, the functions of words are as varied and diverse as the functions of those objects. His point is that there are different uses of language that fit different activities: telling a story, thanking people, greeting and so on, and within postmodern thought there is a tendency to deprive language of its functions.

Christians, in contrast, should approach the toolbox of language as a gift. Language can sometimes operate on the level of social construction (i.e. the social construction of the teenager), but it means that the meaning of language is much deeper and may signify things that are behind and beyond the tool of language used, something that our poems,

---

5. Vanhoozer, *First Theology*, 20.
6. Ibid., 33.
7. Ibid., 32.

songs and prayers point to; the reality of the creator and created order.[8] To explore the analogy of the toolbox further requires us to see that there are many things that can be done with words, texts and sentences. The move from seeing language as a tool, to seeing speech as a way of doing things is a small but important step. Words do not only represent the world—speaking and writing are part of communicative action. Therefore, if language is a form of action it is worth considering how words are used. As people speak they have communicative responsibilities. As the world of the youth ministers is examined and investigated through narratives of practice, the practitioners interviewed can be seen to embody and enact their faith, as they speak to young people they embody communicative action. It is this lived practice that is under exploration.

With this is mind, C.S Lewis[9] uses a simple story to reveal the nature of knowledge: "A certain man (Lewis) goes into a tool-shed and the door closes behind him. It is very dark inside, apart from a single beam of light. At first, he looks at the beam and sees only specks of dust floating in it. Then he steps into the light; instantly the whole previous picture vanishes. He sees neither the tool-shed or the beam of light, but green leaves moving on the branches of a tree outside, and beyond the sun, framed in the irregular cranny at the top of the door."

The significance of this story is about how epistemology is understood—and this depends on the point of view and what is being examined and investigated. Our knowledge changes depending on the perspective taken. In Lewis' parable looking *at* the beam of light is very different to looking *along* it. The beam, of course, could be analyzed, the specs of dust investigated—if this was the only position taken—looking *at*—it would be a fragment of the picture. As Lewis steps into the light he looks along the beam, through the crack in the shed, past the trees, beyond to the Sun 90 odd million miles away, he seeing the bigger picture.

Lewis draws a distinction between looking *at* and looking *along*. Vanhoozer[10] argues that Biblical scholars have been very good at looking *at*. Looking *at* means to raise questions, so the Bible is looked at via its authorship, composition and questions asked about its historical reliability. However, Wright[11] argues that by only looking *at* we have fragmented

---

8. Ibid., 33.
9. Ibid., 18.
10. Ibid.
11. Wright, *How God Became King*, xiv, 24.

the story, concentrated so much on the details that we have lost sight of the bigger picture. What the Gospels are actually saying about how God became King. To return to the idea of language, a word is used within a sentence in a particular way, the meaning of a sentence is its use within a paragraph, and the meaning of the paragraph is its use in the larger document to which it contributes. It is important to not only look *at* the individual words, but also *along* the entire document.

An example of Biblical fragmentation is given by Wright,[12] who is particularly critical of Bultmann's approach to demythologize the Gospels through his form criticism approach. As Bultmann practiced this approach it was predicated on the assumption that if you could discover the forms, the characteristics, and the shape of the small anecdotes you could observe the early church expressing its own faith. Wright[13] argues, that for Bultmann, "this is why the Gospel traditions were passed on: not to remember or celebrate something that had happened in the past" (i.e., in Jesus' public career, but to celebrate and sustain the continuing life of faith of the early community). For Wright, the focus on the detail through Bultmann's[14] particular lens of the non-historicity of the Gospels loses sight of the bigger and wider story. In my language, this is the fragmentation of theology, the whole is lost. Furthermore, this fragmentation is not only found with the Bultmannian tradition. Ironically, some conservative evangelicals end up on the same page as Bultmann, as they read and interpret a lot of the Gospel stories as signposts towards the cross and the faith of the early church.[15] Here the story is fragmented into signposts that end up only pointing to the saving death and resurrection of Jesus. This is a reduction of the whole, this is the Gospel or part of the Gospel in theological shorthand, it is only part of the picture.

Vanhoozer's[16] project seeks to challenge Bultmann's ideas through his notion of remythologising. Therefore, only looking *at* leads to a reduction of reality, stories and traditions become fragmented, resonating

---

12. Ibid., 21–24.

13. Ibid., 22.

14. Wright, *How God Became King*, 23, notes this is not the same thing as careful judgment about this incident or that incident. Part of Bultmann's whole agenda was that the gospels—or at least the early parts of the gospels should not point to or offer history since that might represent an attempt to base Christian faith on something provable and solid—to turn "faith" into a "work."

15. Ibid., 23.

16. Vanhoozer, *Remythologizing Theology*.

acutely with MacIntyre's[17] work on the virtues, in this process is the belief that our theories see all there is to be seen, all there is to be known.[18] Looking *along* takes in the bigger picture, or to put it another way the bigger story or grand narrative.[19] In this book, the idea of looking *at* (the examination of theological shorthand) is used to enable us to look *along* (that the fragments of theology seen can act as icons of epistemology), to see that we actually take part in a bigger story, we are part of the theodrama.[20] This raises questions of Biblical interpretation. Genuine interpretation is not just looking *at* scripture through critical reason (source, history, grammar etc.), but looking *along* scripture, it involves a process of creative imagination, to enter into different ways of seeing, experiencing and thinking. To do this, is to see the Bible as a book of diverse literary forms, a library in conversation with itself and us, to see the world and ourselves through the world of Biblical history, prophecy, law, Gospel and the apocalyptic. This begins by recognizing God as Triune communicative agent and Scripture as the written locus of God's communicative action. For Vanhoozer,[21] the rubric of communicative action embraces a plurality of specific construals, to do justice to the many ways in which God is present and active within his world and word. As the doctrine of the Trinity is explored within chapters 8 and 9, it seeks to open up new vistas that enable wisdom, human flourishing and abundant life. Wisdom is more than information, more than propositional language, it is lived knowledge and the performance of faith. To do this requires us to look *along* the grain of scripture rather than just *at* it. It is faith seeking understanding.

Language, Fragmentation and the Bigger Picture

However, this is only part of the theological picture, this fragmentation and shorthand seen in the arena of Biblical interpretation is part of a much wider and deeper conversation. To help begin to illuminate this we turn to MacIntyre.

17. MacIntyre, *After Virtue*.
18. Vanhoozer, *First Theology*, 18.
19. Walker, *Telling the Story*.
20. Vanhoozer, *Remythologizing Theology*.
21. Vanhoozer, *First Theology*, 38–40.

MacIntyre suggests that we live amid fragments, fragments of past realities that compete for our loyalty. He articulates in this way:

> Imagine that the natural sciences were to suffer the effects of a catastrophe. A series of environmental disasters are blamed by the general public on the scientists. Widespread riots occur, laboratories are burnt down, physicists are lynched, books and instruments are destroyed. Finally, a Know-Nothing political movement takes power and successfully abolishes science teaching in schools and universities, imprisoning and executing the remaining scientists. Later still, there is a reaction against this destructive movement and enlightened people seek to revive science although they have largely forgotten what it was. But all they possess are fragments: a knowledge of the theoretical context which gave them significance has been lost.[22]

MacIntyre's[23] key argument concerns a dissatisfaction with late 20th century moral philosophy,[24] which in respect to its moral language the actual world we inhabit is very similar to the disordered state in his imaginary world. He continues,

"What we possess are the fragments of a conceptual scheme, parts that now lack those contexts from which their significance is derived. We possess simulacra of morality; we continue to use many of the key expressions. But we have—very largely, if not entirely—lost our comprehension, both theoretically and practically, of morality."

In the real world, competing philosophies (Marxism, liberal individualism etc.) embody the ethos of the modern and modernizing world. Therefore, nothing less than a rejection of that ethos will provide us with a rationality and morally defensible standpoint from which to judge and act, to evaluate various rival and heterogeneous moral schemes that compete for our allegiance.[25] MacIntyre's key thesis is that the Aristotelian moral tradition is the best example we possess of a tradition whose adherents are rationally entitled to a high measure of confidence in its epistemological and moral resources. MacIntyre's framework is helpful for illuminating the fragments within which we live due to the lack of

---

22. MacIntyre, *After Virtue*, 1.
23. Ibid., 2.
24. Much has changed in the academic field in twenty years because of his book, though not in the wider world of popular discourse.
25. Ibid., x.

telos and virtue, but challenging on two key issues.[26] Firstly, it is problematic due to MacIntyre seeking to create a sense of tradition and history of which Aristotle would not have been aware.[27] Secondly, MacIntyre does not adequately address the relationship between the Biblical narrative, theology and his articulation of Aristotle's virtues.[28] That said, Hauerwas draws on MacIntyre's idea of Aristotelian virtues and Hauerwas[29] sees that the fragmentation of our world is not only "out there," but that it is also in our souls. He argues that when living amid fragments, it is extremely hard to maintain our moral identity as we are pulled in different directions by our various roles and convictions, unsure whether there is any coherence to our lives.

Furthermore, Aristotle's concept of *phronesis* has formed the basis for much practical theological enquiry.[30] Dykstra and Bass[31] are also deeply indebted to MacIntyre's concept of social practices.[32] Moreover, Vanhoozer[33] develops Aristotle's key idea of *mythos* in a way in which MacIntyre does not. As noted above, *mythos* is understood in the way that truth and meaning develop in definition and relationship to divine action through the *mythos* of Christ. This is an important framework for piecing the fragments back together.

There is a deep resonance between the ideas of fragments, theological shorthand, thin theology within youth ministry, Biblical interpretation and the language of contemporary worship songs. We have not lost our theological way to the extent that MacIntyre[34] and Hauerwas[35] argue

---

26. Ibid., 264–78 there are other areas of concern, e.g., the relationship of philosophy to history, the virtues and the issue of relativism, but these lie outside the realms of this study.

27. Ibid., 146, 277.

28. Stout, "Virtue Among the Ruins."

29. Hauerwas, *The Peaceable Kingdom*, 6.

30. See Swinton and Mowat, *Practical Theology and Qualitative Research* and Browning, *A Fundamental Practical Theology*.

31. Dykstra and Bass, *A Theological Understanding of Christian Practices*.

32. Bass, *Practicing Theology*, 6. MacIntyre's virtue ethics emphasizes that practices pursue the good in a coherent, traditional way, while social scientists influenced by Marxist thought stress the constant negotiations over power that give shape to practices in certain situations.

33. Vanhoozer, *Remythologizing Theology*.

34. MacIntyre, *After Virtue*.

35. Hauerwas, *The Peaceable Kingdom*.

within ethics,[36] but these thoughts echo and chime within this analysis, perhaps giving clues and pointers before we drift too far off course. Therefore, the central argument is that something similar is happening within our use of language—either in the use of theological shorthand within youth ministry, Biblical interpretation, as observed in the Resource Guides or as seen in the worships songs under investigation. That, "*what we possess* (how we talk about youth ministry, the Bible or what we sing) *are the fragments* (theological shorthand) *of a conceptual scheme* (a deeper understanding of the Christian narrative and story), *parts that now lack those contexts from which their significance is derived.*" (The language and the words separate theological thought from its context and story—adapted from MacIntyre[37]) Furthermore, the leap is not as large as it first appears. Healy[38] provides us with a theological bridge. Healy argues that instead of constructing "blueprint ecclesiologies," which foster disjunction between ideal ecclesiology[39] and the concrete church,[40] we must always be responding to what Christ and the Spirit are doing in a particular context, while at the same time taking account of the historic shape of the church within that context. For Healy,[41] this is constructed via ecclesiological bricolage and experimentation as the contemporary is brought into conversation with earlier patterns and forms of worship. Yet, this is deeply problematic. The evangelical charismatic church has been good at responding to what Christ and the Spirit are doing in a particular context, the event in which the worships songs where used is a good example of this, as discussed below.

However, what is not seen, within the songs, some of the moves made within Biblical interpretation or in some of the youth ministry literature is a more profound engagement with a particular tradition and with the depth of the Christian story. Bretherton,[42] is also critical of Healy, seeing that bricolage results in the tradition being broken down into discrete elements (we could call these fragments or theological shorthand). This is

---

36. I recognize that this is false distinction, because Christian ethics are always theological, but I am seeking to show that the words within the worship songs are not (quite) in the same situation.

37. MacIntyre, *After Virtue*, 2.

38. Healy, *Church, World and the Christian Life*, 25–51.

39. Webster, *In the Society of God*.

40. Ward, "Blueprint Ecclesiology," 2.

41. Healy, *Church, World and the Christian Life*, 25–51.

42. Bretherton, "Beyond the Emerging Church," 47.

more problematic than it first seems, as it is further compounded by the declining influence of religious institutions and organizational structures which are crucial to sustaining the integrity of belief and practices over time,[43] enabling belief and practices to shape behavior, and our worldview.[44] Therefore, it is important for practices to connect the articulation of theological shorthand and theological fragments into a deeper understanding of the Christian narrative and tradition, be it Anglican, Baptist or Pentecostal etc.

Language and Mystery

With this in mind, and as the language within the narratives of practice, the Resource Guides and the songs are examined, it is important to understand the limits of language. Any description of someone else's (or one's own) theology is always provisional, all theology be it formal, espoused, operant or normative[45] is both selective, perspectival and therefore limited: it cannot be otherwise.[46] Our understanding of who God is, is partial and the voices of the mystics need to be heeded. Mystics assume rightly that humans are unable in and of themselves to put God into words adequately. As Migliore[47] sees "Christians are confronted by mystery in all the central affirmations of faith: the wonder of creation; the humility of God in Jesus Christ; the transforming power of the Holy Spirit; the miracle of forgiveness of sins, the gift of new life in communion; the call to the ministry of reconciliation; the promise of the consummation of God's reign. To the eyes of faith, the world is encompassed by the mystery of the free grace of God." Furthermore, Marcel[48] sees mystery as being very different to a problem. While a problem can be solved, mystery is inexhaustible, a problem can be held at arm's length, but mystery encompasses us and won't let us keep a safe distance.

---

43. Dykstra and Bass, *A Theological Understanding of Christian Practices*, 13–32 and MacIntyre, *After Virtue*, 221.
44. Bretherton, "Beyond the Emerging Church," 47.
45. Cameron et al., *Talking about God in Practice*.
46. Christie, *Ordinary Christology*, 191.
47. Migliore, *Faith Seeking Understanding*, 3.
48. Ibid.

A different articulation of mystery is found in Otto's[49] notion of the holy that focuses on what he calls the "*numen*," this is a mystery that lies beyond words and concepts, it is a matter of feeling rather than belief. Therefore, it is important to keep the limits of language and the provisional way we talk about God in mind and in the midst of the critical conversations that make up this book. However, Vanhoozer[50] notes, that Otto's idea of the Holy is compatible with Wittgenstein's mandate to maintain a respectful silence before those things we cannot speak. Yet, God does speak and communicate to us via the Biblical mythos and in a way that requires us to keep a sense of mystery, but at the same time, recognize that through the New Testament term *mysterion* God is revealed (at least in part) in the life, death and resurrection of Jesus Christ. It leads Vanhoozer,[51] to put it like this, "the lifetime of the man Jesus is the 'schema' of the mystery of God, but this schema only becomes intelligible when viewed in the light of the canonical schemata that identify the LORD of the covenant as the Creator of all, the Holy one in Israel's midst." The Biblical mystery of how God fulfils his covenant with Abraham has been revealed, yet, the theological mystery persists, for our understanding is partial and dim and it requires many canonical voices and points of view to explore the theodrama. The reality of God, surpasses any one theologian's attempt to grasp and conceptualize it. Scripture outpaces the attempt of any one interpretive scheme to capture its meaning. The process of faith seeking understanding is dialogical, it requires wrestling and grappling with what it means to talk about God and follow Jesus. In the midst of this process it means that one can offer provisional pictures that seek to preserve the richness of canonical and catholic testimony, while at the same time seeking to address the concerns of contemporary contexts. However, although it is important to try and preserve the richness of canonical and catholic testimony there are times when this might be challenged from contemporary thought. To do this requires prayerful insights. If critique and challenge is not brought the Gospel can be used to oppress and not liberate as has been seen in the Christian story over apartheid and in some sections of the church with the ongoing debate with LGBT+ Christians. Therefore, the exploration of the fragments and theological shorthand has the possibility to open people up to the rich-

---

49. Otto, *The Idea of the Holy*.
50. Vanhoozer, *Remythologizing Theology*, 472.
51. Ibid., 473–74.

ness of the Christian story, to help people see beyond the boundaries of their own particular experience and particular part of the story. This is a process of theological education as long held views or assumptions may well be challenged, but it is an important process to try and see beyond one's own particular view point (as far as this is possible), to look beyond the parapet to the *long* view. To seek to try and understand the foibles and particular idiosyncrasies of the particular tradition in which ones sits. As the language of the youth ministers, the Resource Guides and the worship songs is investigated, it could be said that all that is seen is the language of "insiders," terms that are familiar to a particular group although there are certainly elements of this, there is much more going on. Consequently, because this study is seen through an evangelical lens and begins to critique and raises questions how evangelical language operates this study falls within Cataphatic rather than Apophatic theology.

Four Voices of Theology

Cameron et al.[52] develop a typology for understanding theology in ethnographic studies; this is to be seen as a working tool and has a particular focus on theology as action research. Action research is not the focus of this book; however, the articulation of the four voices of theology is helpful in illuminating how the words used within youth ministry and the songs can be analyzed. The theological voices that Cameron et al. outline are not to be seen as discrete and separate from one another for the voices can never be heard without the echoes and reverberations of the others. Cameron et al.[53] see the theological voices as: a) Operant—the theology that is embedded in the practices of a group, what is done. b) Espoused—what we say we do, the articulation of beliefs. c) Normative theology—the theology named by a group that will allow challenge to the former two voices. d) Formal theology, the theology of the theologians, the academy and dialogue with other disciplines.

The normative voice of theology is concerned with what the group names as its theological authority, this theological authority stands to correct, as well as inform the operant and espoused theologies. Cameron et al.[54] see that the normative voice is often related to ecclesial identities,

---

52. Cameron et al., *Talking about God in Practice*, 54.
53. Ibid.
54. Ibid., 54–55.

scripture or the creeds. This is a varied and complex process and the normative voice can be part of an independent dynamic of scholarly readings of church history, doctrine or approaches to scripture.

Within the practice of the youth ministers, and foundational for my argument, it is the youth ministry literature that functions as the normative voice in relation to practice, rather than doctrine, scripture or the Anglican or Baptist traditions of which the youth ministers are part. The youth ministry literature informs the operant and espoused theology of the youth ministers. This is profound and problematic, due to the theological expression of Christian youth ministry and its relationship to the church. Existing literature (e.g. Borgman;[55] Pimlott and Pimlott;[56] Savage et al.;[57] Sudworth et al.;[58] *Youth A Part*[59] tends to present lightweight, thin and shorthanded expressions of theological thought on relationships. Herein, there appears very limited verbalization of relational richness. Much youth ministry canon appears to lack theological depth and ignores the potentialities of relational theological capital within the Christian tradition—it operates as theological shorthand. Nevertheless, Ward[60] begins to offer a deeper definition of relationship—locating it within *Missio Dei*. Dean[61] advances a fuller understanding of relationships through the act of "being there." It is perhaps Root,[62] by drawing on Bonhoeffer's Christology, who gives the most articulate expression of relationships within Christian youth ministry. At the level of articulated practice, there remains, however, a disconnect between some of the deeper theological expressions on relationships articulated by Dean,[63] Root,[64] Ward,[65] and the reality of praxis.[66] This is a crucial for the argument this book is seeking to make and is explored further below.

---

55. Borgman, *When Kumbaya Is Not Enough*.
56. Pimlott and Pimlott, *Youth Work after Christendom*.
57. Savage et al, *Making Sense of Generation Y*.
58. Sudworth et al., *Mission Shaped Youth*.
59. Church of England Board of Education, *Youth A Part*.
60. Ward, *Youthwork*, 43.
61. Dean, *Practicing Passion*, 91.
62. Root, *Revisiting Relational Youth Ministry*.
63. Dean, *Practicing Passion*.
64. Root, *Revisiting Relational Youth Ministry*.
65. Ward, *Youthwork*.
66. Bright and Bailey, "Youth Work and the Church."

Language and Theological Shorthand

As youth ministry is investigated via the youth minister practitioners, the Resource Guides and through the worship songs, theological shorthand is expressed through the language of: *relationships, like Jesus, being there,* and *time* and *journey.* These words articulate a complex and nuanced practice that carry, communicate the Gospel, and the faith of youth ministers amongst young people. When examined, the practice of youth ministers resonates with echoes and fragments of theology from the Christian tradition (*marturia, diakonia* and *kerygma*). Paradoxically, these echoes and fragments of theology sustain the spiritual life of the youth minister, they can be found in the diet of worships songs, and some of the Biblical material that some of the youth ministers employ.

Theological shorthand reveals an embedded theology that evokes and has a connection with the wider theological picture of the Christian Tradition, but this broader tradition is not expressed. This is a thin[67] description of practice, this is thin theology. What I mean by this is that what is expressed reveals an enacted theology that evokes and has a relationship to a wider, deeper, richer set of beliefs from within the Christian Tradition, but this is expressed as shorthand, like a series of motifs and marks; it is a partial, a thin interpretation and theological description of the complexity of actual practice. Within youth ministry, these motifs and marks are the terms of relationship, like Jesus, being there and time and journey, but paradoxically these descriptions are very meaningful in the animation of practice, and they point and are connected to a deeper theological reality.[68] Therefore, the theological shorthand expression of the complexities of practice is like a pencil sketch; this can be beautiful, meaningful and communicative. Yet, if examined closely, the complexities of enacted and lived theology embedded within practice can be seen in full–color, rich in depth and texture.

---

67. Following Ryle, Geertz, *The Interpretation of Cultures,* holds that anthropology's task is that of explaining cultures through "thick description" which specifies many details, conceptual structures and meanings. This is opposed to "thin description"; this can be a factual account without any interpretation. Therefore, a thin description for Geertz is not only an insufficient account it may also be a misleading one.

68. The "four point" expression of the gospel and Biblical story is an example of this. See: www.the4points.com. The four points represent, not very well in my opinion, the good news of the Christian message: God loves me, I have sinned, Jesus died for me, I need to decide to live for God.

To return to the idea of an icon is helpful. Within the Christian tradition icons operate as windows into the story and life of God. They remind us and help us see from our often-mundane realities, that life is richer that we ever thought, that God is at work, drawing us in and helping us see a fresh. Icons operate in liminal spaces existing between two worlds, they add color, light, and shade and texture to what can/cannot be grasped by the intellect—helping to render the invisible, visible. Rublev's painting is an example of this.

To move to a more contemporary metaphor, theological shorthand operates like the icons on a tablet or smart phone, the icons are the theological shorthand, the fragments and motifs. If you press an icon you explore the richer, deeper, wider world of the app, if you can explore the fragments they lead you to a more profound understanding of the Christian story, to a more coherent theology, to a richer description of the grand narrative. The icons[69] act as windows of epistemology, ways of developing theological literacy. The core argument of this book is that the theological shorthand expression of practice is thin, within ministry generally, but particularly in youth ministry, where it operates in a world of fragments[70] and the theology embedded within practice is much more complicated than the language used to describe it. Yet, as mentioned, these fragments (the words) can be used as windows and icons that when reflected and dwelt upon can illuminate the Christian tradition, heritage, and story of which we are part, bringing richness and full color to our theological expressions. Through this process the words become icons of epistemology. However, the tension for youth ministry is that youth ministers live amongst these fragments and there is a level of disconnect between what is espoused, what is expressed, how the Bible is interpreted, what is sung, and the richness of theology within the Christian narrative and story.[71] Now the scene has been set, it is time to explore these tensions in more detail, to do this requires the wrestling of where theology is within practice, it is now time to turn to this important question.

---

69. Just like traditional icons within the Christian tradition, when reflected upon the words, for example, like Jesus can reveal layers of meaning and become a way of deepening knowledge about the Christian narrative.

70. MacIntyre, *After Virtue*.

71. The disconnect between doctrine, theology and "ordinary" Christians resonates with a growing area of study through the work of Christie, *Ordinary Christology* and Astley, *Ordinary Theology*.

Chapter 2

Youth Ministry and Practical Theology

Youth Ministry: Where Is Theology?

Rublev's icon facilitates a process of reflection on who God is and how God makes space for us to participate within the relationships that make up Father, Son and Spirit. The question of how is explored in chapters 8 and 9, but these questions are deeply theological and require theological reflection and consideration to move towards some answers. This requires theological thought. From my experience of teaching and when students are asked if they are theologians there is often some hesitancy in their reply. When asked what theology is they often respond with the basic and stock answer; "the study of God." After all, isn't this right? Does not the discourse about theology live in the ivory towers of the academy? Yes and no. At a basic level, theology is about the study of God, but this is only a partial understanding; it is not the whole picture. For theology is not just an academic enterprise, whose study is God and God's relation to the world, the purpose of theology is not simply to deliver knowledge, or study God, but to serve a way of life. Theology is lived, performed[1] and embodied within the pursuit of this way of life.[2] Theology is not just academic, it is enacted within our relationship with God and in its outworking with others.[3] Just like in Rublev's icon, we take part in a story, a

---

1. Ward, *Participation and Mediation*.
2. Volf, "Theology as a Way of Life."
3. Augsburg, *Dissident Discipleship*.

story and grand narrative[4] that has a rich and deep history, we take part in a theological drama.[5]

Performed theology is most obviously seen in contemporary worship. The performance of the band and the relationship between the band and the audience and the performance/audience aspect of this is explored further below. Yet, performed theology can also be seen in the celebration of Mass at a Catholic church, or in the explicit liturgy within Anglican Church, or even in the implicit liturgy of a Free Church. The relationship between text, audience and context is well documented through cultural studies.[6]

Theology embodied as a way of life falls within the discipline of practical theology.[7] Practical theologians seek to wrestle with and understand what it means to follow Christ and live out the Christian life within the dynamic relationship and dialogue between the Bible, the Church and the world. As Christians we live amongst, negotiate and ask questions from within this complex and nuanced arena. The discipline of practical theology facilitates a focus on the lived experience of faith and enables a community to employ a richer, deeper theology in its life together. Practical theology enables intentional and critical theological reflections on the embodied expression of faith, as Christians live in and join with God's mission in and for the world. Practical theology examines faith in practice, theology in action, as Christians seek to be faithful to the differing aspects of the Gospel story[8] and as a community looks for God's divine action.[9] Practical theology helps to develop theological literacy.

The discipline of practical theology has a focus on the interpretation of human experience and the nature of human practices from

4. Walker, *Telling the Story*.
5. Vanhoozer, *Remythologizing Theology*.
6. Barker, *Cultural Studies*.
7. The term practical theology finds its origins with the German theologian Schleiermacher (b. 1768) who coined the phrase in the eighteenth century. At the time, the German research university model was conceived and the work of theology broken up into what is called the "theological encyclopedia." The volumes in that encyclopedia were 1) biblical studies, 2) systematic theology, and 3) church history. Schleiermacher proposed that a fourth discipline be added, called "practical theology," the aim was to develop "rules of art" for Christian life and ministry. Practical theology is related to these other disciplines within theological education and may draw on these areas (systematic theology, biblical studies and others) to inform and guide practice.
8. Swinton and Mowat, *Practical Theology and Qualitative Research*.
9. Root, *Christopraxis*.

a theological point of view.[10] It is essentially reflection on both divine and human action[11] and how divine reality and human reality relate at the level of experience. Swinton and Mowat[12] define practical theology as "Critical, theological reflection on the practices of the church as they interact with the practices of the world, with a view to ensuring and enabling faithful participation in God's redemptive practices in, to and for the world." Swinton and Mowat[13] see practical theology as dedicated to the enabling and faithful performance of the Gospel and to exploring and taking seriously the complex human encounter with God. Practical theology, therefore, finds itself located within the uneasy, but critical tension between the script of revelation given to us in Christ and formulated historically within Scripture, doctrine and tradition, and the on-going innovative performance of the Gospel and theology as it is enacted, performed and embodied in the practices of the church as they interact with the world.

Consequently, it could be said that *all* Christians (whatever age), who seek to follow Christ and live this out, embody a theology; they are theologians, and theology is in play. From a six year old's bedtime prayer through to the academic systematic theologian, our understanding of God is partial and limited, there is still mystery to behold and explore. Root[14] sees the tensions of exploring what practical theology is, who does it and how is it done. Root articulates how practical theology seeks to connect scholarly discipline with the activity of faith—seeking to make sense of the world for the human agents within it. Yet, in doing so has not attended enough to revelation.[15] Furthermore, within the academic community there has been a turn to examine the reflective God-talk of the "ordinary" Christian,[16] and to investigate how Christians talk about God in practice.[17] Therefore, perhaps the question is not: Are we all theologians? But, how good are we at thinking theologically? This leads to further questions, such as, how disciplined are we in the art of theological

---

10. Ballard, "Pastoral and Practical Theology," 8, and Ballard and Pritchard, *Practical Theology in Action*, 12.

11. Root, *Christopraxis*.

12. Swinton and Mowat, *Practical Theology and Qualitative Research*, 6.

13. Ibid., 4.

14. Root, *Christopraxis*, 27–34.

15. Ibid., 29.

16. Christie, *Ordinary Christology*, and Astley, *Ordinary Theology*.

17. Cameron et al., *Talking about God in Practice*.

reflection?[18] Do we facilitate theological reflection with and amongst communities, either through the pastoral cycle[19] or as a spiritual discipline and practice[20] to articulate more emphatically why we do what we do from a theological perspective?

Theological reflection is an art rather than one approach.[21] With this in mind, our practices, the things we do in action, are filled with theological content[22] and, when reflected upon, are found to be rich in meaning.[23] Therefore, one of the tasks of practical theology is to enable theological reflection on practice. It is this that is important for exploring the theological shorthand under investigation.

Practical Theology as Critical Faithfulness

So far so good, but, Rublev's icon reveals that there is more going on within the painting and how icons function than it first seems. It is the same with the question—where is theology? In particular, questions circulate about the relationship between practice and theology, the relationship between theological revelation and ways of knowing about reality through empirical research. How is this complicated relationship navigated and explored? Swinton and Mowat[24] see that practical theology converts different ways of epistemology, for example, aspects of qualitative research and discourse analysis into its service. Further to this, Root,[25] who is critical of this approach, reminds us that we have to consider the place of divine action, human encounter of the divine (how they relate) and the human condition and reality. It is now time to explore this negotiated space in more detail, to go deeper, because it is at the heart of the theological enterprise.

---

18. Graham et al., *Theological Reflection*.

19. This is a common cycle within practical theology. Ward's, *Participation and Mediation* offers a critique of this saying that it has a tendency to isolate theology to a particular moment (when in fact theology is in each part) and can break up a situation into component parts in a way that is not helpful or intuitive.

20. Ward, *Participation and Mediation*.

21. Graham et al., *Theological Reflection*.

22. Volf, "Theology as a Way of Life."

23. Browning, *A Fundamental Theology*.

24. Swinton and Mowat, *Practical Theology and Qualitative Research*.

25. Root, *Christopraxis*, 34.

To help navigate differing aspects of epistemology and theology, practical theology rotates around the notion of correlation.[26] Swinton and Mowat[27] develop a revised model of mutual critical correlation with a focus on critical faithfulness. To do this, they draw on the work of Tillich,[28] Tracy,[29] and Pattison,[30] with a Christological and a Chalcedonian perspective given through the work of Van Deuson Hunsinger.[31] Swinton and Mowat's[32] model finds its origins in the work of Tillich,[33] and it is also heavily influenced by Browning[34] but, like Anderson,[35] the framework is heavily revised through a Christological perspective and held within a Trinitarian hermeneutic of mission, although this Trinitarian hermeneutic is not explicit. Tillich[36] sought to correlate existential questions which are drawn from human experience with theological answers offered by the Christian tradition. Therefore, the questions that emerge from human experience (the product of rational reflection) find their answers in Scripture and tradition. Through this method, Tillich sought to achieve a degree of relevance for the Christian tradition within a rapidly changing secularizing social context. Tracy[37] expands the critical dimension of Tillich's model and incorporates a dialectical element which enables the correlation between scripture, tradition and experience to be mutually correlative and critical. This bias towards equal dialogue partners leads to a largely existential understanding of faith, as Pattison[38] sees.

---

26. Browning, *A Fundamental Theology* and Anderson, *The Shape of Practical Theology*.
27. Swinton and Mowat, *Practical Theology and Qualitative Research*, 88.
28. Tillich, *Systematic Theology*.
29. Tracy, *Blessed Rage for Order*.
30. Pattison, "Some Straws for the Bricks."
31. Van Deusen Hunsinger, *Theology and Pastoral Counselling*.
32. Swinton and Mowat, *Practical Theology and Qualitative Research*, 77–88.
33. Tillich, *Systematic Theology*.
34. Browning, *A Fundamental Theology*.
35. Anderson, *The Shape of Practical Theology*.
36. Tillich, *Systematic Theology*.
37. Tracy, *Blessed Rage for Order*.
38. Pattison, "The Use of Behavioural Sciences," 79, and Pattison, "Practical Theology," 77, and Browning, *A Fundamental Theology*, 14.

Within Pattison's[39] conversation model that Swinton and Mowat[40] focus on to develop their revised model of mutual critical correlation, the practical theologian identifies a situation within the practice of the church or the world which requires further reflection and exploration (in this book this is youth ministry and its expression, the fragments of theology and theological shorthand). This is then explored through other sources of knowledge, for example, qualitative research, and discourse analysis; through this, the hidden meanings within the situation and the practices that participants take part in can be uncovered. The research data is then brought into conversation with scripture, doctrine and tradition with a view to developing revised forms of practice that will impact and transform the original situation. The intention within this model is to broaden, deepen and, if necessary, challenge both ecclesial practice and theological understandings in the light of current practice. Pattison[41] seeks to embrace perspectives on practice that offer a more stringent and even contradictory explanation of current practice. This, in his view, helps enhance the critical reflection upon the situation under investigation. Within this model, as Swinton and Mowat[42] argue, the data acquired through qualitative research has an equal voice within the conversation and can challenge theology and tradition in exactly the same way as theology and tradition can challenge its findings; this is symmetrical and finds its foundations in Tillich's,[43] Tracy's,[44] and Browning's[45] work. The problem here, is that reality becomes flattened and there is little space for the articulation of divine action as an independent and free reality.[46] In the language of Vanhoozer[47] there is no space for divine communicative action. Swinton and Mowat[48] are sympathetic to this model but see that in principle the epistemological function of social

---

39. Pattison, "Some Straws for the Bricks" sees that an "open and dangerous" conversation takes place between the Christian tradition, the social sciences and the particular situation that is being explored.
40. Swinton and Mowat, *Practical Theology and Qualitative Research*, 81–83.
41. Pattison, "Pastoral Studies," 249.
42. Swinton and Mowat, *Practical Theology and Qualitative Research*, 82.
43. Tillich, *Systematic Theology*.
44. Tracy, *Blessed Rage for Order*.
45. Browning, *A Fundamental Theology*.
46. Root, *Christopraxis*, 56.
47. Vanhoozer, *Remythologizing Theology*.
48. Swinton and Mowat, *Practical Theology and Qualitative Research*, 83.

sciences can be given priority over theology, the theological task can be overwhelmed, or perhaps obscured and this is particularly problematic.

With this in mind, as theological shorthand is investigated and the lived experience of youth ministers practice is interpreted, it is Trinitarian theology as communicative action, through the work of Vanhoozer[49] that provides a normative voice. This is to understand how relationships as communicative acts, theological shorthand and the fragments of theology can be enriched and deepened to be more authentic and faithful to the Gospel. Therefore, formal theology[50] through the work of Vanhoozer[51] acts as the normative voice for practice.

Through the work of Vanhoozer, Trinitarian theology acts as the guiding framework for illuminating and enriching practice. This theology acts as a lens to view the fragments, to magnify and bring clarity to them. What is important is to be able to premise truth and revelation, whilst, at the same time, holding onto the interpretive dimensions of the way enacted youth ministry practice interacts with Scripture and tradition.

Developing Van Deusen Hunsinger's[52] ideas, Swinton and Mowat[53] note how the idea of hospitality is crucial. Here, hospitality is shown towards the research method the practical theologian is working with. In this book, it means that a context and space where the voice of the practitioners (through the qualitative interview), the analysis of Biblical interpretation within the Resource Guides and the investigation of the theological language within worship songs can be heard, respected and taken seriously. The space created acts as a lens for investigating practice and theological shorthand, it is like examining Rublev's icon in much more detail—seeking to interpret and explore the aspects and facets of the painting that are not immediately obvious.

To enable this to happen, Swinton and Mowat[54] argue that qualitative research and discourse analysis need to undergo a process of conversion. What they mean by this is that qualitative research and discourse analysis moves from a position of fragmentation and without a specific goal or telos, to a position where it is grafted into God's redemptive

49. Vanhoozer, *Remythologizing Theology*.
50. Cameron et al., *Talking about God in Practice*.
51. Vanhoozer, *Remythologizing Theology*.
52. Van Deusen Hunsinger, *Theology and Pastoral Counselling*.
53. Swinton and Mowat, *Practical Theology and Qualitative Research*, 91.
54. Ibid., 92–94.

intentions for the world. Therefore, God converts the field of intellectual enquiry outside of theology and uses it in the service of making himself known within the church and then on into the world. This approach resonates with the Trinitarian theology adopted from Vanhoozer[55] as divinely authored communicative action, as both, at least in part, are influenced by the theology of Barth and reverberate with insights from the reformed tradition. It means, in my work, that the interview develops its critique from the inside and the epistemological framework becomes unalterably theistic, but always open to the possibility of the new. This approach is marked by critical faithfulness. In this research, such faithfulness acknowledges the divine given-ness of Scripture, how God speaks and acts, as seen in the work of Vanhoozer,[56] and the genuine working of the Holy Spirit in the interpretation of this, whilst simultaneously taking seriously the interpretive dimensions of understanding revelation within the voices of the practitioners. However, this entire enterprise is held within God's Triune communicative action as this joins with human agency in, to and for the world as charted in chapters 8 and 9.

Practical Theology as Critical Theological Reflection

To enable this to happen requires a process of reflection. Browning[57] argues that, as we approach the theological task of understanding the practices of the church in the world, we do so with questions shaped by the secular and religious practices in which we are implicated. These practices are meaningful or *theory-laden*. For Browning[58] this means that theory is not distinct from practice. All our practices have theories behind and within them. Yet, we may not notice these theories in our practices. We are so embedded in our practices that we take them for granted and view them as so natural that we do not take time to examine and reflect upon them. Drawing on Browning's[59] thoughts, Swinton and Mowat[60] see that there is no such thing as a value-free form of practice. In a very real sense, belief is in the act itself and is seen in the faithful performance of the Gospel. Like Rublev's icon, our practices are filled

55. Vanhoozer, *Remythologizing Theology*.
56. Ibid.
57. Browning, *A Fundamental Theology*, 6.
58. Ibid.
59. Ibid.
60. Swinton and Mowat, *Practical Theology and Qualitative Research*, 20.

with theological content[61] and, when reflected upon, are found to be rich in meaning, even if the expression of these are fragmented, thin or in theological shorthand.

Therefore, the practical theological task enables theological reflection on practice. In this book, the task of practical theology is to mediate the relationship between the current understanding of enacted youth ministry practice as seen in the data, and the Christian tradition through the normative voice of Trinitarian theology. The research moves from practice to theological reflection on practice to suggestions for re-imagined youth ministry practice, an idea that resonates with Browning's[62] thoughts; however, the approach adopted differs from Browning in that Swinton and Mowat[63] premise theology over the social sciences. Therefore, in the approach adopted from Swinton and Mowat[64] theological reflection is facilitated by the social sciences as it seeks to discern, critique and illuminate discrepancies in the practices of the church and point to more authentic and faithful alternatives, an idea that echoes Anderson's[65] thoughts. Here the task of practical theology is to remind the church of the ways in which it differs from the world and to ensure that its practices remain faithful to the script of the Gospel.[66] The theological reflection on current youth ministry practice is carried out from the position of a critical friend, a friend who wants to bring challenge and bring out the best in the other. Therefore, in this research, theological reflection is to be seen as theoretical enquiry seeking to interpret current youth ministry practice, to evaluate, critique and importantly serve and help express what is done and what is said, to enhance current practice.

For Anderson[67] and Root[68] and within this piece of research, the activity of theological reflection is held within the divine work of God. Here, practical theology has a particular focus on the continuing pursuit of competence through critical theological reflection. However, this competence does not merely arise through repetition and practice of meth-

---

61. Volf, "Theology as a Way of Life."

62. Theological reflection begins when a community of faith hits a "crisis" in its practice. Browning, *A Fundamental Theology*, 6.

63. Swinton and Mowat, *Practical Theology and Qualitative Research*.

64. Ibid., 111.

65. Anderson, *The Shape of Practical Theology*.

66. Swinton and Mowat, *Practical Theology and Qualitative Research*, 10.

67. Anderson, *The Shape of Practical Theology*, 53.

68. Root, *Christopraxis*.

ods, as seen in Browning's[69] work, but, importantly, is gained through participation in the work of God. Anderson[70] calls this Christopraxis. For Anderson,[71] Christopraxis "is the continuing ministry of Christ through the power and presence of the Holy Spirit." This becomes the authoritative grounding of an objective reality. This is consummated "in Christ" and continued through the power and presence of the Holy Spirit in the body of Christ, an idea that resonates with Vanhoozer's[72] thinking. For Anderson[73], the decisions made in ministry situations are in line with Christ's own purpose as he acts and stands within the situation and with us. This is similar to Swinton and Mowat's[74] thoughts on the faithful performance of the Gospel, but he gives this greater theological depth, as God acts through our human actions to reveal truth. Yet, it raises the question, "What does it mean for Christ to stand in the situation with us?" Root[75] addresses some of these concerns as he builds on and augments Anderson's thoughts through his framework of Christopraxis. Root[76] is critical of practical theology's over reliance on an Aristotelian understanding of action and sees ministry as going beyond the functional to being located and participating in the being of God. For Root[77] Christopraxis is anchored in the crucifixion of Jesus Christ and this offers the promise of being able to speak meaningfully about the realities of divine action in human life. It means that practical theologians can discern the ongoing ministry of God in human life. For Root,[78] his Christopraxis as a practical theology of the cross, seeks to turn practical theology from *imitation Christi* to *participation Christi*, believing in doing so, that divine action is freed from an inert tradition of interpretation of practice and becomes a living reality. Root,[79] seeks to free divine action through a theology of

69. Browning, *A Fundamental Theology*.
70. Anderson, *The Shape of Practical Theology*.
71. Ibid., 29.
72. Vanhoozer, *Remythologizing Theology*.
73. Anderson *The Shape of Practical Theology*, 39, sees that St Paul has a profound grasp of the Trinitarian relations. This has an impact on Browning's model because Paul's theological foundation is more substantive than mere ethical instruction or practical reasons.
74. Swinton and Mowat, *Practical Theology and Qualitative Research*.
75. Root, *Christopraxis*.
76. Ibid., 53–75.
77. Ibid.
78. Ibid., 81.
79. Ibid.

the cross and sees this not just for interpretation, or to do practice better, or to provide a doctrinal voice, but sees it instead as an existential encounter with the reality of God through Christological participation. While there is much to be said for being anchored in the crucifixion, this carries the danger of neglecting the life and ministry of Jesus that led to his crucifixion.

Vanhoozer[80] also develops the idea of Christological participation (although this differs from Root).[81] For Vanhoozer,[82] human agency is seen as participation in Christ's *mythos* and history. This foundational point about Christological participation is addressed in this book through the work of Vanhoozer[83] and the issue of doctrine navigated through the differing views on the *perichoresis* and the operant mode of participation through the theology of Moltmann,[84] Kilby,[85] Fiddes,[86] and Vanhoozer.[87] As this subject of theological reflection is considered, Graham et al.[88] add a note of caution, arguing that theological reflection is easier said than done and see that theological reflection is largely narrow and under-theorized and too often fails to connect adequately with Biblical, historical and systematic scholarship. Graham[89] continues that theological reflection is often weak in its use of traditional Christian resources and doctrine and has had an uneasy relationship with the Bible.

Practical Theology as *Phronesis* and Faithful Living

Central to the argument within this book is how do the theological reflections embarked upon facilitate and enable faithful living. Swinton and Mowat,[90] as discussed, see the task of practical theology as ensuring faithful living and Christian practice in faithfulness to the Gospel. This is to enable a personal and communal *phronesis*, a form of practical

---

80. Vanhoozer, *Remythologizing Theology*.
81. Root, *Christopraxis*.
82. Vanhoozer, *Remythologizing Theology*.
83. Ibid.
84. Moltmann, *The Trinity and the Kingdom of God*.
85. Kilby, "Perichoresis and Projection."
86. Fiddes, *Participating in God*.
87. Vanhoozer, *Remythologizing Theology*.
88. Graham et al., *Theological Reflection*, 1.
89. Ibid, 7.
90. Swinton and Mowat, *Practical Theology and Qualitative Research*, 6.

wisdom combining theory and practice in the praxis of individuals and communities. This idea of *phronesis* is evident in Browning's[91] work, as it aims for an embodied practical knowledge that enables a particular form of God-oriented lifestyle. Swinton and Mowat[92] see this as resonating with Farley's[93] concept of habitus; although they differ, they both include an orientation devoted to the practical but critical living out of faith. Within this critical living out of faith, Swinton and Mowat[94] argue that practical theology is fundamentally a missiological discipline that receives its dynamic from acknowledging and working out what it means to participate faithfully in the mission of the Trinitarian God, as echoed in Anderson's,[95] Vanhoozer's,[96] and Root's[97] work, but is missing from Browning's[98] ideas. For Swinton and Mowat,[99] it is this mission that provides the hermeneutic which guides practical theology in each dimension of its task. The task, therefore, of practical theology is not simply to understand the world but also to change it, seeking not only, "What difference will this make in the pulpit and pew?" but also, "Who is God and how does one know more fully His Truth?"

Within Browning's[100] thinking, this form of *phronesis* is therefore, particularly problematic, as his work echoes with enlightenment thinking and is Kantian in foundation, as Browning[101] goes beyond Kant to certain strands of Aristotelian teleology. This opens up Browning to accusations of relying too much on human thought and not enough on divine activity. Therefore, reason becomes a source and not just a tool. Related to this is that Browning places *phronesis* on the same footing as theology, therefore theology is not given logical priority, as it is within the work of Swinton and Mowat[102] and Root.[103] As Anderson[104] argues,

91. Browning, *A Fundamental Theology*.
92. Swinton and Mowat, *Practical Theology and Qualitative Research*, 26.
93. Farley, *Theologia*.
94. Swinton and Mowat, *Practical Theology and Qualitative Research*, 27.
95. Anderson, *The Shape of Practical Theology*.
96. Vanhoozer, *Remythologizing Theology*.
97. Root, *Christopraxis*.
98. Browning, *A Fundamental Theology*.
99. Swinton and Mowat, *Practical Theology and Qualitative Research*, 27.
100. Browning, *A Fundamental Theology*.
101. Ibid., 11.
102. Swinton and Mowat, *Practical Theology and Qualitative Research*.
103. Root, *Christopraxis*.
104. Anderson, *The Shape of Practical Theology*, 30.

whilst Browning[105] does include Christology, he does so primarily as a component of systematic theology that belongs to his "outer envelope." This is positioned as "part of the community of memory" with its "historical consciousness" expressed as creed and dogma. However, Anderson argues that the ministry of Jesus (through the Holy Spirit) is as authoritative as the teaching of Jesus. Therefore, for Anderson, Christology must be related to Christopraxis. This means the present reality of Christ, through the power of the Holy Spirit, stirs us to theological reflection and also locates our practice in the on-going activity of the Trinitarian God. Anderson,[106] therefore, argues that practical theology needs a solid theological foundation so that the practical does not overwhelm and determine the theological. Alongside this, the subject matter of theology is not located just in the "historical consciousnesses" of the community in the form of its creeds and dogma, rather, theology must continue to reflect on the contemporary work of the Holy Spirit as the praxis of the risen Christ. Anderson[107] sees praxis as involving tasks but, in the performing of those tasks, meaning is discovered and not merely applied. In this, he relates to and follows Browning's[108] theory-laden model above. This lack of objective reality within Browning's framework is taken up through Anderson's[109] Christopraxis approach. It grounds a practical theological methodology in Christopraxis as the inner-core of its encounter with the Spirit's on-going ministry in the world. Anderson's approach resonates and compliments Vanhoozer's[110] theology, but Vanhoozer provides a more convincing and robust argument for Trinitarian theology as communicative action that becomes pivotal in exploring the overarching themes discovered in the data and the expression of this as theological shorthand.

Furthermore, in Anderson's[111] thinking, Browning's[112] model is adopted and modified and the questions, "How then should we live?" and

---

105. The difference is that Anderson, *The Shape of Practical Theology*, places Christopraxis at the center, rather than experience, foregrounding Christology, interrelated to a Trinitarian foundation.

106. Ibid., 46.

107. Ibid., 47.

108. Browning, *A Fundamental Theology*, 6.

109. Anderson, *The Shape of Practical Theology*, 22.

110. Vanhoozer, *Remythologizing Theology*.

111. Anderson, *The Shape of Practical Theology*.

112. Browning, *A Fundamental Theology*.

"What should we do?" become inherently theological and Christological, as well as ethical, when asked with respect to what God has revealed through his Word and what God is doing through the power of his Spirit. For Anderson,[113] this becomes the on-going hermeneutical task given to the church in its practice of practical theology. Anderson[114] describes a hermeneutical practice of theology as beginning with theological reflection on the context and crisis of ministry in relation to reading the text of Scripture in light of the "text of lives" that manifest the work of Christ through the Holy Spirit. This is why Anderson can replace experience as central to Browning's[115] model with Christopraxis, because Christopraxis holds experience in the on-going activity and work of God and human actions reveal this truth. Anderson's[116] thoughts are important, in particular how the activity of practical theology is placed in the on-going activity of God and also gives it a Christological focus interrelated to a Trinitarian foundation.

However, Anderson's framework raises two points. Firstly, and in line with Swinton and Mowat,[117] Anderson[118] sees it is the role of Scripture that becomes normative, resonating with Vanhoozer.[119] Although normative, and this differs from Swinton and Mowat,[120] but echoes with Vanhoozer,[121] is shown through the on-going Christopraxis, there is still a difficult tension to explore; who decides what is normative and how is such an interpretation reached? In this book, this is approached through Vanhoozer,[122] who adopts a Canonical approach. Secondly, and relevant to the research question, is how do we interpret living texts and situations in the light of Christopraxis.[123] This is not altogether clear and as such Anderson's[124] hermeneutic of practical theology has a particular bias to Biblical interpretation and divine action within ministry rather

113. Anderson, *The Shape of Practical Theology*, 52.
114. Ibid, 38.
115. Browning, *A Fundamental Theology*.
116. Anderson, *The Shape of Practical Theology*.
117. Swinton and Mowat, *Practical Theology and Qualitative Research*.
118. Anderson, *The Shape of Practical Theology*, 30.
119. Vanhoozer, *Remythologizing Theology*.
120. Swinton and Mowat, *Practical Theology and Qualitative Research*.
121. Vanhoozer, *Remythologizing Theology*.
122. Ibid.
123. Anderson, *The Shape of Practical Theology*, 37.
124. Ibid.

than the empirical interpretation of particular situations and practices that is found within Swinton and Mowat.[125] That said, Root[126] sees that "practical theology is not concrete and lived because it is empirical but because it seeks to discern (hermeneutically) the concrete and lived reality of God's becoming in ministry," resonating strongly with Swinton and Mowat.[127] Therefore, Root[128] draws heavily on Anderson[129] in the construction of his Christopraxis, put pushes this further by exploring and seeing that Christopraxis gives people within difficult and traumatic ministerial situations a language to talk about God's presence, helping ministers interpret the divine action of God within human situations. Therefore, for Root,[130] practical theology becomes inseparable from ministry, not only because ministry is practical reason (*phronesis*), but because it takes part in the being of God. To do this, Root[131] connects his theology of Christopraxis with an actualist ontology of the Godself through the work of Jungel and his concept of justification. This is what begins to separate Root[132] from Anderson.[133]

Additionally, Root[134] argues, that practical theology has relied too heavily on Aristotle's thinking and teleology, it lies behind the frame works of Browning,[135] Anderson[136] and Swinton and Mowat.[137] What he means is that through the Aristotelian framework of *actuality* to *possibility* people reflect on past actions/or present reality with a telos towards new actualities—to create new forms of practice. Yet, although this is helpful for reflection on practice and new forms of action, Root[138] argues that it does not allow enough space for divine action or for the practical theologian to articulate with as much depth and richness the work of

---

125. Swinton and Mowat, *Practical Theology and Qualitative Research*.
126. Root, *Christopraxis*, 100.
127. Swinton and Mowat, *Practical Theology and Qualitative Research*.
128. Root, *Christopraxis*, 114.
129. Anderson, *The Shape of Practical Theology*.
130. Root, *Christopraxis*, 114.
131. Ibid., 117–46.
132. Ibid.
133. Anderson, *The Shape of Practical Theology*.
134. Root, *Christopraxis*, 139.
135. Browning, *A Fundamental Theology*.
136. Anderson, *The Shape of Practical Theology*.
137. Swinton and Mowat, *Practical Theology and Qualitative Research*.
138. Root, *Christopraxis*, 139.

God *and* human agency. This is a salient point, and is addressed in this piece by drawing on the work of Vanhoozer.[139] That said, it is recognized, that the process of reflection adopted draws on the actuality to possibility framework, but at the same time, it sees this framework as a theological tool to interpret the work of God within the practices under investigation. Therefore, the reflective process opens up theological enquiry, intentionally investigating, exploring and seeing where divine action is in play. To excavate and interpret the lived experience of youth ministry as enacted mission, qualitative research is placed in an appropriate cycle of reflection. This is the subject that is examined next.

Qualitative Research and Discourse Analysis within a Theological Hermeneutic

Through the methodology adopted from Swinton and Mowat,[140] qualitative research, the interview and discourse analysis can be used to interpret the practice of youth ministry and the insights generated can lead to a deeper understanding of practice—this is the actuality to possibility framework. This is a hermeneutical and descriptive process, and is important as I seek to articulate the practice and theological expression of the youth ministers, the language within the Resource Guides and the use of words within the worship songs. It is approached with empathy, patience and great care as a place of ministry, and divine communicative action.[141] With this in mind, as explored above,[142] there are tensions between qualitative research and theology, especially around the issues of epistemology and truth which leads to a tension that needs to be resolved. This is done in such a way that the constructivist nature of qualitative research enquiry or the epistemology held within some aspects of discourse analysis does not overwhelm the theological. This is negotiated through conducting research within a theological hermeneutic and by placing qualitative research within an appropriate cycle of reflection. An outline of how this hermeneutical journey structures this book is given below.[143]

---

139. Vanhoozer, *Remythologizing Theology*.
140. Swinton and Mowat, *Practical Theology and Qualitative Research*.
141. Vanhoozer, *Remythologizing Theology*.
142. Swinton and Mowat, *Practical Theology and Qualitative Research*, 73
143. Ibid., 26, 94–96. See that qualitative research has the potential to be faithful

Developing a Narrative and Discursive Approach to Exploring Practice

Stories are important and we live by narratives. Vanhoozer,[144] argues that we are part of a theological drama, a theological story—through which we join in with God's communicative action. Walker[145] argues that we are storytellers of a grand narrative. In this work, a mixed methods approach has been adopted involving narrative and discourse analysis. Firstly, the telling of stories by the youth ministers formed an epistemology through narrative and as Swinton and Mowat[146] argue, the telling of stories and the accurate recording, transcription and analysis of this data forms the heart of the qualitative research enterprise. Furthermore, this is investigated by placing qualitative research and the interview in an appropriate cycle of reflection and is held within the practical theological hermeneutic adopted from Swinton and Mowat.[147] This facilitates theological reflection on the embodied acts of mission by the youth ministry practitioners. The results of this are essentially a descriptive and exploratory study, rather

and illuminating in providing a rich and deeper understanding of Christian practice that is derived from empirical enquiry. There are differences between quantitative and qualitative research that highlight why qualitative research is more suitable for answering the research question. This is a well-rehearsed debate. For the difference between quantitative and qualitative research see ibid., 73.

Qualitative research enables the researcher to explore the social world in an attempt to access and understand the ways that individuals and communities inhabit it. It searches for meaning in specific situations and social contexts where subjectivity is valued. It involves an inductive approach, often utilizing small groups with intensive research, with data captured through observation, participant observation and interviews from which a detailed description of events can emerge. Here, qualitative research becomes, not a quest for objectivity, but for meaning, a deeper and richer understanding of situations. Furthermore, Swinton and Mowat, *Practical Theology and Qualitative Research*, 47, see that doubts over generalization can be alleviated, if we think in terms of identification and resonance. This means that, whilst a qualitative research project may not be immediately transferable, there should be a degree of identification and resonance with others working in similar circumstances which may not be identical, but hold enough similarity to create a potentially transformative resonance. Thus, generalization is not a goal for qualitative research; however, the data captured and produced can frequently have implications beyond the immediacy of the research context. There is a tension here that needs to be acknowledged between the purposive sampling method adopted and the generalization of the data.

144. Vanhoozer, *Remythologizing Theology*.
145. Walker, *Telling the Story*.
146. Swinton and Mowat, *Practical Theology and Qualitative Research*, 38.
147. Ibid.

than a hypothesis-testing one. It follows an inductive rather than deductive approach[148] and the outcome of this is a thick[149] description of the enacted and lived faith of the youth ministers being studied. The selection of the participants followed a Purposive Sampling[150] approach and the data gathered from the interview, the start of the analytical process, is further analyzed through Narrative Analysis founded on the work of Riessman.[151]

This method of narrative analysis, shaped and formed the foundations for the data analysis. To investigate the actions and practice of the youth ministers and their meaning, required the investigation of themes that are developed, and found in the stories told by the youth ministry practitioners. Here, the informal interview questions formed the frame, and the stories told provide the color, texture and form of the theological picture. The use of stories is important in the methodology as it gives an immediate response to the interview questions and reveals an embedded theological position. This is because it eliminates, at least in part, the participants giving what is thought to be the correct and right theological answer. This enabled and revealed a deeper and more real theological expression amongst the messiness and realities of practice. Therefore, as Riessman[152] argues, stories tell us not only about past actions but also, importantly for this study, how individuals understand those actions and their meaning. As a mode of analysis, I then identified segments of the stories that held together the relevant themes. By studying the sequence of stories in an interview, and the thematic and linguistic connections between them, it could be identified how the individual youth ministers tied together significant events within their practice. It is the discovery of particular events, stories and practice of how the youth ministers enacted mission amongst young people. This led to key words, themes and ideas that capture the essence of the enacted mission in relation to their stories of practice. The themes and linguistic connections made across the

---

148. Christie, *Ordinary Christology*, 12 sees all empirical research is a conscious process of comparing and evaluating and contains inductive as well deductive moments and the inductive and deductive methods of research do not exclude each other rather they make room for each other.

149. Geertz, *Interpretation of Cultures*, 5–6, 9–10 a "thick description" of a human behavior is a detailed and thorough exploration that seeks to investigate and explain not just human behavior, but its context as well, so the behavior becomes meaningful.

150. Cohen et al., *Research Methods in Education*, 115.

151. Riessman, *Narrative Analysis*.

152. Ibid.

stories, act as heuristic devices of discovery.[153] The exploration of lived practice is important, for, as Moschella[154] sees, theology and practice are an intertwined phenomena and it is possible to study practices in the hope of being able to read and see the theology they enact and evoke as well as the values they suggest. As analysis of the stories[155] was undertaken, the themes found in and developed from the data were explored. Here, relationships, like Jesus, being there and time and journey are the theological shorthand expression of the complexity of practice and articulate the idea that relationships function as communicative acts.[156]

Secondly, discourse analysis is converted and adopted into the theological task through the framework of critical faithfulness drawn from Swinton and Mowat.[157] Critical faithfulness facilitates theological reflection on the chosen songs and Biblical material found in the Resource Guides without discourse analysis overwhelming the theological task. Discourse analysis is based on the understanding that there is much more going on when people communicate than simply the transfer of information. It is not an effort to capture literal meanings; rather it is the investigation of what language does, what individuals or cultures accomplish through language. This area of study raises questions about how theological meaning is constructed. In a useful distinction, Gee[158] describes the differences between discourses with a lowercase "d" and discourses with an uppercase "D." For Gee, lowercase "d" discourses are invoked in localized settings and may pertain to the isolated context where the discourse is being shared. On the other hand, uppercase "D" discourses are integral parts of the culture in which they are used, and can be found across diverse texts. While the same text may have both lowercase and uppercase "ds," the functions of those discourses are different and their analysis is treated differently. This theological study falls

153. Coffey and Atkinson, *Making Sense of Qualitative Data*, 30.

154. Moschella, *Ethnography as Pastoral Practice*, 49.

155. The exploration and description of someone else's practice and theology is a hermeneutical process, as Christie (*Ordinary Christology*, 14) sees. It involves the theological presuppositions of the researcher and this theology becomes the "lens" through which they view the practice and theology of others.

156. Habermas also uses this term (communicative action) in relation to human interaction, relating this to rationality. For Habermas this rationality is inherent in language, however, in the lives of the youth ministers communicative action moves beyond language to lived action and practice.

157. Swinton and Mowat, *Practical Theology and Qualitative Research*, 91.

158. Gee, *Introduction to Discourse Analysis*.

into Gee's lowercase "d" discourse and in particular within critical discourse analysis (CDA). Wetherell et al.,[159] argue that it is not possible to isolate only one philosophical tradition or epistemology that informs the study of discourse. Therefore, this study is illuminated through the philosophical enquiry of MacIntyre[160] and the theological frameworks of Hauerwas,[161] Ward,[162] and Vanhoozer.[163] These authors act as the voice of formal theology.[164]

This is an insider piece of research. I'm involved in the training of youth ministers, before this I was a volunteer and then a full-time youth minister so I inhabit the youth ministry world. I have been a subscriber to *Youthwork* magazine from which the ready to use meeting guides are drawn from and I participated within the worship event over a period of two years (two weekends). I was present in the worship when the songs were sung, field notes were taken on the songs and how they were used in context during the event. This study has limited generalizability, but strong transferable resonance.[165] Crucially, through Critical Discourse Analysis the Biblical material and the songs are analyzed in reference to themselves, seeing how key words have theological meaning within the structure of the Resource Guides and songs.

With this in mind, it is important to note that exploring someone else's practice and theology is a hermeneutical process, as Christie[166] sees. It involves the theological presuppositions of the researcher and this theology becomes the lens through which they view the practice and theology of others. As Astley[167] argues "in describing your theology I am implicitly engaged in a conversation between my theology and yours, at least to some extent. My perspective influences what comes to my attention as I listen to you talk about your practice and faith." Therefore, as Christie[168] sees, the personal religious and cultural history of the researcher, including their theological presuppositions, commitments and

159. Wetherell et al., *Discourse as Data*, 5.
160. MacIntyre, *After Virtue*.
161. Hauerwas, *The Peaceable Kingdom*.
162. Ward, *Participation and Mediation*.
163. Vanhoozer, *Remythologizing Theology*.
164. Cameron et al., *Talking about God in Practice*.
165. Swinton and Mowat, *Practical Theology and Qualitative Research*, 47.
166. Christie, *Ordinary Christology*, 14.
167. Astley, *Ordinary Theology*, 15.
168. Christie, *Ordinary Christology*, 15.

preoccupations are all relevant to what they hear and interpret in the conversations with the research subjects. These personal characteristics form the interpretative paradigm which contains the researcher's epistemological, ontological and methodological premise.[169] This set of beliefs guides the researcher in action. Therefore, the involvement of the researcher is a very necessary and constructive dimension of the interpretive process and forms an integral part of the theological hermeneutic. Within this research, as the enacted practice and the voices of the youth ministers are interpreted, I am able to listen and paint a theological picture that is an interpretation of their embodied practice because of my involvement and experience within the discipline of youth ministry. All of this is guided and interpreted by my own Christian convictions and theological presuppositions, of which I can be aware, but cannot step beyond. It is worth declaring that my interpretive paradigm is in line with the broader Canonical Narrative Theology within which this research sits.

Therefore, the idea of narrative can be used as a framework to help explore the lived experience and voices of the youth ministry practitioners through narratives of practice. The idea of narrative has a long history within practical theology, as Graham et al.[170] argue. Ballard and Pritchard[171] see how narrative can be used within a theological hermeneutic of reflection, by using the fundamental category of narrative which is the primary language of human experience, the process of hermeneutical reflection is able to tap into some of the richest insights available; this resonates with the adopted approach. As Swinton and Mowat[172] argue, the telling of stories and the accurate recording, transcription and analysis of this data forms the heart of the qualitative research enterprise. As Punch[173] sees, there is a storied character to much qualitative data. Thinking about the stories can enable us to think creatively about collecting and interpreting data. This enables us to provide a narrative context which is valuable in studying lives and lived experience. This approach to narratives within qualitative research can give a uniquely rich and subtle understanding of life situations which is ideally suited to this research as relationships as communicative acts are explored. Therefore, through exploring practice as narrative, it is possible to argue that each

---

169. Lincoln and Guba, *Naturalistic Enquiry*.
170. Graham et al., *Theological Reflection*, 47–109.
171. Ballard and Pritchard, *Practical Theology in Action*, 128.
172. Swinton and Mowat, *Practical Theology and Qualitative Research*, 38.
173. Punch, *Introduction to Social Research*, 217.

story described, each experience recorded, reveals a different perspective on the particular reality that is being investigated.[174] As the experiences and voices of the practitioners are explored and as narratives of practice are developed, these stories and lived experiences, taken together, lead to a closer approximation of what the reality of practice looks like. Interpretations of these stories and enacted mission told by the practitioners, through relationships as communicative acts and the theological shorthand expression of these, are maps of reality which the youth ministers use to interpret and navigate their experience. The use of stories is important in the methodology as it gives an immediate response to the interview questions and reveals an embedded theological position. This enabled and revealed a deeper and more real theological expression amongst the messiness and realities of practice.

Swinton and Mowat[175] propose a framework which will bring together the things that have been discussed. They create a four-stage interrelated model which is based on the pastoral cycle. This finds its origins in the work of Browning[176] and is helpful in locating the place and function of qualitative research within a theological hermeneutic. This framework is adopted, but it has been adapted to suit the research question.

Stage One

As mentioned above, the starting point for this study derives from my experience of professional practice with a desire to explore the lived experience of youth ministers in their enacted mission amongst young people not connected to church. Furthermore, the research explores the notion of theological shorthand within this, within the Resource Guides, and the theological expression of language within a number of worship songs. To trace how the centrality of relationships within youth ministry has developed the evangelical tradition is examined in chapter 3.

Stage Two

In this phase, qualitative research has been adopted to develop narratives of practice. Through the interview, the stories of actual enacted mission

---

174. Swinton and Mowat, *Practical Theology and Qualitative Research*, 36.
175. Ibid., 94.
176. Browning, *A Fundamental Theology*.

amongst young people are collected. This begins a disciplined and patient investigation, a slowing down of the various dynamics that are taking place within current youth ministry practice. As this is explored, and the voices heard, a process of analysis begins to develop, forming a deep and rich understanding of the complex dynamics of each situation, thus creating narratives of practice. Through engaging with the complexities of these narratives of practice, new insights about their structure and nature begin to appear. Some of this confirmed initial, intuitive reflections, but new ideas and thoughts emerged from the data that challenged and enhanced what is known about youth ministry as enacted mission. The data is explored and presented in chapters 4 and 5. As the data is explored, relationships are affirmed as an overarching theme expressed by the practitioners. These function as communicative acts and can be seen as theological shorthand. Furthermore, the theological shorthand expressed in these narratives of practice, can also be seen within the Resource Guides and worship songs under investigation, operating as fragments and thin theology, this is explored in chapter 7.

Stage Three

In chapter 6, the data analysis continues, as the narratives of practice are brought into conversation with the youth ministry literature. This explores further the idea of relationships as communicative acts and the resonance of this through the literature. Current youth ministry practice can be seen to be guided by the normative voice and expression of relationships that is articulated through the literature on youth ministry. This discussion is framed through the work of *Youth A Part*,[177] Ward,[178] Borgman,[179] Green and Christian,[180] Dean,[181] Sudworth et al.,[182] Root,[183] Savage et al.,[184] and Pimlott and Pimlott.[185] Following Swinton and Mowat,[186] this analysis is

---

177. Church of England Board of Education, *Youth A Part*.
178. Ward, *Youthwork*.
179. Borgman, *When Kumbaya Is Not Enough*.
180. Green and Christian, *Accompanying*.
181. Dean, *Practicing Passion*.
182. Sudworth et al., *Mission Shaped Youth*.
183. Root, *Revisiting Relational Youth Ministry*.
184. Savage et al., *Making Sense of Generation Y*.
185. Pimlott and Pimlott, *Youth Work after Christendom*.
186. Swinton and Mowat, *Practical Theology and Qualitative Research*.

undertaken within the theological hermeneutic that has been adopted. Therefore, to situate this within a theological methodology requires a focused stage of theological reflection. As Swinton and Mowat[187] see, theology has not been absent, but here, reflection is more intentional and carried out in a more formal manner. Here, through this further stage of analysis, it can be seen how the literature has shaped current practice and this leads to critique the limits of this. Chapter 7 continues the analysis of theological shorthand by examining the fragments and thin theological expression within the Resource Guides and the theological expression found with a number of contemporary worship songs. This is carried out through discourse analysis and it augments and begins to paint a picture of the wider use of theological shorthand found within the arena of youth ministry.

Stage Four

In chapters 8 and 9, the insights from the data (chapter 5) and the further analysis of the data (chapter 6), the analysis of the Biblical material and the language of the worship songs (chapter 7) are drawn together and brought into conversation with the literature on the Trinity. This adds another level of analysis and Trinitarian theology acts as a normative voice in seeking to serve and critique enacted youth ministry practice and add richness and insight to the analysis of the Biblical material and the theology within the songs. Yet, for the Trinity to provide a normative voice for this practice, the differing ideas around the *perichoresis* and the Trinitarian discussions require critique—this is the process of developing theological literacy.

Here, in critical conversation with Moltmann,[188] Kilby,[189] Fiddes,[190] and Vanhoozer[191] the overarching theme from the data of relationships as communicative acts, and the theological shorthand discovered within the Resource Guides and the language within the songs is reimagined. This begins to move practice that is expressed and seen as theological shorthand, to practice that can be more authentic and faithful to the Gospel. This is primarily achieved by locating this in God's divine authorship and

187. Ibid., 96.
188. Moltmann, *The Trinity and the Kingdom of God*.
189. Kilby, "Perichoresis and Projection."
190. Fiddes, *Participating in God*.
191. Vanhoozer, *Remythologizing Theology*.

communicative action through the work of Vanhoozer.[192] This stage is augmented as youth ministry can start to be reimagined, seeing how the art of theodramatic dialogical reflection can help use the words seen as theological shorthand and fragments can act as icons of epistemology via the development of intellectual virtues. This process deepens theological literacy and facilitates youth ministers as dialogical guides. In chapter 10 these discussions continue and the implications for the arguments of this book are noted and explored.

This process is important in facilitating theological reflection on the different elements of practice under investigation and this chapter has considered the question: Where is theology? The discussion has focused on the lived, enacted and performed nature of this. As this has been explored, the chapter has set out a practical theological methodology that correlates the voices of the practitioners, the youth ministry literature, the analysis of the Resource Guides and the songs and it has argued for the normative voice of Trinitarian theology. To do this, qualitative research and discourse analysis has been accommodated within a theological hermeneutic and situated within an appropriate cycle of reflection. This shapes the hermeneutical journey of this book.

The next chapter explores the shape of Christian practices and sets up how theology, through the work of Vanhoozer,[193] provides the normative voice for practice. Furthermore, it is argued that a contemporary understandings of youth ministry, as seen in the data, collapses the traditional Christian practices of *kerygma*, *diakonia* and *marturia* into the relational. Therefore, the pivotal place of relationships within the evangelical tradition is investigated and how these act as the central place of mediation and transmission is analyzed.

---

192. Ibid.
193. Ibid.

Chapter 3

Christian Practices and the Mediation of the Evangelical Tradition

Youth Ministry and Christian Practices

Rublev's icon is focused around the bowl and the table. The table takes center stage, it is both the place of Abraham's hospitality to the angels and a picture of God's openness and hospitality to us. This ambiguity and mystery lies at the heart of communion and at the center of worship. It is a liminal space that is open to us as we participate in what God is doing. This liminal space is important in the practice of the youth ministers interviewed, but this does not take place within the practice of communion, or within the walls of a church, but in the practice of relationships. As the youth ministers spoke about their work amongst young people the traditional practices of *diakonia*, *kerygma* and *koinonia* are collapsed into relationships—relationships become a new practice that is guided by the literature on youth ministry. Yet, to explore how Trinitarian theology can act as the normative voice of practice, rather than the youth ministry literature, the relationship between theology and practice needs to be considered.

Before this is investigated, it is important to note the difference between ontology and epistemology. This can be illuminated via critical realism. Although this study does not adopt this philosophy, it is helpful in distinguishing the difference between ontology and epistemology. Critical realism is made up of ontological realism, epistemic relativism, and judgmental rationality.[1] Ontological realism acknowledges that

---

1. Wright, *Critical Realism*, 10–13.

there is difference between knowledge and the real, so objects exist and events occur in reality whether we are aware of them or not. Therefore, a distinction can be made between ontology and epistemology and once this is established it becomes possible to create a rich description and account of the shape and contours of reality. Because ontology has primacy over epistemology, because reality precedes the knowledge of that reality, our knowledge is always epistemologically relative. Therefore, epistemic relativism resist both the certainty of the enlightenment and the skepticism of postmodernity.

Therefore, as Ward[2] sees via Wright[3] the affirmation of epistemic relativism acknowledges the limits and fragility of our knowledge, but does not deny or remove either the actuality of genuine knowledge or the possibility of establishing better knowledge in the future. Moreover, judgmental rationality sees that not all accounts of reality are the same, indeed, one is required to make reasoned judgments about and between different expressions of knowledge. For Wright[4] "the priority of ontology means that we must adapt our epistemic tools in response to the objective demands of reality, rather than adjust reality to bring it into conformity with our epistemic tools." It means within critical realism that there are no secure foundations for knowledge (enlightenment certainties) but the possibilities for reasoned rational discussion are essential and necessary (avoiding postmodern skepticism).

The Normative Voice of Theology in Serving and Critiquing Practice

This debate is vital for thinking about the normative place of theology within practice. It essentially means that the Trinitarian theology, through the work of Vanhoozer, is offered as a normative voice in a rational discussion, not necessarily to be used as a theological blueprint,[5] but as a provisional guide to help illuminate our way, a way of developing theological literacy. Therefore, the objective reality of God is not denied, but it is recognized that this is just one way to talk about the knowledge

---

2. Ward, *Liquid Ecclesiology*, 22.
3. Wright, *Critical Realism*, 13.
4. Ibid.
5. Ward, "Blueprint Ecclesiology," 11.

of God and it is offered in the awareness that Vanhoozer's[6] theology is a robust and rigorous framework that relates well to Canonical theology.[7]

With this in mind, historically, practical theology has tended to focus on the techniques of the church rather than their theological content and intent. Within this understanding the term practice is related first and foremost to particular technical procedures which ministers must learn in order to minister effectively. This forms the basis for the applied model of practical theology, as Ballard and Pritchard[8] note. Swinton and Mowat[9] continue, that the applied model of practical theology is when Biblical studies, historical and philosophical studies are taken by the practical theologian and used to develop techniques for ministry. Here the task is simply to apply doctrine worked out by other theological disciplines to practical situations. Within this understanding, it is assumed that practice is something that individuals do to one another. The individual and the action carried out may not have any connection with the wider community or the social and historical context within which the practice emerges. This means that when the effect of the action is understood only as a goal and end to itself, as a function, practices can become dislocated from their historical and theological roots, becoming a partial expression of their true meaning and purpose. This is important as it finds expression in the data in this research as theological shorthand, it reverberates as fragmented theology through the literature on youth ministry, and it is also seen in the Resource Guides and worships songs as theology is short circuited.

As the question about the normative voice of theology is explored, Cahlan[10] raises a note of caution, seeing that when doctrine is used in inappropriate ways it can diminish dialogue, questioning and experience, and if presented inappropriately, doctrine can lack historical perspective and be over rational. Furthermore, as Ward[11] argues, there is a sense of ambiguity about the process and how theology and doctrine are used that needs to be acknowledged. Expanding on this, Ward[12] argues that "God

---

6. Vanhoozer, *Remythologizing Theology*.
7. I recognize the tensions between canonical theology and critical realism.
8. Ballard and Pritchard, *Practical Theology in Action*, 58–59.
9. Swinton and Mowat, *Practical Theology and Qualitative Research*, 17.
10. Cahlan, "Introducing Ministry," 107.
11. Ward, "Blueprint Ecclesiology," 10.
12. Ibid.

is who God is in Jesus Christ," however, it is the theologian's attempts to express and make sense of what has been revealed that gives rise to perilousness and ambiguity. Therefore, in the talk about God and the place of theology in serving and critiquing practice, it is important to accept the contingent reality and fragility of language and words as discussed above.

That said, Swinton and Mowat[13] see that tradition and doctrine offer a store house of critical perspectives for contemporary and situated practices; through specific settings practical theology opens a window onto this larger tradition. Thus, theology serves, illuminates, critiquing situations and practices providing clarity and the indispensable core of ideas which animate and bring to life the community's witness of faith. The witness of faith is mediated through Christian practices and a fuller understanding of the term "practice" is provided by Dykstra and Bass.[14] They describe practices that together constitute a way of life. By Christian practices, they mean "things people do together over time to address fundamental human needs in response to and in the light of God's active presence for the life of the world." It is possible to see the reverberation of these ideas in the voices of the practitioners as they articulate practice through the notion of relationships as they work amongst and respond to young people.

As the shape of Christian practices is explored, it is possible to see differing intellectual traditions at work. Within the work of Dykstra and Bass,[15] Swinton and Mowat,[16] and Volf,[17] it is possible to see the influence of the moral philosophy of MacIntyre, as Dykstra and Bass[18] are indebted to MacIntyre's concept of social practices. Also, Swinton and Mowat[19] and Volf[20] use Dykstra and Bass'[21] definition of practice, whilst Tanner[22] and Graham[23] draw on the social theorist Pierre Bourdieu. This is important because MacIntyre's virtue ethics emphasize that practices

---

13. Swinton and Mowat, *Practical Theology and Qualitative Research*.
14. Dykstra and Bass, *A Theological Understanding*, 18.
15. Ibid., 13–32.
16. Swinton and Mowat, *Practical Theology and Qualitative Research*.
17. Volf, "Theology as a Way of Life."
18. Dykstra and Bass, *A Theological Understanding*.
19. Swinton and Mowat, *Practical Theology and Qualitative Research*.
20. Volf, "Theology as a Way of Life."
21. Dykstra and Bass, *A Theological Understanding*.
22. Tanner, "Theological Reflection."
23. Graham et al., *Theological Reflection*.

pursue the good in a traditional way, while social scientists, influenced by Marxist thought, stress the negotiations over power that give particular shape to practices in specific social situations, as seen outworked through Tanner's[24] and Graham's[25] related theological approaches.

Christian Practices and a Way of Life

Dykstra and Bass,[26] argue that Christian practices constitute elements of a way of life that becomes incarnate when human beings live in the light of and in response to God's gift of life; Christian practices have a normative and theological dimension. When participation in such practices occurs, people taking part in God's work of creation and re-creation grow into a deeper understanding of God. Therefore, normatively and theologically understood, Christian practices are the human activities in and through which people co-operate with God in addressing the needs of the other and creation. Root[27] is sympathetic to Dykstra and Bass' view of practice, particularly in how practice itself becomes a means of grace, because our practices are gifts given to humanity—drawing us into divine action. But Root[28] notes, that the outworking of participation within the divine life operates almost completely on the plane of humanity. This allows great opportunity for practices and concrete actions to bring life in its abundance to communities and for these practices to have great theological depth, yet, Root[29] suggests, that it may miss the potential for divine encounters outside the practice itself.

In line with this, Dean[30] sees the word "practice" comes from the Greek root meaning "to do" and "to act"; practices knit us into the long history of Christian "doing" and strengthen us for the active mission that God lays before us. Yet, as Dean argues, practices do not transform us, *grace* does, but practices can be God's multifaceted means of grace in the material world of human interaction. They become conduits of love that enliven and animate our witness.

24. Tanner, "Theological Reflection."
25. Graham et al., *Theological Reflection*.
26. Dykstra and Bass, *A Theological Understanding*, 20–22.
27. Root, *Christopraxis*, 70.
28. Ibid., 70.
29. Ibid., 71.
30. Dean, *Practicing Passion*, 151.

Dean[31] lays out a constellation of classical Christian Practices. The practices in focus for this book are: *marturia*, witnessing to the self-giving love of God in Christ; *koinonia* fellowship and hospitality; *diakonia*, serving and helping others; *kerygma*, proclaiming the love of God and *doxology* worship.[32] These are interwoven, but have distinct elements. Dykstra and Bass[33] argue, that Christian practices can provide a normative understanding of what God wants for us, how we can discern God is at work, and how we are to be faithful and responsive to God's Spirit.[34] This is beneficial when traditional Christian practices are considered (e.g. Communion or Baptism), but is also problematic, because in the data there is a disconnect from more traditional Christian practices. In reality, the traditional practices are collapsed into the relational; furthermore, the theological language used to describe these is fragmented and thin. Therefore, a methodology is being developed in which theology provides the normative voice for shaping practice, recognizing the fragility and contingent reality of this. This is done to illuminate, add richness, depth and color to the practices under investigation. This is an alternative view to the normative role of practice as provided by Dykstra and Bass,[35] Tanner,[36] and Graham.[37]

Volf,[38] who emphasizes a different side of the same concern as Dykstra and Bass[39], argues how theology and beliefs normatively shape Christian practices. By beliefs he means the core Christian doctrines, as the ideational side of the act of faith. Volf[40] recognizes the shaping place of doctrine, but this is different from Cahlan,[41] as doctrine provides the normative voice of theology with which she disagrees. Volf[42] argues that theology should serve practice through its normative dimension, there-

---

31. Ibid., 154.
32. These practices have been chosen because of how they link and interrelate to the themes within the data.
33. Dykstra and Bass, *A Theological Understanding*, 20.
34. Sheppard, "Tryin to Be Christian," 38–42.
35. Dykstra and Bass, *A Theological Understanding*, 20.
36. Tanner, "Theological Reflection."
37. Graham et al., *Theological Reflection*.
38. Volf, "Theology as a Way of Life," 258.
39. Dykstra and Bass, *A Theological Understanding*, 7.
40. Volf, "Theology as a Way of Life," 247.
41. Cahlan and Nieman, "Mapping the Field," 85.
42. Volf, "Theology as a Way of Life," 263.

fore, helping us to see, illuminating, and critiquing specific situations and practices.[43] Ward,[44] would see this as the gravitational pull of the Church that seeks to move towards a blueprint ecclesiology. In contrast, within Swinton and Mowat's[45] approach, primacy is given to Scripture, tradition and revelation in how they provide a normative voice for the faithful performance of the Gospel; in the work of Vanhoozer,[46] this finds explicit expression. At the same time, Swinton and Mowat[47] recognize that the ways in which revelation is interpreted, embodied and worked out are deeply influenced by specific contexts and traditions. These contexts, histories and traditions profoundly impact the types of practices that are developed in response to revelation and how these remain faithful to that revelation. This then is a creative tension between Scripture, doctrine and tradition that leads to a flexible integrity rather than unbending rigidity.[48] In line with this, Jones[49] also sees how doctrine can serve and enrich practices. Jones sees the normative voice of these and argues how doctrine can be an imaginative landscape that serves as the conceptual territory within which Christians stand to get their conceptual bearings on the world and on the reality of God. In this sense, doctrines are imaginative spaces which we occupy—we inhabit them and learn to negotiate the complexities of our living through them.

However, in a similar way to Swinton and Mowat,[50] they are not walled off, but their borders are permeable, yet within them, distinct theological landmarks can be found.[51] Therefore, Jones[52] also sees that doctrines are dramatic scripts which Christians perform, again resonating with Swinton and Mowat.[53] Here, with doctrine as a script, this

43. Osmer, *Practical Theology*, 139–60.
44. Ward, "Blueprint Ecclesiology."
45. Swinton and Mowat, *Practical Theology and Qualitative Research*, 89.
46. Vanhoozer, *Remythologizing Theology*.
47. Swinton and Mowat, *Practical Theology and Qualitative Research*, 89.
48. Pauw, "Attending to the Gaps," 42.
49. Jones, *Graced Practices*, 74–75.
50. Swinton and Mowat, *Practical Theology and Qualitative Research*.
51. Jones, *Graced Practices*, 75. These are the truths found within revelation, such as, "God is the creator of the universe and wills to be in covenant relationship with humanity, but humanity has turned from God in sin. God sent Jesus Christ into the world to redeem humanity from sin and promises the world forgiveness of sins and life eternal."
52. Ibid.
53. Swinton and Mowat, *Practical Theology and Qualitative Research*, 4–5.

unfolding occurs according to ruled patterns of thought and action. Therefore, doctrine provides a scripted code for the motions of the Christian life. This highlights Ward's concerns about blueprint ecclesiologies that collapse the ontological with the epistemological. Yet, doctrines cannot be conceived apart from their relationship to patterned forms of practice because, as imaginative landscapes and dramatic scripts, they are always occupied by the authoring motions of those who live within them, an approach that resonates with Volf's[54] thoughts and with Vanhoozer[55] as part of the divinely authored action; the theodrama.

The Normative Voice of Practice

A different view of normativity is given by Graham.[56] As Graham approaches practices, she argues that issues of normativity should be approached reflexively and not prescriptively, as dialogue and reflection arise out of the practical wisdom of communities; resonating with Ward's[57] thoughts. For Graham,[58] truth and value are not conceived as transcendent realities but as provisional—yet binding, and form strategies of normative action. This is in contrast to Swinton and Mowat,[59] Anderson,[60] Volf,[61] Dykstra and Bass,[62] Cahlan,[63] Jones,[64] and Vanhoozer.[65] In Graham's[66] approach, Osmer[67] argues that normativity means that the idea of "transforming practice"[68] is pivotal because it becomes the

54. Volf, "Theology as a Way of Life."
55. Vanhoozer, *Remythologizing Theology*.
56. Graham, *Transforming Practice*, 6–7.
57. Ward, "Blueprint Ecclesiology."
58. Graham, *Transforming Practice*.
59. Swinton and Mowat, *Practical Theology and Qualitative Research*.
60. Anderson, *The Shape of Practical Theology*.
61. Volf, "Theology as a Way of Life."
62. Dykstra and Bass, *A Theological Understanding*.
63. Cahlan, "Introducing Ministry," 107.
64. Jones, *Graced Practices*.
65. Vanhoozer, *Remythologizing Theology*.
66. Graham, *Transforming Practice*, 205–7.
67. Osmer, *Practical Theology*, 159.
68. Graham, *Transforming Practice*, 7, sees "practice" as the place of transformative action and the place of divine activity. Related to both of these, we can see in existing practices new forms of practice that may challenge and critique the received tradition.

generative source of new knowledge, values and social patterns.[69] Graham[70] argues primarily that the point of "transforming practice" is to disclose God. In this, the faith community, through its practices, becomes a way of enacting and naming the divine presence in the world. Therefore, the faith community becomes the medium, symbol, model and witness of such transcendence, an idea that finds resonance with Tillich,[71] Ward,[72] in the voices of the practitioners and in the literature on youth ministry. Furthermore, Graham's[73] approach locates itself as the "critical inquiry into the validity of Christian Witness." It, therefore, opens up the study of the whole mission of the church as expressed within the diversity of its practices as the church seeks to communicate and mediate faith. For practice to become transformative, Graham[74] sees that this involves searching for ways of enacting and performing consistently and authentically a tradition of values. These recognize their own contingency but, at the same time, seek to create new forms of practice that still have some degree of discipline, transparency and coherence. Osmer[75] sees that it means theology must find new ways of developing truth claims and values that will be persuasive to a skeptical, postmodern world, an idea that chimes with the critical realist approach put forward by Ward[76] and Wright.[77]

Graham's[78] thinking is both important and problematic. It is important, because it takes context and the lived experience seriously. Yet, it is also particularly problematic, because Graham[79] discounts the normative function of Scripture as the primary foundation for the formation of a

69. Within this, she offers three criteria with which to guide and assess transforming practice in the church. Firstly, does this contribute to human liberation as an expression of the Christian commitment to love and freedom? Secondly, does this attend to women's experience without essentializing this? Thirdly, does this support a reflexive consolidation of practical wisdom that emerges out of practice, which is held within a commitment to alterity?

70. Graham, *Transforming Practice*, 205–7.
71. Tillich, *Dynamics of Faith*.
72. Ward, "Blueprint Ecclesiology."
73. Graham, *Transforming Practice*.
74. Ibid., 112.
75. Osmer, *Practical Theology*, 154.
76. Ward, *Liquid Ecclesiology*, 22.
77. Wright, *Critical Realism*.
78. Graham, *Transforming Practice*.
79. Ibid., 7.

community of faith and practice. Furthermore, she seems to take into account but then discounts the value of the Christian tradition. Moreover, if, as Graham[80] argues, there is no universal and over-arching metaphysical guarantee for principled living—no "god given," as it were, then on what basis is truth constructed and contested, if values are no longer axiomatic and founded upon the grand narrative of history? If this is the case, then what stops a community's practice becoming introspective and self-serving? These questions are partly answered by the critical realist approach put forward by Ward,[81] but by forgoing the notion of blueprint ecclesiology and by resisting the gravitational pull of the church, one is left too far adrift, despite Ward's concept of abiding and relying on "structured feeling"[82]

Furthermore, Pauw[83] who, in contrast to Graham,[84] argues that, in fact, a religious community's best insights into the possibilities and deformity of its beliefs and practices often come from outside, as critical reflection is required in order to unmask the perennial human tendencies of triumphalism and self-description that those within the community may not be aware of and not sufficiently alert to these tendencies within their midst. In addition, Graham's[85] thoughts are again problematic because of the placing of so much emphasis on whether it is possible to speak about the "infinite" and "undetermined world" of God in the language of the "contingent" and "finite" world of practice,[86] a point echoed by Vanhoozer.[87] Subsequently, relating to the argument of Graham's[88] positioning within a post-modern context, concern is expressed that exposure to post-modernism means we are in danger of descending into nihilism. Finally, another problem is that it is possible to see this kind of postmodern practical theology as elevating practice as the guiding criterion of Christian theological identity, as something entirely antinomian, spontaneous and led by the spirit of the age, rather than being rooted

---

80. Ibid.
81. Ward, "Blueprint Ecclesiology."
82. Ibid., 15.
83. Pauw, "Attending to the Gaps," 43.
84. Graham, *Transforming Practice*.
85. Ibid.
86. Graham et al., *Theological Reflection*, 195.
87. Vanhoozer, *Remythologizing Theology*.
88. Graham, *Transforming Practice*.

in Christian revelation and tradition.[89] As Root[90] sees, a problem with postmodern Bourdieuian practical theologies, is that knowing about God is conflated to the cultural and held within the cultural expression of practice. Root[91] continues, that a well-developed practical theology should attend deeply to the human through the incarnational humanity of Christ but also search for the otherness, the divine, that stands outside of the cultural in the person of Jesus.

That said, Graham[92] argues that the proper focus of practical theology is not the pastoral agent, or theological ethics, or applied theology, but the practice of the faith community itself, an important point as the enacted practice of the youth ministers is investigated. Graham[93] sees that, by focusing on the reality of practice, we are able to recognize that theory and practice do not exist independently. Here, she follows Browning[94] to see that the arena of Christian praxis is value-directed and theory-laden action. This idea is pushed further as the medium through which the Christian community embodies and enacts its vision of the Gospel. Here theology is conceived as an enacted performed discipline in which the criterion of authenticity is deemed to be "orthopraxis" or authentic transformative action, rather than just orthodoxy (right belief).[95] As the theological shorthand expression of relationships is explored, this distinction is important. The practice of the youth ministers has a focus on right action (orthopraxis), on performing a function, on relationships, on being like Jesus, and being there for young people. This evokes and has a connection to deeper set of "right" beliefs (orthodoxy) from the Christian tradition, but this is only partially expressed through the language of theological shorthand and is at risk of drifting away from the grand narrative.[96]

89. Graham et al., *Theological Reflection*, 198.
90. Root, *Christopraxis*, 65.
91. Ibid.
92. Graham, *Transforming Practice*.
93. Ibid., 7.
94. However, Graham is critical of Browning's emphasis within practical theology as the production of ethical perspectives derived from the practice of communities. Rather, she seeks to interpret the contingent and enacted nature of theology that is located within the practice of communities. Within this, she argues, it is possible to capture glimpses of divine activity amidst human practice.
95. Chung, *Struggle to be the Sun*.
96. Walker, *Telling the Story*.

Developing the ideas of orthopraxis and orthodoxy, Volf[97] recognizes the normative place of beliefs and doctrine in shaping practice, yet, he also sees that engaging in practices can lead to acceptance and a deeper understanding of these beliefs and that these lead to transformation. Volf[98] argues, engagement in practices helps us to see how core beliefs and doctrines are to be understood and critiqued as Christians live in ever changing situations. This is because beliefs are always held in situational and contextual rendered forms, a point echoed by Swinton and Mowat.[99] Moreover, as we have seen, it is possible to suggest, at least in part, that even when given logical priority, theology itself can be the subject of critical reflection and challenge.[100] This is important, but as Volf[101] argues, the whole way of life with all its practices is supported and shaped by something outside of this way of life—by what God has done, is doing and will do. Therefore, more than just normatively guiding practices, Christian doctrines narrate the divine actions by which humanity is constituted as agents of practices, a point that connects and runs like a thread through Vanhoozer's[102] theology.

Therefore, as Swinton and Mowat[103] argue, the practical theological task is the quest for truth and the development and maintenance of faithful and transformative practices that enable the church to perform faithfully to the Gospel as it participates in God's Triune mission to the world. This echoes Anderson's,[104] Vanhoozer's[105] and Root's[106] work, placing the on-going activity of practical theology in the on-going activity of God. It differs from Graham,[107] as it locates truth and value as transcendent realities that go beyond that of culturally bound practice.

---

97. Volf, "Theology as a Way of Life," 258.
98. Ibid.
99. Swinton and Mowat, *Practical Theology and Qualitative Research*, 90.
100. Ibid.
101. Volf, "Theology as a Way of Life," 254.
102. Vanhoozer, *Remythologizing Theology*.
103. Swinton and Mowat, *Practical Theology and Qualitative Research*, 25.
104. Anderson, *The Shape of Practical Theology*.
105. Vanhoozer, *Remythologizing Theology*.
106. Root, *Christopraxis*.
107. Graham, *Transforming Practice*.

The Fluid Shape of Practice

An alternative view for the place of Christian practice is provided by Tanner.[108] This differs from Volf[109] and Jones,[110] but resonates with the normative nature of practice as seen through Dykstra and Bass.[111] Tanner[112] sees that theology is important in everyday Christian life. For Tanner, theological inquiry is forced by the vagaries of Christian practices themselves, and is, therefore and consequently, a necessary part of their ordinary function. What this means is that theological reflection does not merely come to Christian practices from the outside, as articulated through Volf's[113] and Jones'[114] approach, but arises within the ordinary workings of Christian lives to meet pressing practical needs. For Tanner,[115] and here she differs from Dykstra and Bass,[116] Christian practices do not require much explicit understanding from believers to inform and explain their performance, neither do they require much agreement from the participants, and often Christian practices are open-ended rather than undefined.

Therefore, for Tanner,[117] through engagement in a critical and reflective way with Christian practice, we are called to be active witnesses to what God has done for us in Christ and to be active disciples. Being witnesses means, through effort-filled deliberation, we can understand what Christianity stands for in our own lives and for our own time and circumstances. It is not simply an immersion in established practices. However, this requires the ever-renewed and renewing of personal and church-specific decisions about how to deepen insights which come through the way of Christian practices and how to make into a coherent whole the various things we believe and how we act as Christians. Moreover, it includes how we are to interact and interrelate with the wider

---

108. Tanner, "Theological Reflection."
109. Volf, "Theology as a Way of Life."
110. Jones, *Graced Practices*.
111. Dykstra and Bass, *A Theological Understanding*.
112. Tanner, "Theological Reflection," 228.
113. Volf, "Theology as a Way of Life."
114. Jones, *Graced Practices*.
115. Tanner, "Theological Reflection," 229–30
116. Dykstra and Bass, *A Theological Understanding*.
117. Tanner, "Theological Reflection," 233.

changing world. Tanner[118] sees Christian practices as the way in which communities of faith define themselves as Christian. This is through both historic Christian practices, as seen in the thoughts of Dykstra and Bass,[119] and seeing practices that bring about a new purpose and direction for a Christian community. This leads Tanner[120] to see how Christian communities are more open to interpreting how practices should be done in pursuit of God's praxis, rather than being dependent on engaging in certain actions in certain ways.

For Tanner,[121] this leads to a fluid and flexible perception of Christian practices, accommodating both the reality of the messiness of the social organizational life and engaging in acts that are significant and historically meaningful. Within such a community, theological reflection becomes central and this means that rather than adopting an "internal property" of practices, Christian practices become meaning-making and distinct in the way that Christians understand and act in their activity and relation to the world. Tanner's[122] thoughts are important, because she does not discount the place of historical practices but opens and widens these to the scope of empirical enquiry that have the possibility for new forms of practice, rather than towards specific historical reinterpretations. Therefore, as the voices of the practitioners are explored through narratives of practice, we can see when relationships that function as communicative acts are held within God's communicative action, as seen through the work of Vanhoozer,[123] they can be adopted as an authentic contemporary practice undergirded and guided by the rigorous thought of both tradition and theology. Relationships move from being guided by the normative voice of the literature on youth ministry, to being guided by the normative voice of Trinitarian theology as communicative action; they move from not *only* having a focus on orthopraxis, but this practice can be informed and enriched by the wider Christian tradition. Furthermore, the language used within the narratives of practice (like Jesus, relationships, being there and time and journey) and the theological shorthand and fragments discovered in the Resource Guides and wor-

---

118. Ibid., 30.
119. Dykstra and Bass, *A Theological Understanding*, 18.
120. Tanner, "Theological Reflection," 230–33.
121. Ibid, 233.
122. Tanner, "Theological Reflection."
123. Vanhoozer, *Remythologizing Theology*.

ship songs can act as icons of epistemology, as windows into a deeper world that can be explored in relation to orthodoxy. This will be explored in chapters 8 and 9, but now it is time to consider the place of mediation within the evangelical tradition.

Mediation and the Evangelical Tradition

As the place of theology and Christian practices have been explored, it has begun to be argued that relationships have become a new practice within youth ministry. These have collapsed the traditional practices of *diakonia, marturia* and *kerygma* into the relational. This will be explored in more detail in below, but before this, the place of relationships within the evangelical tradition needs to be investigated. As will be seen, the relationships of the youth ministers with young people function as conduits of communication, they act as places of mediation. In their relationships with young people youth minsters are acting as communicative acts; they mediate their care, concern, and Christian witness to young people by being there. This rich and complex practice is expressed simply through the theological term of relationships, this is theological shorthand in action. Furthermore, as has been noted, current youth ministry practice can be seen to be guided by the normative voice and expression of relationships that is articulated through the literature on youth ministry, this is explored in more detail in Chapter 6. Therefore, it is possible to see relationships as a construct, a practice that is supported by the discourse on relationships within the youth ministry literature, relationships are meaningful and meaning making, they are the medium and at least in part, the message.[124]

This rotates and pivots around the notion of mediation. Mediation, like culture, is a complex and rich term, it can act as an accordion word; you can squeeze in as much or as little meaning as you like. Central to its understanding is the role of an intermediary.[125] The internet is an example of this, allowing communication between people as it acts as mediation and functions as an intermediary. Rublev's icon also functions this way, mediating or communication something about who God is and the story the painting seeks to represent. This is multi-faceted and layered with meaning. For example, you have the composition that fo-

---

124. McLuhan, *The Medium Is the Message*.
125. Ward, *Participation and Mediation*, 107.

cuses on the table—inviting us in, but you also have the colors within the painting. These, through reflection, can communicate or mediate the different characteristics of the Godhead. This is multidimensional, complex, and open to interpretation and construction. The painting acts as an intermediary and a conduit of mediation that has the possibility to open up spaces for meditation. The Holy Spirit, on the right, is wearing a garment of blue, draped and wrapped over a robe of green, suggesting how the Spirit hovers over the waters of creation and breathes life into us and the earth. The Son is clothed in a heavy garment of reddish brown and a cloak of blue, holding the possibility of representing heaven—pulling together heaven and earth, the gold interwoven through the earthly cloth, opening up spaces of imagining, enabling reflection on his divinity in the midst of his humanity. The Father seems to be wearing a mixture of shimmering colors, almost translucent and dancing with light.

Rublev's icon acts as an expression of theological thought. Ward[126] sees that theological transmission is also an expression; it animates the life of the church. He argues that theological writing and publishing have acted to shape academic theology through the transmission of ideas. Theology is also limited by the expression it may take, as limitations act on the text as ideas are communicated; written words can only tell part of the story. In the youth ministers' work amongst young people their practice is shaped by the literature on youth ministry, this is acting as the normative voice, it has taken on the role of formal theology[127] and this voice is louder than the church traditions of which they are part. The youth ministry literature operates as a place of transmission, here ideas about what youth ministry should be like is a process of theological expression. This animation[128] relates to the way that theology, through mediation, finds expression and is set in motion. This process of transmission moves and carries theology, as the circulation of theology is transmitted between people and across distances.

This animation and circulation is not only seen in the youth ministry literature and its transmission of ideas to the youth ministers, but it can also be seen in the construction and mediation of the theology within the worship songs and in the Resource Guides. Therefore, transmission operates as communication and culture, but it also operates as a means of

---

126. Ibid., 110.

127. Cameron et al., *Talking about God in Practice*, 54.

128. Ward, *Participation and Mediation*, 110.

encounter.[129] In the practice of the youth ministers it is through relationships that they open up liminal spaces of encounter amongst the young people they serve. In the worship songs, the songs become narratives of encounter,[130] as the experience of an act of worship mediates God's presence. The medium of the songs act as an active agent in theological animation and transmission, not simply in the circulation of expression but also in determining theology's shape. Yet, through this process of transmission, animation, expression and encounter-fragmentation occurs. This is the process of theological shorthand. It is seen in the youth ministry literature, in the expression of practice by the youth ministers, in the theological transmission of the songs and in the Resource Guides. This fragmentation relates to MacIntyre's[131] thoughts discussed above, but pushes these ideas further as it begins to see what shapes that fragmentation—what leads to the expression of practice, bible reading and worship as theological shorthand. In some sense, this is completely normal, for as theological ideas are transmitted, mediated and animated, there will be change. But a key point is that this is not intentional or is not expressed and seen. It happens by missiological and ecclesiological accident, the youth minister's expression of the complexity of practice through theological shorthand is not recognized, the words used in the worship songs and Resource Guides are not seen as fragmented expressions of a much larger story.

One of the key conduits of mediation and transmission within youth ministry is relationships. These have a long, complex, and rather untidy history within youth ministry in the UK and North America. The transmission and mediation of these ideas between people, across distances and continents has shaped contemporary youth ministry. Therefore, it is now time to turn and consider the place and intermediary role that relationships play within the evangelical tradition as faith and ideas are mediated.

---

129. Ibid.
130. Ward, *Selling Worship*.
131. MacIntyre, *After Virtue*.

The Relational Hermeneutic and the Evangelical Tradition

As the theme of relationships as communicative acts is explored through the voice of the literature (chapter 6), it is possible to locate the literature within the evangelical tradition. Here the influence of the evangelical tradition within the literature and the echoes and resonance of this within the voices of the practitioners can be observed and noted. The work of Young Life is central, because as this organisation developed its work amongst young people the incarnation was adopted as a framework for ministry justification. The incarnation became a pattern for ministry rather than a theological explanation.[132] Furthermore, the incarnation as a model of ministry begins to find its voice in the UK through the work of Ward[133] and in the publication *Youth A Part*.[134] The echoes and resonance of this thinking has infused relational youth ministry in the UK and can be seen through the relational narratives of the youth ministers and their practice amongst young people. This is observed through three interconnected areas: relationalism,[135] plastic hermeneutics,[136] and the mediation of the evangelical tradition.[137] As the data shows, the idea of relationships as communicative acts is central to the participants' expression of mission amongst young people. Relationships can be seen as a central part of evangelicalism and are foundational in its mediation of the Gospel in the UK[138] and North America.[139]

Relationalism

Ward[140] sees relationships as being evident in the CSSM camps run by Eric Nash and the first of these ran in Seaford in 1929. "Bash" camps as they came to be known had an emphasis on the quality of relation-

---

132. Root, *Revisiting Relational Youth Ministry*, 53.
133. Ward, *Youthwork*.
134. Church of England Board of Education, *Youth A Part*, 23–38.
135. Root, *Revisiting Relational Youth Ministry*.
136. Rogers, "Reading Scripture."
137. Ibid.; also Bebbington, *Evangelicalism and Cultural Diffusion*.
138. Ward, *Youthwork*.
139. Root, *Revisiting Relational Youth Ministry*, also Shepherd, *Faith Generation*, 38–42.
140. Ward, *Growing Up Evangelical*, 37–39.

ships with young people that were outworked through "personal work." Root,[141] argues that this emphasis on relationships forms part of the evangelical's cultural tool kit, seeing that evangelicalism has perceived itself as living in unsettled times since the nineteenth century. This resonates with Ward,[142] who argues, that within the UK evangelicals hit upon a "grand strategy."

This "grand strategy" aimed at securing the future for evangelicals by concentrating on building relationships with young people to win "keymen" for Christ. The work amongst young people was promoted by Bishop Taylor Smith who saw young people as a means whereby evangelicals might hold back the liberal offensive. This "grand strategy" had an entrepreneurial spirit that grew out of the work of CSSM, IVF, Crusaders and VPS[143] and Ward[144] sees that this focused on success with the wealthy, educated and middle classes which was evangelicalism's most natural context. Furthermore, this entrepreneurial spirit drove evangelical mission in urban areas. As Ward[145] observes, in the 1950's a generation of evangelicals moved the focus of evangelism from the youth fellowship and the grammar school, to the open youth club as they sought to reach young people within secondary modern schools. This entrepreneurial spirit resonates and echoes throughout the work of Oasis and CYM and these training providers have a focus on relationships as the primary means of reaching young people, not only within church contexts but also beyond the church. This focus on relationships, as Root[146] argues, is enacted as personal influence and reverberates through the literature; *Youth A Part*,[147] Ward,[148] Borgman,[149] Green and Christian,[150] Senter et

---

141. Root, *Revisiting Relational Youth Ministry*, 69–70.

142. Ward, *Growing Up Evangelical*, 45.

143. CSSM was the Children's Special Service Mission, this later became Scripture Union. IVF was the Inter Varsity Fellowship—later called UCCF (Universities and Colleges Christian Fellowship). VPS was the Varsity and Public-School Camps.

144. Ward, *Growing Up Evangelical*, 41.

145. Ibid., 63.

146. Root, *Revisiting Relational Youth Ministry*, 70.

147. Church of England Board of Education, *Youth A Part*.

148. Ward, *Youthwork*.

149. Borgman, *When Kumbaya Is Not Enough*.

150. Green and Christian, *Accompanying*.

al.,[151] Passmore,[152] Sudworth et al.,[153] Dean,[154] Savage et al.,[155] Root,[156] Pimlott and Pimlott,[157] and Shepherd.[158]

Root,[159] by drawing on the work of Smith and Emerson[160] traces this emphasis on relationships within the evangelical tradition to a core and foundational evangelical theology; a theological commitment to a personal relationship with Christ. This relationship is so central that it forms the center of the evangelical universe; it distinguishes them from non-evangelicals and non-Christians and personal relationships guide strategies of engagement across all other structures of culture, whether in family, government or larger society. Therefore, this method is strategic in that it consciously attempts to influence others; it is relational in that it relies on interpersonal relationships as the primary medium of influence. Moreover, through personal connections and positive example, evangelicals believe they can influence others towards the benefits and joys of being in a personal relationship with Jesus. As Ward[161] argues, this idea is also central to the historical nature of youth ministry in urban contexts within the UK and can be seen within the work of the Mayflower in Islington in the early 1960's and especially through the work of George Burton who pioneered this relational style. The development of this work has been documented by Ward,[162] and traces the friction between the wider evangelical tradition and the developing Frontier Youth Trust (FYT). However, within the midst of this tension the incarnation is adopted as a key motif of presence and ministry justification, resonating with the work of Young Life.[163]

---

151. Senter et al., *Four Views of Youth Ministry*.
152. Passmore, *Meet Them Where They're At*.
153. Sudworth et al, *Mission Shaped Youth*.
154. Dean, *Practicing Passion*.
155. Savage et al., *Making Sense of Generation Y*.
156. Root, *Revisiting Relational Youth Ministry*.
157. Pimlott and Pimlott, *Youth Work after Christendom*.
158. Shepherd, *Faith Generation*.
159. Root, *Revisiting Relational Youth Ministry*, 20.
160. Smith and Emerson, *Evangelical*, 188.
161. Ward, *Growing Up Evangelical*, 64.
162. Ibid., 65–77.
163. Root, *Revisiting Relational Youth Ministry*, 70.

The Influence and Reach of Young Life

It is worth pausing here and noting the influence and reach of Young Life. The methodology of Young Life and its adoption of the incarnation and relationships as a key way to mediate and make the Gospel attractive to young people in America has resonance that reaches across time and beyond the shores of America.[164] This is the transmission, animation and mediation of theology between people and across distances that Ward[165] highlights. For Young Life, the incarnation becomes a model for ministry that undergirds all of their work as they seek to embody Christ for young people. For Young Life, relational ministry came from earning the trust of young people through friendship,[166] an idea that runs strongly through Ward's[167] and Passmore's[168] work. Tanis[169] continues, through the foundation laid by Jim Rayburn, Young Life established incarnational theology by building relationships with young people out of love. Here, Rayburn followed the pattern of loving first in order to evangelize later. Relationships functioned as a place of mediation and the incarnation gave them a theological example to copy, it drove the workers of Young Life to be where young people are, it enabled Young Life to penetrate youth subculture.[170] As Tanis[171] sees, Young Life developed this idea of incarnational theology through building relationships in order to mediate and communicate the message of the Gospel into the world of young people. Furthermore, this relational idea becomes central to the doctrinal values of Young Life: "A relationship with Christ is the most important relationship you could have, sin is the sign of a broken relationship with God, through love and discipleship it is experienced more deeply in relationship."[172] Here, relationships become the lens through which all doctrinal understanding take place. What is important here, as Tanis[173]

---

164. Tanis, *Making Jesus Attractive*, 3.
165. Ward, *Participation and Mediation*, 110.
166. Tanis, *Making Jesus Attractive*, 73.
167. Ward, *Youthwork*.
168 Passmore, *Meet Them Where They're At*.
169. Tanis, *Making Jesus Attractive*, 75.
170. Ibid., 76.
171. Ibid.
172. Ibid.
173. Ibid., 150.

sees through the work of Anderson,[174] is that it is actually the praxis of ministry that shapes the beliefs of Young Life. This is then transmitted and mediated back towards doctrinal belief and forms a hermeneutic of relational understanding for practice and for the Christological understanding of ministry; proclaiming Christ as the most important person is a central focus of all Young Life ministry. This concept of incarnation and presence, as seen in Young Life, echoes through the data and is especially seen through the articulation of practice as relationships, like Jesus and being there. Furthermore, these ideas resonate with the theology of the early days of FYT, where links were made between the incarnational language of relationships, presence, the kingdom of God and Shalom. As Ward[175] argues, this was expressed by Jim Punton and was fundamental in helping evangelicals journey into urban mission. Yet, the theological frameworks of the Kingdom of God and Shalom are lost and not articulated in the stories of the youth ministers interviewed. A key reason for this is the influence of the literature on contemporary youth ministry that reverberates with the theology of Young Life and the incarnation as ministry justification.

There are three key points here; firstly, the incarnation as a pattern of youth ministry has been widely adopted and the motif of relationships runs through youth ministry as a foundational way of mediating the Gospel. Secondly, however, the emphasis on the doctrinal side of relationships and the proclamation of Christ is not as clearly articulated—especially in the work of the practitioners. Here, the clear doctrinal roots of Young Life as articulated by Tanis[176] have been replaced by a more overarching theme of presence and being there. Thirdly, the doctrinal articulation by Young life of the Gospel in purely relational terms is articulated in theological shorthand and fragments. The depth and richness of the Gospel story is reduced in order to enable its cultural mediation and transmission. This redaction of the Gospel through the emphasis on Christocentric relationships, Christ's divinity, and his death can be seen to distort the wider Gospel message.[177]

Furthermore, the relational emphasis is not unproblematic; the evangelical relational approach that is advanced in the youth ministry

---

174. Anderson, *The Shape of Practical Theology*.
175. Ward, *Growing Up Evangelical*, 76–77.
176. Tanis, *Making Jesus Attractive*, 76.
177. Perrin, *The Bible Reading of Young Evangelicals*, 78.

literature and within the data can offer a one size fits all approach. Root[178] argues, that because evangelicals view the complex, socially structured world, through the simplifying lens of relationalism, they often offer straight forward and simple solutions to complex multidimensional problems. This resonates with the practitioners as they seek to use relationships to help young people deal with complex problems. Within the expression of youth ministry within the data this simplification can be seen as theological shorthand in action, because the term relationship becomes a straight forward description and the simplification of the complexities of practice.

Evangelicals and Plastic Hermeneutics

The second influence from the evangelical tradition that echoes through the data is the idea of plastic hermeneutics. This is seen in how the youth ministers related their practice to being like Jesus. Rogers,[179] through the work of Malley,[180] argues that evangelical hermeneutics in regard to Biblical interpretation can have a very flexible or plastic[181] conception. Here the tradition presents the text as an object for hermeneutic activity, but the goal of that activity is not so much to establish the exegetical meaning of the text, but to establish transitivity between text and beliefs.

This point is worth considering in more detail because of the implications of the hermeneutical activity on the embodied world of youth ministry. Perrin[182] sees that young evangelicals recognize the gap between the world of the text and their own. Here they focused on seeking to understand the cultural world described within the text, before then exploring theological themes and appropriating principles for their own lives. Sometimes these principles where doctrinal, but more often focused on individual behavior and a polyvalence of such readings (within interpretative limits) appeared perfectly acceptable. Furthermore, Perrin[183] notes, the priority within how young evangelicals read the Bible was how the world in the text related to and played out within the readers' world

---

178. Root, *Revisiting Relational Youth Ministry*, 71.
179. Rogers, "Reading Scripture," 95.
180. Malley, *How the Bible Works*, 73.
181. Rogers applies this term to Malley.
182. Perrin, *The Bible Reading of Young Evangelicals*, 107.
183. Ibid.

and horizon. Perrin[184] argues, that whilst some of her research participants made vague reference to authorship in the New Testament, none recognized or wrestled with the authorship of the Old Testament texts. The authors of the Biblical books seemed invisible. This jump between the text of the Bible and the reader's contemporary world is in part due to the hermeneutical world of the young evangelical. Perrin[185] sees that evangelicals usually practice a common-sense reading. Drawing from the work of Harris,[186] they typically understand that a text appears to say what the narrative voice within in it presents. This is seen as a trustworthy report of actual events. Therefore, they often ignore or are unaware of literary theories of interpretation and resistant reading is unlikely—unless texts cross certain lines. Therefore, evangelicals behave as compliant readers and operate on a hermeneutic of trust.[187]

This supports what Rogers[188] sees, as texts are shaped and molded to the readers' context without enough time spent, or naiveté shown, in understanding the process of textual transmission and authorial horizons. Furthermore, Perrin,[189] draws on Malley,[190] to see the importance evangelicals place on English translations being faithful representations of what they understand as "ancient revelation events." Perrin,[191] sees that Malley,[192] suggests a misunderstanding about the origins of the Biblical text and the process of its documentation that leads Barr[193] to note that evangelicals have a largely socialized rather than logical doctrine of Scripture. As the notion of theological shorthand is considered a number of these points are relevant. Firstly, the notion of a polyvalence of interpretation,[194] means that there is fragmentation taking place as the text begins to mean different things to different people. This points to a complex world of circular transmission, animation and mediation based on a largely socialized view of scripture. Yet, within this socialized view,

---

184. Ibid.
185. Ibid., 77.
186. Harris, *Fundamentalism*, 281.
187. Perrin, *The Bible Reading of Young Evangelicals*, 77.
188. Rogers, "Reading Scripture," 95.
189. Perrin, *The Bible Reading of Young Evangelicals*, 80.
190. Malley, *How the Bible Works*, 49.
191. Perrin, *The Bible Reading of Young Evangelicals*, 80.
192. Malley, *How the Bible Works*.
193. Barr, *Fundamentalism*, 81.
194. Perrin, *The Bible Reading of Young Evangelicals*, 101.

Perrin[195] argues, that there did not seem to be a pressing need for doctrinal closure or indeed seeking some sort of definite answer; implying that relationships and inclusiveness between readers is often a higher priority than resolving theological dilemmas. It means, that if a process of fragmentation has already occurred with the socializing understanding of scripture, finding a different or deeper exploration of a particular doctrine that is different to the recognized status quo is difficult. Theology within the socialized world operates like a series of mirrors reflecting back established, perhaps thin and fragmented understandings of doctrinal thought and theology. This is what, at least in part, is happening with the adoption of relationships and like Jesus as the key motifs of transmission and mediation within the data. This can also be an uncomfortable place because if alternative views on established theology, perhaps seeking to deepen some elements are seen to challenge established theologies then a process of ostracization can take place.[196]

Secondly, the tension here, is that evangelical reading strategies are informed above all by the overriding principle of inerrancy,[197] and this has become a socialized norm. Therefore, the terms of infallible or reliable become socially defining theology as evangelicals seek to defend the authority of the Bible and this is central in shaping evangelical reading practices. Therefore, as Perrin[198] sees, the Bible must be interpreted in such a way as to avoid any admission that it contains any kind of error. In order to avoid the recognition of error, fundamentalists twist and turn, backward and forward between literal and non-literal interpretations. Furthermore, Perrin[199] notes that Conservatives do avoid literal readings at times, and opt for other ways of interpreting the text, including allegorical ones, particularly to avoid conflict with scientific evidence.[200] This process of oscillation results in the harmonization of conflicting passages, some vagueness over textual difficulties, inconsistency of attention and interpretation, and the glancing over of certain passages while other texts are emphasized. It is these inconsistencies that lead to fragmentation and

195. Ibid.

196. Steve Chalke is an example of this through his efforts to acknowledge a different view on the atonement and on human sexuality within the evangelical world.

197. Perrin, *The Bible Reading of Young Evangelicals*, 76.

198. Ibid.

199. Ibid.

200. Ibid. The evangelical/fundamentalist relationships are complex and a number of schemas to differentiate between them exist.

the Bible being broken up into proof texts and theological shorthand. As Perrin[201] argues, despite their core value of Biblical authority, evangelicals can be guilty of selective reading; of being devoted admires of the Bible, but not daily Bible readers.[202] Therefore, despite claims about the authority and centrality of scripture, the amount of engagement with the Bible for the average evangelical is minimal.[203]

If avoiding inerrancy is one paradigm for evangelical reading of the Bible, then a second pattern embraced by a majority of evangelicals is the emphasizing of the salvific hermeneutic and the centrality of Christ's atoning sacrifice for humanity. For some evangelicals Christocentrism is an evangelical priority, and crucicentrism a core belief.[204] Importantly, as seen above, it is this insight that illuminates how Young Life sought to position the incarnation as presence and ministry justification. This idea then becomes played out as model within the literature (Ward,[205] Pimlott and Pimlott[206]) and this model is mediated through relationalism as personal influence. This is what is seen in the outworking of the term like Jesus, where this becomes a theological shorthand expression for the animation of those beliefs and actions that are inspired by the acts and stories of Jesus. Furthermore, the idea of model within the literature and within the data of being like Jesus, become a plastic hermeneutic that is molded and shaped to a wide variety of different situations and missional activity amongst young people.

Ideas and Mediation of the Evangelical Tradition

The echoes of evangelical thinking can also be seen in a third interrelated area; how the literature is the louder voice in the guiding of practice. This resonates with how the evangelical tradition has historically tended to mediate ideas. Here, Rogers[207] via Bebbington[208] argues, that the overriding pattern was for ideas to spread from above to below. It can be

201. Ibid., 87.
202. Ibid.
203. Ibid.
204. Ibid., 78.
205. Ward, *Youthwork*.
206. Pimlott and Pimlott, *Youth Work after Christendom*.
207. Rogers, "Reading Scripture," 94.
208. Bebbington, *Evangelicalism and Cultural Diffusion*.

seen as evangelicals have wrestled with the idea of Biblical hermeneutics and how this has gained ground since the 1970s. Perrin,[209] suggests that hermeneutics became a focus for evangelical churches in Britain at this time, as Thiselton introduced Gadamer's theories of interpretative horizons to evangelical vocabulary. This had the effect of putting the hermeneutical cat among the Bible believing pigeons, as what had once seemed obvious was no longer what it seemed and hermeneutics became a divisive issue. This debate lies outside the scope of this work, but it is important to note that Thiselton's work became popularized by John Stott and he began to challenge readers and preachers to recognize that they viewed the text through cultural glasses. Therefore, Stott encouraged his readers to hold a conversation between Scripture and context that was then applied to the faith and life of the believer as the fusion of horizons took place at the point of application.[210]

What is important here, is how Perrin[211] sees that these ideas have trickled down into how "ordinary" people read the Bible and that this has become established as normative practice for exegesis and preaching. This resonates and has parallels with the "grand strategy" and the work of the youth fellowship. As Ward[212] sees, this is largely the story of a movement downwards as the approaches developed in work amongst middle classes are adopted in work with those further down the social scale. Therefore, as Bebbington[213] notes, ideas and practices spread from groups with greater advantages to a wider consistency. Bebbington[214] highlights three characteristics that facilitate this process: a) education, b) the well to do and c) the young. It is possible to see resonances of this in this study, for as Bebbington[215] sees, literature is one of the key forms of mediation. Therefore, ideas of the educated or academic can be passed on and mediated to a wider constituency through the literature, as seen through the work of Stott and the process of hermeneutics. Just as these ideas have trickled down within Bible reading, this process can also be seen in how relationships, the incarnation, like Jesus, being there and

209. Perrin, *The Bible Reading of Young Evangelicals*, 74–75.

210. Ibid., 75.

211. Ibid.

212. Ward, *Growing Up Evangelical*, 45.

213. Bebbington, *Evangelicalism and Cultural Diffusion*. See also, Rogers, "Reading Scripture," 94.

214. Ibid.

215. Ibid.

the idea of model that occupy a central place within the literature, are then mediated and passed onto the wider constituency of youth ministry practitioners through the work of Oasis and CYM.

The ecumenical and entrepreneurial nature of these youth ministry training providers play down the differing ecclesial traditions and the youth ministry literature becomes the common uniting factor and thus the louder voice in guiding the youth minister's practice. This is louder than the Anglican and Baptist traditions and contexts of which the youth ministers are part. It is the youth ministry literature, animated by the theology of Young Life, which mediates how relationships function as the transmission of faith. This process is intertwined and underpinned by an evangelical view of the Bible that has been formed socially. This has, unwittingly, been mediated through a fragmented, thin and shorthand reading of the Bible, that views life through a Christocentric lens. This has distorted or downplayed wider aspects of the Gospel story and Christian tradition.

This chapter has sought to explore the shape of Christian practices and has set up how theology, through the work of Vanhoozer,[216] (explored in chapters 8 and 9) provides the normative voice for practice however tentative that may be. Furthermore, it is has been argued that a contemporary understanding of youth ministry collapses the traditional Christian practices of *kerygma*, *diakonia* and *marturia* into the relational. Following this, the pivotal place of relationships within the evangelical tradition has been investigated and how these act as the central place of mediation and transmission has been explored. With the building blocks in place it is now time to introduce the youth ministers.

---

216. Vanhoozer, *Remythologizing Theology*.

PART TWO
Echoes of a Coherent Theology:
Theological Shorthand and Current Practice

Chapter 4

The Youth Ministers

This short, but pivotal chapter introduces the youth ministers. This gives, at least in part, some context to the data and stories. It reminds us that these are real people in time and place and there is a fragility to these accounts. What is seen is the long term, dedicated, sacrificial service amongst young people. It is a reminder of the paradox at the center of this study—the transferable, portable theology that is assimilated by the youth ministers from their theological education and articulated as theological shorthand is enough to fuel this life changing work amongst young people. These brief introductions sketch and highlight key aspects of the youth ministers interviewed, where they worked, what denominations they have been in, are still within, and foundational elements of their work amongst young people.[1]

The Youth Ministers

Andrew

In his interview, Andrew's stories are about his work amongst very vulnerable young people. They involved young people on the fringes of the church community connected to a Friday evening outreach group. The focus was not on a talk or an epilogue, but on relationships and

---

1. The youth ministers interviewed were all professionally trained within degree programs, either by the Centre for Youth and Mission or by Oasis College in the UK and could be classed as "veterans" due to their experience of working amongst young people.

conversations with a particular group of lads and their friends. Some of these young people were on the margins, living difficult lives that often-involved drug or alcohol abuse. There is great disparity between the middles class church and its values and these young people. The club provided an opportunity for the leaders and volunteers to get alongside the young people through football, pool and table tennis. The relationship between Andrew and the young people acted as a bridge, leading to informal meetings and activities outside of the group. Andrew helped them in practical ways; to find employment and with difficult situations within their wider relationships and families. Andrew was often the only contact they had with a person of faith. He is employed at a large evangelical Baptist Church within a commuter town and has grown up and come to faith within the Baptist tradition. Andrew's wider practice covers a rich variety of ministry with young people; including, school's ministry, mentoring, the YMCA and the Princes Trust. His practice also includes facilitating the church groups on a Sunday morning and evening for young people aged 11—18, running a youth led worship service, and facilitating eight small discipleship groups.

David

Central to David's practice are conversation and relationships. His interventions were important and he worked amongst some very challenging young people, drug use and anti-social behavior are very prevalent. David runs a drop-in youth club and he estimated that up to 90–95% of young people who came to this had no other contact with the Baptist church or other churches within the town. The drop-in revolves around BMX and skate ramps, this helps David and the volunteers create a space where the young people were happy to hang out and chat. This activity enables David and volunteers to engage in small conversations, but these conversations were often pivotal and changed the course of some the young people's actions. These interventions often helped diffuse violence amongst young people and attacks on property. The stories told in his interview are mainly about the drop-in. David works for a large evangelical Baptist Church in a pleasant suburb of London and he came to faith through the Baptist tradition. David is involved in a number of different projects that engage with young people. His practice is similar to some of the other youth minister interviewed, it involves the facilitating of the

Sunday morning and evening groups, a number of small discipleship groups and youth led worship services. In addition to these, David works on a number of cross town projects including a social action and worship project. He is also heavily involved in Street Pastors.

Jill

Jill's practice centers on work amongst NEET[2] and marginalized young people. The stories told in her interview focus on her work at a drop-in youth club, this opened following four months of detached work by Jill and her team. The focal point of the drop-in is on the relational and conversations facilitated by table tennis, pool, cooking activities and craft. As part of this, Jill and a committed group of volunteers ran an IT project with a range of laptops that young people used to help with homework, C.V. writing and applying for jobs. Often the young peoples' home lives were chaotic and this very practical help was invaluable. Jill's ministry amongst these vulnerable young people often goes well beyond the detached work and the drop-in. Her work involved advocacy and support, for example, she worked alongside a young person and her mum at a drug charity to help prevent further drug abuse within the family. Jill is part of a large evangelical Anglican Church in London and is the full time employed youth minister. She grew up and came to faith within the Baptist tradition. Before her training, Jill worked for an ecumenical detached youth project.

Mark

Mark works for a para church charity within a very difficult urban area. His practice has a particular focus amongst young people who are involved with gangs and violent crime. This work was facilitated by relationships, and like some of the other youth ministers,[3] he saw his work in terms of holistic transformation, moving young people from low aspirations and poverty to have a hope and dream for the future. In the interview Mark spoke openly about his work amongst gangs and very violent young people, helping them gain confidence and supporting them to find work. The reasons why they belong to gangs are complicated, but

2. Not in Education, Employment or Training.
3. Kerry, Kim and Martin.

Mark could see how poverty and a chaotic dysfunctional home life saw them look for a place to belong, a place where their name was known and they received recognition, even if it was for violent or anti-social activity. Before doing this, Mark worked for a Christian school work charity and came to faith within the Baptist tradition.

Rachel

Rachel has worked with a Community Trust that operated in the middle of a difficult estate in inner London, her worked involved helping young people leave gangs. She now works for a para church mission organisation amongst young people on two local estates in a medium sized town. She runs fours projects, including some detached work and a drop-in. The interview reveals stories about her work amongst difficult young men and a few girls who are part of this group. The work centers on conversations about appropriate alcohol use, advising on safe sexual health, helping them with good mental health, finding work or college courses, as well as questions about faith. Rachel came to faith within the Baptist tradition, so she also told stories about her work as a youth minister amongst young people connected to a Baptist Church. Here the focus of her work was on the Sunday morning and evening groups, small group discipleship, youth led worship and activity days that explored issues of faith with young people.

Tom

Tom, like Terry below, runs a café project. The café is located in a parade of shops that has become a focus for the police after some trouble with young people who gather in large groups. The youth café is run in partnership with a para church organisation. Tom also visited a local school as a mentor, ran a football project, and an after-school drop in. As a youth minister, he also facilitates the church groups on a Sunday morning and evening, a youth led worship service, small discipleship groups, and a Friday night youth club. His focus is on developing relationships and holding conversations at different stages of the young people's faith journey. Stories from different aspects of these were told in the interview. This correlation of projects is important for Tom as they provide a way of meeting with young people at different points in their week. Tom is employed full time for a large evangelical Anglican Church within a leafy suburb of London. He came to faith through the Anglican tradition.

Kim

Kim works in a tough urban environment supporting young women who are involved in gangs and subject to gang violence. Her interview brings this work into focus.

Kim held a very inclusive way of working, like the other youth ministers, her attention is on developing relationships that build trust with young people. She saw her mission to young people in the widest sense, helping then make good decisions about sexual health, drug education and appropriate levels of alcohol consumption. Kim works at a project connected to an inner-city church and she seeks to challenge and intervene when the young women make poor choices that affect them and their wider family. Her inventions amongst young people are invaluable, she spoke openly about her conversations, seeing how these had the chance to make a huge difference and with appropriate challenge, and regular support, the lives of these young women could slowly be turned around. Kim also helped out in a variety of other youth projects including a radio station and a café that sought to work and empower young people on the margins. Kim grew up and came to faith within the United Reformed Church in a rural location.

Sam

Sam found himself in the center of a complex and very difficult pastoral situation. He told a story about a young person who rang him just after a failed suicide attempt. Sam was first on the scene and helped get them get to hospital. He then supported the family, seeking to bring the fragile and broken pieces of their life back together. The focus within the interview is his relational work with marginalized young people. Sam is in contact with them through a project that is part of an ecumenical church partnership and he hopes to build trust and to be there for young people as he communicates his faith. Importantly, he seeks to connect his pastoral work in schools to the wider youth provision across the town provided by churches, trying to build support networks for these vulnerable young people. Sam came to faith in his early teens through the work of an evangelical Baptist Church and the youth ministry of that church was pivotal in Sam's journey of faith. He is now the youth minister within an Anglican Church in a small seaside town in the South East of England. Sam also facilities the youth groups on a Sunday morning and runs discipleship sessions with young people.

Kerry

Kerry explicitly talked about relationships, being there, and journeying with young people as being foundational to her practice. She is based in central London and is part of project that works with young people in a local school. The idea of role model is important to Kerry and she notes that young people will not listen unless she has open and positive relationships with them. In her interview she told stories of her work in the secondary school as she helps support young people on the margins of exclusion, using relationships and sport to help engage and communicate with them. Through this process Kerry seeks to create trust between her and the young people, opening up conversations so appropriate challenge can be brought. Kerry is part of the community and her church runs a number of other projects for children, young people and adults - including a food bank and debt advice center. She coordinates a number of groups within the church and works with young people between the ages of 11 and 18. Alongside mentoring, discipleship is important in this work, Kerry grew up and came to faith within the Baptist tradition.

Martin

Martin works as a detached youth worker on an inner-city estate in central London. It is challenging ministry and he uses skate boarding to help connect with young people. Through this he seeks to bring hope to young people whose lives rotate around the estate, a very small and insula geographical area. It has taken a long time to build relationships with the young people and gain their trust. This is a Christian project, and Martin sees his mission in its widest sense seeking to intervene and help young people make good decisions about sexual health, drug use and alcohol consumption. Mentoring is a foundational aspect of Martin's practice. His ministry often goes way beyond the detached work, meeting with the local council, seeking provisions for young people. Martin also acts as a bridge between the local young people and the police, working with conflict resolution and mediation to diffuse tensions between them and explore aspects of faith. He came to faith within the Baptist tradition.

Terry

Terry runs a café project. The café is located in a local parade of shops that is on the edge of a very deprived area. Through this Terry seeks to connect with young people who are often in trouble with the police and who would not normally cross the boundaries of a middle-class church. Terry described these NEET young as being vulnerable, marginalized, but very open to talking about faith. Terry often helped them with a range of issues, from writing C.Vs., discussing mental and sexual health, appropriate use of alcohol and trying to find employment or housing. In his interview Terry told stories about this work and his work amongst young connected to the church. His focus is on developing relationships and holding conversations with the young people, to be there and journey with them, helping them navigate the multiple and complex problems they face. Terry came to faith within the conservative evangelical Anglican tradition and now works as a youth minister for a large evangelical Anglican Church within a leafy suburb of London. Terry also helps run the church groups on a Sunday morning and evening, a youth led worship service, small discipleship groups and a Friday night youth club.

Dan

Dan works within a very challenging urban environment in inner London. He sees relationships to be central to this work. Dan seeks to help the young people he works with make good decisions about drug education, appropriate levels of alcohol consumption, employment and sexual health. His interventions often involve referrals and signposting to other organizations as he helps young people through the complex issues they face. In his interview he told stories about this work and also about his wider work with young people in a church context. Dan came to faith through the Baptist tradition and has also worked for an Anglican Church in a small market town. His current role is a complete contrast to his previous role, running a series of youth and discipleship groups on Saturdays and Sundays for young people aged between 11–18. In his interview he articulated stories from both of these contrasting expressions of youth ministry.

Interpretative Journey and Key Themes

Now the context of the practitioners has been set, the interpretative journey begins by the development of the key themes within the data. As glimpsed in the introductions to the practitioners, relationships are affirmed as an overarching theme expressed by them. These operate as communicative acts, as places of mediation, connection, and transmission and are the threads that run through the stories told. Relationships that function as communicative acts are seen to influence young people and help youth ministers connect with them.

However, this multifaceted and complex practice is summed up through the language of relationship, like Jesus, being there and time and journey; I see this as theological shorthand. The theological shorthand exposes an embedded theology that evokes aspects of the wider Christian tradition and practices (*diakonia, marturia, kerygma*), yet, this wider tradition and associated practices are not overtly articulated. This is important because in the retelling of their stories, in their narratives of practice and their involvement of mission amongst young people, the youth ministers did not even mention (not once!) the traditions of which they are part—be that Baptist, Anglican or United Reformed. Perhaps this is due to the nomadic nature of youth ministry. Youth ministers go where the jobs are rather than staying in a particular tradition, but the overwhelming narrative, the normative voice, is the relational. Relationships with young people guide every aspect of what they do, either by building trust, helping them with interventions, or guiding the youth ministers as they seek to become role models. The cannon of youth ministry literature shapes and frames this relational picture. What they have read or been taught, not surprisingly, gets reflected back and the youth ministers act like mirrors for the training they have received. Due to the mediation of youth ministry, from the top down and across distances and time, the literature functions across denominations and the traditional practices of the church (*diakonia, marturia, kerygma*) are collapsed into the relational (although this is not noticed or articulated). Therefore, the complexities of practice, helping young people navigate complex problems like drug and alcohol use, or difficult social relationships within gangs is expressed as theological shorthand through the terms: relational, like Jesus, being there and time and journey. Through this process theology becomes thin and fragmented.

If the theme of relationships runs through the narratives, then like Jesus can be seen as the theme that the others revolve around. Like Jesus, as model, is how the youth minister practitioners enact mission amongst young people. The third theme of being there is the enacted presence of the second—like Jesus, and becomes an enacted theological moment in time and space through which the youth ministers act as a symbol.[4] As a symbol, they embody qualities of that which they participate in, what they point towards, however, this is not expressed, only the language of model is articulated and this is seen as being like Jesus. This is theological shorthand in action. As symbols, youth ministers, through being there, are meaningful on account of their relationship to Christ. Therefore, it is an act of embodied faith that points towards and models Christ and seeks to be like Jesus. Like Jesus and being there is carried, transmitted and given direction and shape through the web of connections made in the relationships established. But this takes time and is a journey. Through this fourth theme of time and journey, liminal spaces are created through time. These liminal spaces are places where relationships as communicative acts through being there take place; it is the space where being like Jesus is enacted. This is what the practitioners strive for in their enacted mission. These are places of transition, places of waiting and not knowing, places of movement, frustration and life. Within this liminal space, there is an interweaving between the themes, relationships, being there and like Jesus, as all take time and this is either explicit or it is implied through the idea of journey and is an embodied communicative act of faith by the youth ministry practitioners in a series of encounters with young people. Furthermore, through relationships there is a focus on right action (orthopraxis), on performing a function, it evokes and has a connection to a deeper set of "right" beliefs (orthodoxy) from the Christian tradition, yet this is not overtly articulated—and theological expression becomes thin and fragmented. Therefore, there is an association with the traditional church practices of *marturia* and *diakonia* and in a very limited way, evokes the practice of *kerygma*, but these are collapsed into the expression of relationships.

4. Tillich, *Dynamics of Faith*.

Now the youth ministers have been introduced, the key themes and ideas outlined, it is time to continue to explore the interpretive journey as these foundational themes are investigated in more depth and detail.

Chapter 5

Narratives of Practice: Theological Shorthand and Relationships as Communicative Acts

Narratives of practice offer glimpses and capture living experiences, they are like a series of photographs, snapshots frozen in time. This is first and foremost hallowed ground, one treads carefully, entering liminal spaces of encounter with the living God, spaces where youth ministers have faithfully lived out their calling amongst young people. Yet, the paradox at the heart of this study becomes clearer, the tension between their theological language and their sacrificial service amongst young people. This chapter investigates, interprets, and presents the voices and experiences of the youth ministers—it slows down practice frame by frame, word by word, examines, and analyses the qualitative data gathered and captured through the interviews. This is the second step in the reflection cycle and seeks to excavate and discover what is really going on. As explored earlier, the aim is to gain new insights into practice about the way youth ministers enact mission amongst young people. Importantly, it captures words and aspects of speech that demonstrate theological shorthand in action. Through the stories gathered, weight is given to this notion and of how theology becomes fragmented and thin in the complexities of practice.

Rublev's icon tells a story, but, strictly speaking, icons depict visually, rather than tell stories, though the people and situations they depict are part of well-known stories. Rublev's icon, as we have seen, depicts Abraham's guests and suggests participation in Trinitarian relationships—but we only understand the latter from the much more complex

Biblical narrative. In the picture are three staffs that dissect the painting into three connected sections. Why should angels have staffs? Perhaps it is to show how God joins with us on our journey, enters it, and communicates with us in those liminal spaces. It demonstrates God's relational interest in us. Relationships, journey, and liminal spaces are important in the narratives of the youth ministers who were interviewed. Their interviews tell of their journey with God and with young people as they seek to support them in some very difficult circumstances. They are very human accounts, demonstrating their very real love and care for young people. As their voices are heard it is a reminder that we enter sacred places of divine action. The narratives are approached and viewed through the lens of critical faithfulness and as stories of encounters with young people are told they demonstrate a very real and lived faith.

Relationships as Communicative Acts: Connection and Transmission

Within the narratives expressed by the youth ministry practitioners, Kerry, Kim, David, Andrew, Tom, Dan, Mark, Sam, Martin and Terry are explicit about the theme of relationships, whilst for Rachel and Jill the relationships are implicit and implied. Within all the narratives articulated, the implicit and implied act of relationships acted as theological shorthand, a way of summing up the complexities and nuances of enacted practice. Within the theme of relationships, the language of construction is discovered, relationships are built, (Tom, Andrew, David, Dan, Kerry, Kim, Sam, Martin) and connections made (David, Andrew, Terry). However, relationships also have a softer way of being expressed through the notion of sharing of lives (Andrew, Kim, Sam, Tom, Dan, Mark, Rachel, Jill,). This is an interconnected theme which is explored below through being there. Moreover, within the theme of relationships, the relationships that are built and the connections made transmit the faith and these can be seen as circuits of influence and the place of sub-cultural engagement. Relationships can be seen to function as communicative acts as the enacted mission amongst young people, and encompass the traditional church practices of *marturia* and *diakonia*. The idea of relationships as communicative act, as a place of connection and transmission is seen in Andrew, Sam and Dan's articulation of enacted mission. These ideas are present in the way being there and the sharing of lives (Andrew,

Sam, Dan) function as a place of connection between themselves and the young people and as a place for the transmission of their faith. In the verbalizing of Andrews's relationships with young people, he used the term connections and he also uses the term build, articulating that you need to get to know young people and build a relationship with them. For Andrew, he sought to enact mission through this process and through various interactions he aimed to share and communicate something of his life and faith as a Christian. Dan, Kim and Kerry expressed very similar ideas, and for these connections to be made required trust, in fact, for Dan, without this trust the relationships would ultimately flounder, but the creation of trust took a long time.

Furthermore, David, Kerry and Kim also articulate this notion of having to build relationships and they see this as central to the forming and creation of trust between themselves and young people. This term built, used by David, Kerry and Kim, ties into the idea of relationship as a means of connection; moreover, it evokes a sense of time and the idea journey. These are strong themes within the data and will be explored in more depth below. The idea of relationships as a place of connection that is built is also articulated through how Mark expressed himself as a minister who functions like a bridge. Here, this core theme of relationship is seen as a metaphorical bridge, a place of connection, connecting the minister's life to that of the young person. Furthermore, for Mark, the relationship leads to how influence is gained through the level of respect and trust they have for the minister, resonating with the thoughts of David, Kerry, Kim and Dan. Therefore, for Mark, relationships are seen as a place, not only of connection, but of transmission and mediation. Relationships carry the ideas and faith of the ministers as influence. Here they seek to connect with young people and have moral sway, evoking the practice of *marturia*. Pivoting around this place of connection, Mark articulates how these relationships go beyond the sessions the ministers are involved in and this means being there for young people. Therefore, relationships as a place of connection is expressed as being there through the spending of time and this can be seen as intentional (Tom, Dan, Kim, Kerry, Sam). This is seen through how Mark, Tom, Dan, Terry and Kim explicitly articulate the central place of relationships in terms of their practice:

Mark: *'if the relationship isn't at the heart of it and you haven't got time for someone, then you need to create time and if it's outside of the session that's fine—we can sort it.'*

Tom: "*in my practice I have a very strong emphasis on building relationships... in an unlimited amount of spheres... seeking to communicate who Jesus is at various different stages in the young people's faith journey.*"

Dan: "*relationships and trust are fundamental to my practice, ... you have to be as open as possible, otherwise there is no relationship, with no relationship it's a struggle to help change or influence the people you are working with.*"

Terry: "*for me relationships are central, they unlock the potential within a young person*"

Kim: "*relationships help me to act as a role model, here young people trust you—they listen to what you say, you can have an influence.*"

Therefore, for Kim, Mark, Tom, Dan and Terry relationships occupy a central place and are seen as the way in which they can engage with young people. There is intentionality about these relationships in order to help young people articulate and think about their faith. For Tom it's not just about relationships for relationships sake, but these have a purpose of communicating faith and seeing young people's lives transformed by Jesus. For Terry, relationships unlock the potential within a young person. Here then, in a similar way to Mark above, the relationship acts as the place of intentional connection and a place of transmission through which the faith of the youth minister can be demonstrated. Therefore, the role of relationship as connection and transmission becomes a place of sub-cultural engagement; the relationships act as circuits of influence that seek to connect the differing worlds of adults and young people, the connecting of worlds was expressed by all the youth ministers.

This resonates with Mark's idea of a bridge; however, these connections take place over a period of time and as a journey. This demonstration of faith that is built and carried through time and through journey is discovered within the relationships (Tom, Dan, Kim, Kerry, Terry, Martin and Sam). Therefore, it leads Tom and Dan to run groups that are all about building relationships. This is echoed in David's thoughts. Again, faith is communicated and embodied by the relationship and this takes place through the notion of being there and caring for the young person, resonating with the practice of *marturia* and *diakonia*. The relationships are seen as places of connection to carry and transmit the message of faith; relationships function as communicative acts that seek to make faith relevant and act as a place of sub-cultural engagement. This is also found in Jill's expression of enacting mission amongst young people and it is possible to see Jill's relationships as a form of connection and as a communicative act amongst young people. However, the actual term of relationship is not as explicit as in the language and expression of Kim, Kerry, Andrew, David, Terry Tom, Dan, Sam, Martin and Mark, but it is implicit within the work and ministry that she is involved in. The sense of relationships as a place of communication, as a space of connection and mediation is seen in Jill's, David's and Sam's expression.

Jill: *"just by going where they are . . . "I have found myself sitting on a bench . . . in the winter, in the freezing cold . . . and it seems to be there where they really poured their heart out."*

David: *"Christianity is so foreign that actually it needs to be introduced in a different type of way, through connections, through relationships, just by caring really for people."*

Sam: *"Relationships are central as a way of being there for young people—to help them understand the care and concern you have for them."*

For Sam, Jill and David, this relational practice, as communicative act, as connection seeks to transmit, mediate and demonstrate their embodied and lived faith. It is shown in how Jill, Sam and David begin to articulate the sense of suffering the young people felt. Furthermore, for Jill, it is the relationship that acted as the connection and that transmitted the message and enabled her to articulate and speak about a God who has the possibility to change things. Additionally, in the expression of Kim, Tom, Dan, Sam, Andrew, Mark, Kerry and Martin the term relationship sums up this complex and nuanced practice of relationships as a place of communication and can be seen as theological shorthand for the embodied mediation of faith amongst young people. It encompasses the traditional practices of *marturia*, *diakonia* and, in a very limited way, evokes the practice of *kerygma*.

Tensions within Connection and Transmission

Relationships and the connections made were not seen as unproblematic and Rachel, Tom and Andrew articulated some of the problems associated with relationships in their enacting of mission amongst young people. Rachel sees that a relationship with a young person can be very challenging to keep up and when this finishes it is extremely difficult. Rachel sees, in terms of relationships, that youth ministers are not taught about incomplete stories. Within Rachel's thinking, relationships are seen through the lens of a story, being expressed and worked out, a story with twists and turns, with the central plot held between the young person and youth minister. However, when these stories end, they are particularly painful for the minister. Rachel struggled with the fact that perhaps she should have brought things to a completion and that she may have let the young people down. Within her practice, relationships are a place of connection where young people can express their struggles and suffering and are a means to communicate and transmit her faith. Yet, there is also a personal cost to these relationships, for when they seem incomplete, when the connections are broken, when the story ends, it can be agonizing for the youth minister. Consequently, it is possible to see the genuineness of the connections made within Rachel's relationship with young people, due to the emotional investment made and how costly this intentional activity can be.

Tom also expresses this sense of frustration and sadness when the relationship with a young person can end and the place of connection can finish. It again pivots around this concept of investing in and building relationships. Tom sees that through relationships with young people he has shared some very challenging times, times when they have struggled and have been suffering and he has become part of their lives. Here the issue of suffering is raised again, but the tension for Tom is found when young people reach the "end," due to age (year nine), of an open youth club that has been relationally based. Within this particular aspect of Tom's practice, there is no explicit time to speak about God and he needed to bridge the gap between this relational way of working to a more formal and structured group. Subsequently, Tom expresses a limit to how relationships function as a place of connection that can transmit faith. He seeks a more directed and formal means to enact mission and communicate his faith amongst young people. Likewise, Andrew had also wrestled and reflected on the tension of using relationships as a place of connection and method of transmission in the enacting of mission. Andrew says that he had been taught:

"*that relational youth work was about, from a Christian perspective, was trying to get young people to the point of becoming Christians and as much as I wanted that to happen, I felt like a car salesman trying to sell Christianity, trying to get people to buy into Christianity.*"

This has led to a tension that Andrew articulates by knowing that youth work should be relational due to his training and the expression of relationships within the youth ministry literature and to a certain amount of skepticism as to what was happening in those relationships. Here

Andrew is highlighting a problem that exists within the enacted practice of relationships as communicative acts as connection and transmission, the sense that sometimes these can feel forced and unnatural, the feeling that although relationships function as a place of mediation, they may not always be enough. Moreover, both Sam and Kim spoke about the cost of the unpredictable nature of relationships, when relational support of young people takes a lot of time, when they have spent hours supporting a young person that other parts of their job get left undone.

Sam: *"sometimes you spend so much time supporting young people who are going through so much—building those styles of relationships in different environments—it's difficult to balance."*

Kim, spoke openly about how hard this had been for her and on the unfinished nature of relationships (resonating with Rachel), the impact of this on her mental health and on the mental health of other youth ministers she knew who had experienced burn out.

Kim: *"it's so hard sometimes supporting young people, you know, the issues they face are so complex and difficult that it costs you so much time. It feels so unfinished and you never switch off—if fact I burnt out, I struggled with my mental health because of the depth, difficulty and how hard the situations the young people faced were—I did not feel equipped to deal with them, relationships weren't enough sometimes, I needed more support"*

This points to uncomfortable tensions within practice, the perceived isolation of youth ministers as seen in the feelings of Kim and Rachel. They feel like they are on their own. It is a misunderstanding of boundaries and almost the out working of a messiah complex—that they alone have to do the work, they alone have to fix young people's problems. This is an outworking of theological shorthand and a lack of theological literacy because the wider church, the support of the congregation and the working of God's Spirit is not recognized within these moments. It is the belief in seeking to be like Jesus youth ministers have to do it all.

Relationships as Communicative Acts: Like Jesus

The next interrelated theme: like Jesus can be seen as pivotal in the enacted practice of the youth ministers. The youth ministers model and base their actions on being like Jesus. This theme, like that of being there and time and journey, is carried and transmitted through relationships as communicative acts and the connections the youth ministers made with young people. Again, the theme of like Jesus acts as theological shorthand, a relatively uncomplicated theological expression of the complexities of working and enacting mission amongst young people, yet, it resonates with the practice of *marturia*.

The practitioners articulate this in the following ways:

Tom: "*if you look at Jesus,*" "*to be like Jesus*"; Rachel: "*the example Jesus set*"; Andrew: "*I look to the New Testament and the example Jesus sets*"; David: "*I seek to try and mirror God's image,*" *to be like Jesus*"; Jill "*sees that Jesus built relationships*"; Mark: "*I want to be an example of Christ*" and to be "*like Jesus.*" Sam: "*the best I can be in modelling Jesus*"; Terry: "*I try and be like Jesus*"; Martin: "*I can be an example of Christ*": Kim: "*I try and model Jesus.*"

To examine and investigate in more detail the lived theology held in these terms of look, example, mirror and see, the idea of model, of being like Jesus needs to be explored. As this is investigated, the paradox between the complexity and nuances of practice and the theological shorthand description of this is illuminated.

Tom expresses the sense that Jesus spent a lot of time with his disciples and invested in them; here, Tom seeks to model and be with young people in the same way that Jesus did by spending time with them. Yet, Tom's being with young people could be seen as being very different from Jesus' being with his disciples. It could seem that Tom was seeking to make disciples of his own. I don't think Tom means this, but some of Tom's language could raises ecclesiological questions and could point to a lack of theological literacy. This resonates with the thoughts above by the youth ministers seeking to minister on their own and not recognize the wider work of God's Spirit.

That said, there is again an interrelating and correlation of the themes, by seeking to be like Jesus, Tom sees that time spent with young people is important and, through this time spent, the relationship is built. For Tom, being like Jesus and spending time with young people leads to the young people knowing that they are valued and, through this expression of time and being like Jesus, they have value to God. In this process, it is possible to see how, for Tom, being there acts as a symbol that points and directs young people to the value God has for them, a theme explored in more depth below. Rachel also articulates how this sense of value is important and she makes the link between how value can be seen in the example Jesus set. For Rachel, this is in the way Jesus is seen to make friends with those who are outcasts and on the margins of society, an idea also echoed in Terry's thinking. For Rachel, the example of being like Jesus becomes a guiding principle for her ministry, but she is honest in seeing the theological limitations of this as a framework that underpins her practice. Therefore, Rachel expressed a tension between the limits of her theology and the outworking of her practice and there is a tension between her theological understanding and the lived experience and reality of working amongst young people, especially when difficult issues are faced and the boundaries become blurred. Rachel needed to wrestle between what she believed the Bible was teaching and a particular pastoral situation she was facing. This is articulated through how Rachel expressed the nuances of enacted practice as she told a story of how two young people had begun sleeping together. For Rachel, this situation involves theological wrestling as she seeks to use the model provided by being like Jesus to understand a very complicated pastoral situation. Jill also seeks to use the model provided by being like Jesus, as she seeks to bring a young person back into community because of her understanding of how Jesus worked with those on the margins. Moreover, Tom also makes a direct link to the Gospels and his practice resonates with Rachel, Jill, David, Andrew and Mark. Tom is more explicit, seeing that he constructs a theology around his practice and he derives this directly from looking at the example Jesus set as he seeks to be like Jesus in his relationships with young people. However, Tom, like Rachel, wrestles with the tensions and limits of this. The stories involve issues of inclusion, exclusion and young people on the margins, but importantly they have a focus on orthopraxis and express the practice of *marturia*. The tension is seen as Rachel expresses the thought that:

"*Jesus, like totally welcomed everybody, and I am trying to tally that, with the fact that Jesus, you know the story in the Gospels, where Jesus allowed the rich man to walk away—it is so difficult to get the balance between saying you are welcome here and we love you, but your behavior is not according to what you say you agree with.*"

For Jill: "*this is kind of where I am at, that's my passion, to bring those that were out of community back into it and it's the same for Lily, you know, she was permanently on the outside of community, but through a trip and conversations, she was brought back, they feel a part of things. Just like the woman in the Gospels who is bleeding and as she is healed is brought back into community.*"

For Tom: "*I think there is a real danger of doing that with Jesus, that you kind of always focus on the 'woman at the well' and that kind of story, you forget that actually, no sometimes he (Jesus) . . . he did challenge and he did speak up and he didn't just allow people to just get on with whatever they were doing. I think there's a danger you go too far the other way."*

Kim and Terry also spoke about how they sought to model Christ: *"I never seek to put on a front with young people—I seek to help them become the best they can be, to model Jesus to them, especially with the girls I work with. When they have misused drugs or alcohol, to help bring them out of darkness to light."*

Terry continues: *"yes, I try and be like Jesus, like Jesus treated the Women at the well, to show young people I value them, even when they face such difficult times, you know with drugs or whatever."*

These stories begin to narrate complex pastoral situations, and the Gospel stories are a deep resource for dealing with the nuances of pastoral practice, but the language of model and like Jesus in Rachel's practice becomes limited for such an example. The move made from this complex pastoral practice to the story of the rich young man raises question of how Rachel's theology informs and illuminates practice. The richness of embodied faith is also seen in Jill's practice as she seeks to work with Lily. Like Rachel, Kim and Terry she looks to the Gospels to see the example that Jesus sets as she seeks to be like Jesus and like Rachel and Terry, Jill connects this complex pastoral situation to one of her favorite Gospel stories. In Rachel, Terry, Kim and Jill's thoughts the idea of like Jesus can be seen as theological shorthand, as like Jesus operates as a phrase for seeking to express the complexities of the pastoral situations faced in the light of their understanding of certain Gospel stories or metaphors— *"moving from darkness to light"* (Kim).

Furthermore, David again uses the language of being like Jesus and makes a direct link between his practice and the Gospels. David expresses this through how as Christians we seek to be disciples, we try to mirror God's image and to be more like Jesus. For David's enacted mission this is embodied through the need to care for young people and echoes the thoughts of the other youth ministers. David makes a direct link between his practice and the model of being like Jesus. David conveys and makes the explicit link between how he sees that Jesus was very interested in people's physical, mental and spiritual needs. He expresses how this is so interrelated and then makes a move to how he held a holistic view of young people. Therefore, like Kim, Terry, Rachel, Andrew, Tom, Jill and Mark, David made a direct link between how he perceived Jesus treated people and how he treated and cared for young people in his enacted mission. Again, like Jesus is used as theological shorthand to sum up the complexities of practice and resonates with the practices of *marturia* and *diakonia*.

Like Jesus and the Incarnation

That said, a richer and deeper theological description of practice is given by Mark, Terry, Andrew and Kerry. This still revolves around the idea of model and Mark seeks to transform young people's lives through being a living example. Mark uses the word *incarnational* to describe his enacted mission and he sees this as being like Jesus. For Mark, the key is spending time with people, like Jesus did with his disciples. Jesus as an example and model leads to questions that help enact his mission amongst young people. These questions help shape and orientate his practice and he articulates this by asking how did Jesus live and what did he do? This leads Mark to articulate the importance of how Jesus lived amongst and shared his life with people. Therefore, for Mark, it is the sharing of lives that is important. Again, the notion of being like Jesus pivots around the interrelating themes of relationships, being there and time and is worked out in Mark's practice as communicative acts. Terry also sought to articulate a deeper theology—although the language of model is still employed. Terry saw the importance of Jesus and his relationships with the Father and Spirit as key to understanding his mission amongst young people. For Terry, it is Jesus' relationships within the Trinity and with others that are to be modelled to young people. There is deep theology here—not least in terms of our participation in God, but this is still articulated through the lens of model and no explicit theological frameworks of the Trinity are given.

In addition to the idea of being like Jesus and Jesus as a model, Mark saw himself as embodying Christ within his practice. This is a rich, enacted theology and Mark saw his mission amongst young people, not in terms of young people becoming Christians, but about realigning them to what God created them to be—resonating with Kim's thoughts. Within this practice is a robust theology, but again it is in theological shorthand. The language of *incarnation* points to a deep theology of who God is. This is a God willing to locate himself in time and space amongst humanity in Christ, the God who crosses boundaries. This is worked out in the practice of Mark as he crosses boundaries to work amongst very difficult young people. But this complex, nuanced and skilled practice is encapsulated in the theological shorthand expression of *incarnation* and resonates with Rachel, Terry, Kim and Jill's thoughts above in how the language of example and being like Jesus is still the language of model. However, Mark sees himself, through being a living example, as a facilitator for the work of God and this goes beyond the articulated expression in Rachel's, Jill's and David's practice. The use of the word facilitator is important, and the language of facilitator moves toward ideas of participation in God. The embryonic articulation of a deeper expression of theology is also found in Andrew and Kerry. Andrew also articulates the idea of example. For Andrew, when he looks at the New Testament Jesus, he sees Jesus as an example, sharing life together with people. It helps Andrew to understand how people are important and are not just a project; therefore, for Andrew, seeing the example Jesus set leads him to share and communicate his faith.

Andrew articulates this by looking at how Jesus sought to do this, as he seeks to be like Jesus. Here, Andrew expresses how you can journey with young people and crucially he sees that perhaps God is involved and within the relationship, that the Holy Spirit is at work doing more than he can comprehend. There is a link here between the language of example and model to a deeper theological expression of practice, that God is present. This language evokes what it means to participate in God and the sense that God is involved in the relationships is profound and has a deep theological reality that seems, at least in part, to inform Andrew's enacted mission amongst young people. Kerry also begins to articulate a deeper theology, as she seeks to frame her practice through what the Kingdom of God may be like for the young people she works with. At the same time, this is expressed through the language of being like Jesus and being a role model—the use of the word Kingdom operates as a theological fragment, theological shorthand for bringing hope and transformation to the community she serves. It encapsulates the complexities of practice. To start to articulate a Kingdom theology stands in contrast to the other youth ministers but begins to resonate with Mark's thoughts above.

Relationship as Communicative Acts: Being There

The third theme of being there is the enacted presence of the second, like Jesus, and becomes an enacted theological moment in time and space through which the youth ministers act as symbols. As a symbol, they embody the qualities of what they point towards and participate in, but this is articulated through the language of model, of being like Jesus as seen above. As symbols youth ministers, through being there, are meaningful on account of their relationship to Christ. Therefore, it is an act of embodied faith that points towards Christ and seeks to be like Jesus. The expression of the theme of being there is seen in the interrelatedness of this and the others that have been explored so far. Being there as symbol is the theological shorthand expression of pastoral care and the coming alongside young people who are suffering and in very difficult situations. Being there is mediated through relationships as communicative acts in the way the youth ministers made connections with young people and it is how their faith is transmitted and communicated. To be like Jesus is modelled over time and through the narrative structure of journey. There is a direct correlation between how the youth ministry practitioners see their practice and the life of Jesus and how he responded to people. This is embodied through the theme of being there and again has a focus on orthopraxis and resonates with the practice of *diakonia*.[1]

Being there for Jill involved her coming alongside young people who were having a very difficult time and working amongst them. She illustrates this by recalling a moment with young people in which she sat with them in the rain for over an hour and Jill explicitly expressed this as being there for them as she listened to their problems and troubles at home. The theme of being there resonates through Jill's practice and finds acute expression in a story Jill told about a young person called Lily. Jill describes Lily's life as life in the midst of suffering and how this played out through drink and drugs. By fostering a relationship and being there with Lily, Jill began to get to know the complexity of the problems that Lily was facing. Jill, through conversations and over a period of time, worked with Lily and Lily came to the point when she decided to give up drugs. Through this intervention, Jill put Lily in touch with a drug rehabilitation center. From this point, Jill was able to sort out a place in a childcare nursery and Lily became involved in some work experience and went on to attend college. For Jill, being there for this young girl over a period of time led to a transformation of her life through the relationship established. For Jill, being there, this coming amongst and being with young people in the midst of suffering is theological shorthand for

---

1. For a theological exploration of being there see Wells, *A Nazareth Manifesto*.

the complexities of practice, for being like Jesus and communicating the deeper realities of who God is and how he loves, cares and has compassion for people. Being there acts as a symbol that points to who God is. Furthermore, Jill articulates a cost to being there when beginning to express how important the relationship was within this story:

"I think, with young people, if you're not willing to start it, then don't . . . if you are not willing to be there, in it for the long haul, then don't do it. Because actually you can't help a young person, get started and walk away."

There is a correlation with the other theme of time and journey, as being there and the time taken with Lily was crucial in turning her life around. What's more, Jill articulates her mission amongst young people, not in terms of young people coming to faith, but in her work amongst them in difficult situations and helping them in very practical ways—resonating with Kim, Mark, Martin and Kerry. This revolves around the overarching theme of relationships as communicative acts and is enacted through being there and being like Jesus. For Jill, being there was such an important part of her mission amongst young people that she was willing to go beyond what was expected of her in her role as youth minister. Consequently, it was through this willingness to be there for Lily and the other young people for the long haul that led her to communicate aspects of her faith and how she began to see change. This also resonates in the ministry of Kerry, Kim, Dan and Terry. For Kerry, it was the consistency of relationship that was important—being there for young people was explicitly expressed—*"when they needed someone I was there."* For Kim, being there was expressed as time spent with young people as she sought to demonstrate Jesus' compassion and help them with their problems. Dan also demonstrated compassion through being there; again, he saw this as being like Jesus as he sought to offer unconditional love. Terry saw his being there for young people as non- mechanical—he wanted to offer young people time and an approach that was based on relational, unconditional love, because this is how he saw himself being like Jesus. There are echoes of these approaches in how Tom saw his care reflecting and pointing to how God loves and cares for people.

The idea of symbol finds expression through love, care and being there and is articulated in a story Tom told. Tom articulates how he worked alongside two girls and how one of the girls was suffering and facing a very challenging time. This was not an issue that Tom had dealt with alone, the vicar had been involved and so had the previous youth minister. The previous youth minister had met them in a local coffee shop, so Tom adopted this practice. The story of Tom's work amongst these young people pivots around a difficult situation with the group he was working with. The situation involved a demanding young person who needed one-to-one support and the girl Tom had been working alongside had expressed an interest in helping others. Within Tom's enacted mission alongside this girl, the practice of being there was expressed. This is demonstrated through being connected through relationship, and Tom was able to work with this girl who was from a marginalized position on the edge of a community so that she was brought into and given a place within that community. This is similar to how Jill saw her enacted practice with a desire to bring people back into community. For Tom the complexity of this practice, like Jill, Kim, Kerry, Terry and Dan can be seen as theological shorthand, as it is summed up through the straightforward expression of being there. Being there is the demonstration of compassion and unconditional love. Here, Tom acts as a symbol which points towards a God who cares and has compassion and this is demonstrated and lived out in the actual practice of care and concern of being there for this young girl, resonating with the practice of *diakonia*. Moreover, we can see how the other theme of time and journey reverberates through this narrative and shapes this practice.

The theme of being there and the compassion demonstrated in the practice of the youth ministers also echoes within David's enacted mission. For David, being there has a very practical outworking. Illustrated by a story he told of a young woman. This story locates David's idea of mission in a similar vein to Jill, Kim, Kerry, Sam, Martin and Tom. Likewise, it is not only about people coming to faith, but also how that mission is the outworking and expression of practical care, concern and love; therefore, like the others, this has an emphasis on orthopraxis. This is transmitted and mediated through the building of connections and through relationships functioning as communicative acts. This is embodied in being there in the midst of suffering and is rooted in David's understanding of how Jesus related to people.

David expresses this explicitly through his support of a girl who became pregnant which created enormous tensions within the family. For David, being there for this girl and the support he gave her finds direct correlation with the person of Jesus. David articulates this by seeing that Jesus often looked after somebody's physical needs before he talked about the kingdom of God. Here again is an intertwining of the themes. Being there acts as the theological shorthand expression for the complexities of practice and this is embodied in very practical care and concern. However, this theological shorthand in the lived practice of Jill, Rachel, Kim, Kerry, Terry, Tom and David acts through the youth minister being a symbol that points to a God who cares and is concerned about suffering and this is seen as being like Jesus. This again is transmitted through the connections and relationships as communicative acts established by the minister as they enact mission amongst young people and is shaped over a period of time. This practice of being there is also demonstrated in the ministry of Mark, Andrew, Martin, Dan and Sam; again, being there is a theological shorthand expression of the complexities of practice. Here, Mark, Andrew, Dan, Martin and Sam function as symbols that point to how God is interested in the whole of people's lives. Mark expresses this through a story of how he worked with a young person; this is articulated as being there for them in the midst of a very challenging time.

This particular young person was suffering due to the death of his Dad and he had no male role model. Mark became a role model for this young person and it led to the young person wanting to emulate what Mark was living out, resonating with Kerry, Kim and Dan. Mark uses the phrase model to articulate how the young people want to model what he is doing in terms of working amongst other at risk young people. This again is a demonstration of how Mark enacts mission, but this mission is seen in its widest sense, about enabling and helping young people to become participants and contributors to society, chiming with the work of Kim, Kerry, Dan and Martin. For Mark, like the others, this wider sense of mission is expressed by seeing his practice as being concerned about their whole life. For Sam, his holistic care and concern for young people is articulated by being there for them when they face difficult times. Sam tells the poignant story of how he supported a young person through an attempted suicide. When the suicide attempt failed it was Sam who the young person contacted first:

"You know that you have spent quality time with a young person, when the relationship is important and working when you become the first point of contact in an emergency, it was me the young person called and not their family. This was both good, and . . . you know, a bit of worry, as it places additional pressure on you to be there for them"

Being there for this particular young person was an important relational response for Sam (despite his concerns) and for Sam it demonstrated the love and compassion of Jesus, but this complex act was summed up through the simple phrase of being there for them at their point of need. For Martin, being there for young people also acted as a role model, resonating with Kim, Kerry and Dan's thoughts. It was through being there that the young people knew that Martin was a Christian, he explicitly related being there as a concrete example of being like Jesus:

"I meet young people on their turf, I'm a role model, an example of Jesus. Through being there young people know that I'm a Christian. They come and talk to me, ask me stuff and once people know that I'm a Christian, sometimes they ask me to pray for them, you know to try and help them, even if they are not sure what they believe, they trust me you know... it's because of how you are with them"

This very pragmatic example of being there is played out through what Martin could offer young people connected to the detached project he ran. For example, what things could he do to make the young people lives better, what could he do to break down some of the barriers between the young people and the police, how could he help the community? Being there travels on the conduits of relationships that act as places of communication, mediating aspects of the Christian faith, but is articulated as fragments of theology expressed as theological shorthand. Yet, this practice opens up liminal spaces, spaces where God can act and like the practice of Tom, Jill, David, Martin, Mark and Sam has an expressed focus on orthopraxis, evoking and enacting the practice of *diakonia*.

The Cost of Being There

The emphasis on orthopraxis and the practice of *diakonia* is again seen in Rachel's ministry as she articulates her mission amongst young people through being there. Again, Rachel articulates this sense of mission in its widest sense; enabling young people to become more socially responsible, resonating with the ministry of Kim, Kerry and Martin. However, for Rachel, the cost of being there resonates through the narrative. This is expressed in how Rachel began working on an estate in South London where she met a girl called Sarah. For Rachel, being there acted as the vehicle through which a relationship became established and connections were made. The act of being there is an enacted symbol, a committed expression of faith and represented through the act of listening. Within this story, the other theme of time and journey is seen, but this is implied and not made explicit. Through this dedicated act of being there, through a committed act of listening, a relationship began to take shape. Rachel illustrates this by seeing that Sarah needed some attention; she just wanted someone to listen to her problems. This committed act of listening represented a willingness to be present with Sarah, someone willing to give the time and be there with her. Through the act of listening, a relationship was formed. Still, even though a relationship had been established it was not unproblematic.

Rachel says: "*there were occasions when I was in tears and I was like 'Jesus you need to help because I can't give up on her', but she's driving me insane, she would call me at all sorts of hours of the night. It was like two years after I left the estate and I stayed in contact with her, but it was so difficult as I wasn't allowed to go for coffee unless I had her mum's consent.*

Her Mum ended up in hospital and it made it a really difficult relationship to keep up actually and I found that really hard. Although I found it hard, it is why I wanted to be working there, it was from the example Jesus set of making friends with people who no one else wants to be friends with."

Within Rachel's expression of difficult and hard, the act of being there as a symbol of who God is, is costly. Rachel wrestles with this as she enacts her faith as she seeks to be like Jesus within this situation. The tension here is that she feels like she is the only one able to help, it points to a misunderstanding of pastoral boundaries, again, it raises ecclesiological questions—where is the congregation, how is Rachel supported? As above, again, the work of God's Spirit is not given enough attention, youth ministry is seen as an individual pursuit. The outworking of her theology as theological shorthand is enormously costly.

That said, Rachel's sacrificial being there, as a symbol of practice, led Sarah to ask to come to church. Therefore, through this embodied act of mission and Rachel being there for Sarah, it led Sarah to ask questions of Rachel's faith, especially around issues of suffering and sex before marriage. Again, within this enacted story of mission amongst young people, we see in Rachel's reflections the intersecting of the four themes. The encounter flourishes through the relationship established, but it was the committed act of being there through listening that established the relationship as a communicative act. Through this process Rachel acted as a symbol that pointed to God and the deeper realities of her faith. This led to questions being asked by Sarah. Moreover, this story finds theological expression and articulation by Rachel locating the very reason why this piece of practice, to be like Jesus, took place. Here again, we can see the complex nuances of practice expressed in the theological shorthand of the phrase is like Jesus and being there. Again, this encompasses and resonates with the practices of *marturia* and *diakonia* and has a focus on orthopraxis. Consequently, this being there and the establishment of a relationship took time. The journey lasted three years and went way beyond and outside the established boundaries of the original project. It is the theme of time and journey that is explored next.

Relationships as Communicative Acts: Time and Journey

The theme of time and journey expresses the commitment of being there. Being there is an enacted theological moment in time and space through which the youth minister symbolizes and embodies a greater reality, it is an act of faith. This is seen as being like Jesus as model; therefore, as has been discussed, both being there and like Jesus act as theological shorthand. They are transmitted and given direction and shape through the connections made. These are carried by the relationships which function as places of communicative acts, but this takes time and the creation of a liminal space. In this liminal space the youth minister practitioners seek to be like Jesus. This is a place of transition, a threshold, of waiting and not knowing, a place of movement and life. Within this liminal space, there is an interdependence between the themes: relationships, being like Jesus and being there, all take time, and this is either explicit or it is implied through the idea of journey and is an embodied act of faith in a series of moments. Being there as an embodied act of faith is given expression through the words time and journey and is articulated within the thoughts of all of the practitioners.

As the youth ministers told stories and articulated how they enacted mission amongst young people, the sense of time is expressed clearly:

Tom: *"over time, obviously you build relationships . . . actually the biggest gift I can give a young person is time, because actually most adults they encounter can't give them much time, and a lot of them don't get any time with adults,"* Tom continues, *"it's not a time when you are setting an agenda, it's time when they are able to share their own thoughts and their own experiences, and that actually you provide a listening ear"*

Andrew: *"over a period of about three years we got to know them relationally . . . it is all about time to share your life."*

Mark: *"the key is actually spending time with people."*

Martin: *"time is essential in my work amongst young people, it enables me to get to know them, through relationships and the time spent they see me as a role model."*

Sam: *"for me, it's not necessarily about length of time, you know, you could spend years with a young person, at a youth club or something and not get to know them—it is about the quality of time spent."*

In Tom's expression above, he places an emphasis on time as a gift and as a commodity in his enacted mission amongst young people. There is also the sense of space when time is available with no agenda and space is given to be present and provide a listening ear. This resonates with Sam's ideas about the importance of quality time and chimes with Rachel's thoughts above, as the act of being there finds expression through listening. For Tom, this is drawn from how Jesus worked, investing in others, and there is direct correlation between being there for a young person and being like Jesus and the time this takes. For Terry, the importance of time spent with young people is also drawn from Jesus' ministry, and he sees it particularly within the Woman at the Well story and how Jesus made time for her, resonating with Rachel. Terry also sees how time may be earnt:

"you know, you need to spend quality time with young people, sometimes you have to earn it, that said, you can also distinguish between chronos time and kairos moments, you have to discern which is important."

For Terry, the distinction between, being there, earning the right to talk, longevity of time spent and liminal spaces created through kairos moments begins to point to the activity of God. However, this complex and nuanced process is still held in the notion of time and summed up quiet straight forwardly. But the nuances go beyond the use of words and can be seen as theological shorthand for the complexities of work with young people that evokes the practices of *marturia* and *diakonia*.

Moreover, Andrew also sees the value of time and how this acts to create a liminal space. Here, being there for a young person, and the time for conversations becomes a space where Andrew seeks to communicate something of his life. It is being present with a young person and this takes time, builds connections and through a relationship that functions as a communicative act, faith can be seen to be transmitted. Additionally, like Tom and Terry, Andrew makes a direct link to being like Jesus, as he expresses that as Jesus worked with his disciples it took time. Mark also expresses the physical length and amount of time it can take when working with young people and, for Mark, the time spent brings about a change in the young person and, like Andrew, Terry and Tom, there is a direct correlation between this thinking and being like Jesus. Moreover, Mark then links the idea of like Jesus to that of relationship and time. Through this interplay of relationships, being there, time and like Jesus, there is the creation of a liminal space, a place of waiting and not knowing. This is what the youth ministers were aiming for in their enacting of mission. As Mark, Terry and Sam articulate, the key is in spending time with young people; it is time that unlocks their practice as *marturia* and *diakonia*. For Andrew, Martin, and Dan, being there and being like Jesus is also expressed through the idea of journey. For Andrew, this means that you can journey with young people. Here, the sense of journey finds a deeper theological expression as he seeks to trust that God is in the relationship and in the conversations that happen. Here, Andrew, through the notion of journey, begins to express a deeper theology to being like Jesus.

For Andrew, following the work of the Holy Spirit, sees that:

". . . for me anyway, and I would like to think for our team here, it means that we need to trust God . . . but it also takes some of the responsibility away from us. Because whether or not these people end up following Christ or not is actually not down to us, it's down to God's Spirit."

As Andrew adopts this theological view, it leads him to see time as a pivotal part of his enacting of mission amongst young people. Here, Andrew begins to articulate the twinning between relationships as communicative acts and how important the aspect of time is within this process. Andrew sees that the young people who have become interested in Christianity are those young people that he has spent time with and sometimes this time can be seen as wasted. Yet, the sense of wasted time is important as they are allowed space to discover God. This is the creation of a liminal space, a threshold, a time of not knowing, trusting and waiting. The creation of a liminal space again marks out time as a commodity and here are echoes of time as a gift that we see in Tom's thinking. However, for Andrew, this sense of wasting time has serious implications. It leads Andrew to see time as one of the core values of his work and central to his enacting mission amongst young people. It has led him to re-orientate his practice for the intentional creation of space and time to be with people, the intentional creation of liminal spaces. In Martin's and Dan's practice, this sense of journey is also important. For Dan, it makes it easier to work with young people if you have time:

"if you can be constant with them in their journey, demonstrating unconditional love, like Jesus did amongst the Pharisees and tax collectors."

There is a confusion here between Jesus' attitude to Pharisees (of whom he was frequently critical) and towards tax collectors and sinners. This could be a slip of the tongue for Dan, but it could also point to rather vague understanding of Jesus' actual ministry—he didn't often hang out with Pharisees (apart from Nicodemus).

Martin, sees that it is *"how you are with them"* that is important within this and that you are like Jesus with them. Although Martin did not use the word journey, it is implied in how he talks about time and his work amongst young people. Additionally, within Jill's expression of mission amongst young people, the sense of time can also be seen in the creation of liminal spaces. This is again expressed through the notion of being there, such as, on a park bench sharing food or hot drinks for many hours in the freezing cold of winter. Time is again central to her practice and, for Jill, she needed to be in it for the long haul. Again, there is a correlation of the themes also seen in Dan, Terry, and Martin's practice, between being there and time in the enacting of Jill's practice as an act of faith. Moreover, Tom articulates that the sense of time spent is actually part of his enacted mission amongst young people. Tom sees that the time spent with them is mission. It is the creation of a liminal space to allow God to work. This process of time spent as mission, the creation of a liminal space, is worked out and interwoven in the metaphor of journey and expressed through the term relationships and these function as communicative acts. Furthermore, Andrew's thoughts resonate with Tom, Terry, Martin and Dan as he also sees practice as a journey:

Andrew: *"you know all the talk is you journey with people. . . . yet, we get an image of trying to fix people rather than trying to journey with them."*

Tom: *"So it's journeying, relationships, but with a purpose, it's very much a journey and working with them at different stages and bringing in different challenges at various points. I mean our key idea is to journey with young people to see their lives transformed by Jesus Christ."*

Tom quantifies this by telling a story of a young person who he started to work with at a local school. The other themes of relationships and being there reverberate through his narrative, but the element of time and sense of journey is expressed. In this narrative of practice, a young person came to a café and, through the relationship, he joined a football team. Through this he came to a mission group (Tom's adaptation of an

Alpha Course), then to a discipleship group and then he came to faith and was baptized and confirmed. Tom conveys this process as a journey, the young person went from being part of a group to making a commitment and the journey took about eighteen months. Within these ideas of time and journey is the creation of liminal space. To be present to someone, through being there, a liminal space is created, a place of threshold, of waiting and not knowing, it is a place of tension. Within the practice of Andrew, Martin, Terry, Dan and Tom, the theme of time and journey acts as theological shorthand for the complexity and nuances of practice and the communicating of their faith amongst young people; it again evokes the practices of *marturia* and *diakonia*.

Jill and Kim, also express the idea of a liminal space through journey and that sense of not knowing and waiting. Furthermore, for Jill, the journey created opportunities for questions, questions about her faith and why she did what she did. These arose from spending time with a young person in their difficulties and suffering. Within the idea of journey, as Jill expresses it, we again see the interplay of relationships and journey. Here, a relationship is established and, through being there, a connection, transmission and mediation of ideas is found; relationships function as communicative acts. Within this liminal space God is mentioned and pointed towards; here, through being there we see the embodiment of symbol. Jill sees that the young person knew that she was a Christian and through this sense of journey that Jill articulates a liminal space is created as Jill waits for God to act. Moreover, there is a sense of not knowing how events with this particular young person will turn out. Jill expresses this sense of not knowing what will happen and how God will work in the future. The story ends on a note of hope as Jill tells of how this girl's perception changed from having a cynical sense of a Christian as a "*God botherer*" to one where Christians "*aren't that bad.*" Therefore, for Andrew, Tom and Jill, the journey is a process, the creation of a liminal space, a time and place where faith can be enacted and performed, but it comes with no guarantees, it is ambiguous. Kim articulates the frustrations seen within youth ministry when seen through the lens of time and Journey. For Kim, work amongst young people can be:

"*never ending and there is never enough time, you end up working way more than you thought, you have to be so flexible, sometimes it's so hard.*"

Therefore, spending time with young people can bring its own pressure and expectations, often not verbalized, there is a cost for the youth minister in choosing to work this way.

That said, enacting mission amongst young people through time and journey and the creation of liminal spaces is a positive act of faith to be like Jesus and a positive act of waiting amongst the unknown as the youth ministers wait expectantly for God to act. Moreover, in this liminal space the youth ministers seek to move young people on in their journey, either to help them be better citizens (Kim, Kerry, Martin, Andrew, Mark, Jill, Rachel, David) or seeking to move them into relationship with Christ (Terry, Dan, Sam, Andrew, Tom, Rachel, Jill, David). Therefore, this is what the practitioners are aiming for in their enacted practice. It is possible to see time as a place where connections and the transmission of faith is sought, as they seek to be like Jesus through relationships that function as communicative acts. In this enacting of faith the focus is on orthopraxis and resonates with the practices of *marturia* and *diakonia*. This complex practice is summed up through the theological shorthand of time and journey. In the following chapter the data within narratives of practice is brought into conversation with the literature on youth ministry as missionary endeavor, as the practice of relationships is investigated further.

Chapter 6

Narratives of Practice and the Normative Voice within Youth Ministry

The last chapter captured practice frame by frame, it examined how youth ministers told stories of their work amongst young people and the language used to articulate this. These liminal encounters with the living God have been places where the youth ministers have sort to follow Christ and live out their faith amongst young people. These liminal encounters and spaces are difficult places for the youth ministers to be and to inhabit. It is a costly ministry, full of patient sacrifice and simple phrases: relationships, like Jesus, being there, time and journey sum up the complexities of very difficult situations. The narratives explored captured the words and nuances of speech that reveal theological shorthand in motion, the analysis of the stories has demonstrated how theology becomes fragmented in the complexities of practice.

Relationships guide youth ministry as missionary endeavor. Therefore, in the practice and narratives of the youth ministers, relationships are a construction, a constructed practice for ministry. They are, meaningful and meaning making. They are meaningful because they are the medium of the mission and they are meaning making because they mediate the faith, message and acts of mission of the youth minister. Therefore, the overarching theme of relationships, so constructed as practice, becomes the medium and at least, in part, the message. The *acts* of the enacted mission, the energy for the mediation, the transmission and communication of the Gospel amongst young people—all stem from relationships. Here, the collapsing of the classic view of Christian practice as *diakonia*, *kerygma* and *marturia* into the practice of relationships takes place.

In the background within Rublev's icon is a house and a tree, they are not the focus of the painting, but like the staffs create a sense of journey, a place of destination. The door is open to the traveler, the tree a marker on the way. This chapter extends the exploration of the significance of relationships for youth ministers by bringing their stories into critical conversation with the youth ministry literature. One of the arguments has been that the youth ministry literature acts as the normative voice for contemporary youth ministry practice. It is time to explore this in more depth as the interpretive journey continues.

The Youth Ministry Literature as the Normative Voice for Practice

The sense that relationships act as the energy for enacted mission finds resonance in Ward's[1] thinking that "relationships are the fuel on which youth work travels" and beyond this to the model provided by Young Life. Therefore, not only is the theme of relationships central to how the practitioners view their enacted mission amongst young people, it is also central within the literature—*Youth A Part*,[2] Ward,[3] Green and Christian,[4] Senter III et al.,[5] Passmore,[6] Sudworth et al.,[7] Borgman,[8] Dean,[9] Savage et al.,[10] Root,[11] and Pimlott and Pimlott,[12] Griffiths,[13] Shepherd[14] all have relationships as a theme. Therefore, within this new relational paradigm, the term relationships acts as a construct for practice because of the meaning given to them. Here, the term relationships has become part

---

1. Ward, *Youthwork*, 43.
2. Church of England Board of Education, *Youth A Part*, 36.
3. Ward, *Youthwork*, 43.
4. Green and Christian, *Accompanying*.
5. Senter et al., *Four Views of Youth Ministry*.
6. Passmore, *Meet Them Where They're At*.
7. Sudworth et al, *Mission Shaped Youth*, 11.
8. Borgman, *When Kumbaya Is Not Enough*, 30.
9. Dean, *Practicing Passion*, 183.
10. Savage et al., *Making Sense of Generation Y*, 122–35.
11. Root, *Revisiting Relational Youth Ministry*, 62.
12. Pimlott and Pimlott, *Youth Work after Christendom*, 75.
13. Griffiths, *Models for Youth Ministry*, 10.
14. Shepherd, *Faith Generation*, 8–48.

of a discourse within the youth ministry literature and this discourse determines its interpretation and seeks to articulate its meaning and can be seen as a communicative act. In turn, this discourse, at least in part, finds resonance in the practice of the youth ministers. Therefore, current youth ministry practice can be seen to be guided by the normative voice and expression of relationships that is articulated through the literature on youth ministry.

Ward[15] begins to give a deeper definition of the term relationship and importantly locates this in sharing in God's mission to the world, but again, ministry is still seen as a model.[16] Dean[17] also articulates a fuller understanding of this term, and locates this beyond the "role of the individual" as expressed through Ward[18] and in the practice of the congregation. Griffiths,[19] differs from Borgman,[20] Ward,[21] Dean,[22] Passmore,[23] Sudworth,[24] and Pimlott and Pimlott[25] and wants to reframe the notion of relationships through the concept of *kairos* time. Shepherd[26] sees the importance of relational work as underpinning the act of faith generation among young people. However, it is Root[27] who gives the most articulate expression of the term relationship as he engages with this concept through a Christology developed through the work of Bonhoeffer. This is an important move and takes us beyond relationships that are like Jesus as model. Yet, at this level, there is a disconnection between the theological expression within Root's work and the lived practice of the youth ministers interviewed. Importantly, however, this finds deep resonance with Andrew's thoughts about his practice. Andrew crucially sees that perhaps *"God is in that relationship."* It is possible here to see echoes of

15. Ward, *Youthwork*, 43.
16. Ibid., 29.
17. Dean, *Practicing Passion*, 91.
18. Ward, *Youthwork*.
19. Griffiths, *Models for Youth Ministry*, 6–10.
20. Borgman, *When Kumbaya Is Not Enough*.
21. Ward, *Youthwork*.
22. Dean, *Practicing Passion*.
23 Passmore, *Meet Them Where They're At*.
24. Sudworth et al., *Mission Shaped Youth*.
25. Pimlott and Pimlott, *Youth Work after Christendom*.
26. Shepherd, *Faith Generation*, 46.
27. Root, *Revisiting Relational Youth Ministry*.

Root's[28] theology and thinking. Furthermore, Terry explicitly articulates the difference between *chronos* and *kairos* time within relationships, reflecting and articulating, at least in part, the thoughts of Griffiths.[29]

Therefore, there is a connection between what is taught and written about within the missiological task of youth ministry within the new relational paradigm and the practice of the youth ministers as they enact mission amongst young people. There is a level of connection between the theory and the lived-in practice. Yet, that connection only goes so far and what is surprising is the low level at which this is articulated. Within the embodiment of relationships and the articulated expression of relationships, theological shorthand is in action, an uncomplicated way of expressing and articulating the complexities of mission and embodiment of the Gospel amongst young people. It encompasses a richness of ideas and a deep sense of performed theology, but this is simply expressed through the term relationship. There are two interrelated problems here. Firstly, the straight forward use of the term relational is down to the relatively simple expression of this within some of the literature on youth ministry. For example, in *Youth A Part*[30] relationships are expressed as "we communicate through deeds and actions before we communicate through words." This expression of the term relationships resonates clearly with relationships that function as communicative acts, but is a light description in terms of the richness that is found in actual practice that we have seen in the narratives. However, it finds correlation within the thoughts of David who sees that: *"Christianity is so foreign that actually it needs to be introduced in a different type of way, through connections, through relationships, just by caring really for people."* Within this statement from David, there is a richness of thoughts and ideas about how connections are made and about the transmission, mediation and communication of faith, as well as the pastoral care of a person, but these are carried and thinly expressed and pivot around the idea of relationship. In addition, this resonates in the work of Green and Christian[31] and through the notion of Accompanying. Here again, relationships are central to this

---

28. Ibid., 15.
29. Griffiths, *Models for Youth Ministry*.
30. Church of England Board of Education, *Youth A Part*, 36.
31. Green and Christian, *Accompanying*, 33–38.

framework and are discussed, but the theological rationale for these is weak.[32]

Furthermore, in the follow up work to *Youth A Part*,[33] Sudworth et al.,[34] give relationships a limited description. Here relationships "are the only means we have of enabling and encouraging young people to reach maturity in their physical, emotional, social and spiritual lives." These are communicative acts, it is personal relationalism finding expression and there is correlation with how Mark sees the central activity of relationships. He says, *"if the relationship isn't at the heart of it and you haven't got time for someone, then you need to create time and if it's outside of the session that's fine, we can sort it."* In the work of Sudworth et al.,[35] relationships are also seen as central and the only vehicle to carry the holistic development of young people. Questions need to be asked if the limited description of relationships given here can carry the weight of what is expected of them. Furthermore, relationships are seen to be central and are to be made explicit within the post–Christendom paradigm as Pimlott and Pimlott,[36] see. Relationships occupy a central place in the work of Savage et al.,[37] but again this is a weak description and there is no robust theological exploration. Relationships are also given a shallow description by Borgman,[38] although, the essence of his description captures the nature of the enacted mission amongst young people of the youth minister practitioners: "we must live among them and feel the pulse of their lives, the beat of their hearts." In Borgman's expression, a correlation can be seen between this and the notion of sharing of lives (Kim, Kerry, Andrew, Tom, Mark, Rachel, Jill and Terry). Therefore, the narratives of practice, as told by the youth ministers in their enacting of mission amongst young people, are only mirroring, reflecting and constructing the frameworks for practice from what they have observed, read and been taught from the community of practice that is youth ministry.

The second problem is intimately connected with the first. There is a link between this relatively new youth ministry missiological paradigm

32. For a critique of this Accompanying framework see Thomson, *Telling the Difference*, 246–52.

33. Church of England Board of Education, *Youth A Part*.

34. Sudworth et al., *Mission Shaped Youth*, 11.

35. Ibid.

36. Pimlott and Pimlott, *Youth Work after Christendom*, 75–80, 141, 145.

37. Savage et al., *Making Sense of Generation Y*, 122–55.

38. Borgman, *When Kumbaya Is Not Enough*, 30.

and the foundation of this approach within the Young Life frame work. Here the theological tensions and shallowness of this approach[39] have worked their way out into the practice of the youth ministers. They have moved away from a diet of entertainment[40] but have inherited the incarnation as ministry justification and as a pattern for ministry that becomes expressed as like Jesus and as model in the narratives of practice. Although the youth ministry practitioners see themselves as being like Jesus, the term incarnational is only used once by Mark and has been replaced by the overarching term relationship. At the heart of this lies a problem about the theological expression of youth ministry. In the examples given, there is a lightweight expression of theological thought around the term relationship. Within the articulation of mission amongst young people by the practitioners, there is a very limited verbalization of the richness and theological depth of relationships or of the themes and capital of this within the Christian tradition. The richness of this term is not articulated and importantly, not drawn upon or expressed in the practice of youth ministers.

The practitioners have expressed how central relationships are to their practice. It is now time to explore how these relationships function. Not only as places of connection that link the life of the youth minister to the young people, but also how these relationships articulate, mediate and transmit faith and act as circuits of influence and places of sub-cultural engagement. Again, these themes can be traced back into the literature.

Relationships as Communicative Acts: Connection

As the theme of connection[41] is explored and investigated, it echoes in the youth ministry literature. The idea of relationships as communicative acts, as a place of connection is seen in Andrew's articulation of enacted mission. These ideas are present in the way the sharing of lives acts as a place of connection between himself and the young people. It acts as a place for the transmission and communicating of faith. This is explored below. In the verbalizing of Andrew's relationships with young people, he used the term "*connections*." For Andrew, relationships are built, seeing that you need to "*get to know them and try and build a relationship, a*

---

39. Tanis, *Making Jesus Attractive*.
40. Tanis, *History and Influence*.
41. This word also finds expression in the work of Lovejoy, *Making Connections*.

connection." It is possible to trace the echoes of this idea of a connection back into Ward's[42] work. Ward[43] articulates similar ideas of connection, but uses the language of contact. The missional drive within the notion of contact is provided by the youth minister and again reverberates with the strategy of Young Life.[44] It is the intentional meeting of young people in a place that is comfortable for them; it is about spending time with a particular group of young people with the aim of building relationships.[45] Again, we can see Ward's[46] thinking echoing through the narratives the youth ministers told of how they enact mission amongst young people. For example, Tom speaks about building *"intentional relationships"* and *"connections"* and meeting young people where they are, whilst Jill also articulates Ward's[47] notion of contact by expressing her ministry as, *"just by going where they are."* However, the language of contact is not used, but this idea of contact is reframed through the notion of connection. Furthermore, it is possible to see the interrelation of the other themes of time and journey and being there. As Ward's[48] notion of contact and extended contact is considered, he sees "there is no short cut to developing a trusting and mutual relationship with a group of young people." These themes become more explicit through the idea of extended contact as the intentional relationships develop deeper.[49] Moreover, these ideas of contact and extended contact echo through Mark's narrative. Here, this core theme of relationship is seen as a metaphorical bridge, a place of connection and communication, connecting the minister's life to that of the young person, there is interrelation between contact, bridge and connection that is carried through relationships as communicative acts and is expressed through being there.

The idea of connection that is expressed through the narratives of the youth ministry practitioners also resonates through Root's work. Root[50] sees that "ministry is about connection," one to another, about sharing in suffering and joy, about persons meeting persons . . . it is about

42. Ward, *Youthwork*, 46–59.
43. Ibid., 46.
44. Tanis, *Making Jesus Attractive*.
45. Ward, *Youthwork*, 49.
46. Ibid., 53.
47. Ibid.
48. Ibid.
49. Ibid., 52.
50. Root, *Revisiting Relational Youth Ministry*, 15.

shared life." As the stories told by our youth ministry practitioners are explored, these themes shine through. In the stories told by David, Kim, Kerry, Sam, Rachel and Jill, they shared in the suffering of young people, and Jill also took part in the joy and success. The interrelation between the research themes can be seen as connection is made through the sharing of lives that are enacted in being there. Within the idea of connection the personal cost of these connections as expressed through the narratives of Kim, Sam, Rachel, Jill and Tom can be observed. Echoes of the idea of connection and building relationships chime in the work of Green and Christian[51] as they develop their Accompanying motif. They do articulate a difference between counselling, mentoring and befriending, but the notion of connection remains through their expression of being there. In the work of Passmore[52] and Pimlott and Pimlott,[53] the reverberations of this idea of connection that echo in Jill's enacted practice can be seen.

Pimlott and Pimlott[54] express this as being incarnational and they articulate it as being alongside young people in success and in times of suffering and struggle. Moreover, in the language of the youth ministry practitioners, when they use the word connection, it is again used as theological shorthand. It sums up this deeper expression of lived practice that when they meet young people they are engaged in suffering alongside them. This is expressed through being there as they seek to be like Jesus to them when they are hurting, suffering and feeling alone; it is about "persons meeting persons,"[55] but it is not articulated as such. This complex, nuanced and multifaceted practice is summed up through the words connection and relationship; again, this is a partial description in terms of the complexity of practice and evokes and points towards a wider theological picture. What is missing, in all but one (Andrew), in the use of this theological shorthand, is the theological articulation that Root[56] gives to the idea of connection, that Christ is not outside of the relationship, but within it. The idea of relationships as communicative acts as connection has been explored, this reverberates through the narratives of practice and echoes in the youth ministry literature. In the last chap-

---

51. Green and Christian, *Accompanying*, 21–27.
52. Passmore, *Meet Them Where They're At*.
53. Pimlott and Pimlott, *Youth Work after Christendom*.
54. Ibid., 75.
55. Root, *Revisiting Relational Youth Ministry*, 15.
56. Ibid.

ter, the inferred, but interrelated theme of transmission was developed. Transmission is the mediation of faith and is explored next.

Relationships as Communicative Acts: Transmission

This theme is inferred from the data and is found within the practice of the youth ministers as they enacted mission amongst young people. It sees that the youth ministers use and rely on the medium of relationships to transmit and mediate their faith and also to extend influence through their practice. It is possible to see these as circuits of influence—relationships that function as communicative acts. For Andrew, he seeks to enact mission through this process and through the desire to *"share something of our lives and faith which obviously involved us as Christians."* Within the sharing of our lives as Christians, the idea of transmission can be seen, and through relationships influence is sought. Furthermore, for Mark, the relationship leads to how *"influence is granted because of the level of respect and trust"* they have for the worker. Therefore, for Mark and Andrew, these relationships are seen as a place not only of connection but of transmission that can mediate and communicate the ideas and faith of the minister, they act as places of influence, as they seek to connect with young people and have moral sway. The role of relationships as communicative acts, as transmission, becomes a place of sub-cultural engagement.[57] This is articulated by Tom, who sees that *"over time . . . you build relationships with them . . . and that there is an overlap of two worlds."* Furthermore, in David's thoughts above, we saw that *"Christianity is so foreign that actually it needs to be introduced in a different type of way."* Furthermore, Kim, Dan and Sam also articulate the importance of trust as they seek to influence and communicate their faith amongst young people. Again, the desire is that, through relationships, the Christian faith is transmitted and mediated, this happens through the embodied action of the youth minister by being there and seeking to be like Jesus.

Within these aspects of enacted mission the theme of relationships as communicative acts as transmission can be clearly seen. Furthermore, echoes of the theme of transmission can be seen in the cited literature. In the literature, it takes two forms; the first is through the term incarnation. The incarnation is taken as a model or pattern and is adopted to communicate the act of faith from one sub-culture to another, through

---

57. Hebdige, *Subculture*.

the medium of relationships and is articulated in the following, *Youth A Part*,[58] Ward,[59] Borgman,[60] Sudworth et al.,[61] Savage et al.,[62] and Pimlott and Pimlott.[63] The second is interrelated to the first, but the sociological motivations for this are unmasked through the work of Root[64] and his work on the incarnation and relationships working at the level of influence within the paradigm of youth ministry as mission. Firstly, the term incarnation can be considered and the resonance of this can be traced through the narratives of the practitioners. Sudworth et al.[65] describes the term incarnation as "it involves entering the young people's world and honoring them by taking it as seriously as they do." The echoes of this idea ring through the narratives told by the youth ministers as they enacted mission amongst young people and finds particular resonance through the narratives of David, Kim, Sam, Kerry, Tom and Mathew through relationships functioning as communicative acts. There is also a link here between these thoughts and Ward's[66] work. There is a strong correlation with relationships as communicative acts as transmission and connection to Ward's[67] ideas on contact, extended contact and proclamation. In Ward's[68] model these are sequential and each build on the other until a deep enough relationship is established to allow proclamation to take place. In the practice of the youth ministers, very little verbal proclamation actually took place. What is seen is a very strong commitment to the relationship and the embodiment of faith and being there like Jesus. Therefore, there is a focus on and a strong commitment to orthopraxis.

The relationship becomes the place of connection and transmission but the transmission, the communicative acts, are the embodied faith of being there and being like Jesus in deed and action. Although this is important, it is limiting in terms of the classical practice of *kerygma*, of spoken proclamation. However, being there in deed and action finds

58. Church of England Board of Education, *Youth A Part*.
59. Ward, *Youthwork*.
60. Borgman, *When Kumbaya Is Not Enough*.
61. Sudworth et al., *Mission Shaped Youth*.
62. Savage et al., *Making Sense of Generation Y*.
63. Pimlott and Pimlott, *Youth Work after Christendom*.
64. Root, *Revisiting Relational Youth Ministry*.
65. Sudworth et al., *Mission Shaped Youth*, 12.
66. Ward, *Youthwork*.
67. Ibid., 43–59.
68. Ibid.

deep resonance in the thinking of Savage et al.[69] and is expressed through the term "prior mission."[70] Although this concept of "prior mission" is not articulated in the narratives of practice, this is the arena of the youth minister's mission. Pimlott and Pimlott[71] adopt the incarnation and this is expressed through having a focus on "being, on relationships, on seeking to flesh out the Gospel through identifying with people as Jesus did." The phrase "as Jesus" resonates with the idea of model that is articulated through the narratives of practice and again, within Pimlott's and Pimlott's[72] thinking, the incarnation is adopted for the transmission of the Gospel into particular sub-cultures. However, no in depth theological explanation of this is given, but this transmission happens as relationships act as circuits of influence as communicative acts and are established by the workers amongst groups of young people.[73] Shepherd[74] highlights the importance of this development with youth ministry– seeing how the incarnation is adopted as a means of boundary crossing in order that Christ and the Gospel might become known in that context. Passmore's[75] work also highlights this as youth workers should "meet them where they're at" and, as can be seen, resonates strongly with Ward[76] and Borgman.[77] Again, it is this incarnational theology that underpins and guides the complex and nuanced work of the youth ministers interviewed, yet, this is not explicitly expressed. The theological notion of the incarnation becomes fragmented, it is summed up through the word relationships and functions as theological shorthand.

The second point is interrelated to the first, incarnation, but this finds expression as influence. As seen in the work of Jill, Kim, Kerry, David, Sam, Mark, Dan, Martin and Rachel the youth ministers used relationships as places of transmission and mediation, as communicative

---

69. Savage et al., *Making Sense of Generation Y*, 121, 162.

70. Ibid., see prior mission, by drawing on the work of Ann Morrisey, as appropriate contact and seeking an appropriate starting point with those who have little or no knowledge of the faith.

71. Pimlott and Pimlott, *Youth Work after Christendom*, 75.

72. Ibid.

73. Ibid., 66–67.

74. Shepherd, *Faith Generation*, 40–41.

75. Passmore, *Meet Them Where They're At*.

76. Ward, *Youthwork*.

77. Borgman, *When Kumbaya Is Not Enough*.

acts, as circuits of influence. As explored above, Root [78] sees that evangelicals have tended to use relationships for engaging in the sub-cultural world of young people. We can see this echoed in the thinking of *Youth A Part*,[79] Ward,[80] Borgman, [81] Passmore,[82] Savage et al.,[83] Sudworth et al.,[84] and Pimlott and Pimlott,[85] and we can see this thinking embodied in the way youth ministers enact mission amongst young people. Importantly, this is how the youth ministers saw the medium of relationships. To act as the transmission of embodied faith, as communicative acts, as the message, to seek to be an influence (Mark) on the young people they minister amongst. Here, relationships as mediation and transmission can been seen in the narratives of all the youth ministers and are used as instruments of personal influence.

Therefore, "prior mission," or moving young people into more constructive roles within the community (Mark, Kim and Kerry) is sought through relationships as places of connection and transmission, as influence amongst young people. Here again is an interrelation between the themes. It is possible to see in the relationships which are established within the practice of the youth ministers that they have credibility amongst young people; they are seen by young people to "get it." Here, the care that the youth minister shows for a young person by being there translates or is transmitted as sympathy for the young person's situation. This observation echoes through the literature and finds particular expression in the work of Dean,[86] Ward,[87] Borgman,[88] and Pimlott and Pimlott.[89] Shepherd[90] sees this pastoral care for young people as a particular development within youth ministry, he calls these transformational practices and he highlights how it interrelates to youth ministry

---

78. Root, *Revisiting Relational Youth Ministry*, 78–79.
79. Church of England Board of Education, *Youth A Part*.
80. Ward, *Youthwork*.
81. Borgman, *When Kumbaya Is Not Enough*.
82. Passmore, *Meet Them Where They're At*.
83. Savage et al., *Making Sense of Generation Y*.
84. Sudworth et al., *Mission Shaped Youth*.
85. Pimlott and Pimlott, *Youth Work after Christendom*.
86. Dean, *Practicing Passion*, 180.
87. Ward, *Youthwork*, 59.
88. Borgman, *When Kumbaya Is Not Enough*, 32.
89. Pimlott and Pimlott, *Youth Work after Christendom*, 75.
90. Shepherd, *Faith Generation*, 42–47.

as missionary endeavor. Within the idea of relationships that function as places of influence, a deep interrelatedness with the other themes of time and journey can be seen. This is because influence takes place over a long period of time as has been expressed within the narratives of practice. Again, within the narratives of the youth ministers, we can see the complexities of practice but this all gets summed up in the theological shorthand description of relationship. Within this correlation of the themes of relationships as being there and time and journey, it is possible to see that they pivot around what it means to be like Jesus. This essential theme is the one explored next.

Relationships as Communicative Acts: Like Jesus

The next interrelated theme, like Jesus, as noted above, can be seen as a pivotal theme in the practice of the youth ministers. The youth ministers modelled and based their actions on being like Jesus. This theme, like that of being there and time and journey, is carried by relationships as communicative acts, and the connections the youth ministers had made with young people. Again, the theme of like Jesus acts as theological shorthand, a relatively simple theological expression of the complexities of working and enacting mission. As seen above, this theme finds expression, through the work of Kerry, Tom, Rachel, Sam, Andrew, Martin, Kim, David, Terry, Dan, Jill and Mark. To continue the examination and investigation of this theme, the lived theology held in these terms of look, example, mirror and see, the idea of modelling, of being like Jesus is explored in more detail. To do this, the paradox between the richness of practice and the theological shorthand description of this can be illuminated. Furthermore, the data continues to be brought into conversation with the literature. How the youth ministry practitioners understand their enacted mission amongst young people is seen in the use of language reflected in the terms "*look*" (Andrew, Tom) "*example*" (Rachel, Kim, Dan, Kerry, Mark), "*mirror*" (David, Terry) "*see*" (David, Andrew) and "*like*" (Tom, Sam, Kim, Terry, Mark, David). This is theological shorthand, a partial description of the richness of the practice which transmits, mediates and embodies the story of faith. Therefore, in the youth minister's stories, the theological expression and language is of a spectator and an observer. The words, look, example, mirror and see, are the language of being like, the language of imitation, with Jesus and his ministry as a model for their own. Moreover, Jesus evokes the idea of something to copy and observe and put into practice. However, what is seen in the practice of the youth ministers is a reflection of what they have inherited, read and been taught. As noted above, through the work of Root[91] and Tanis,[92] Young Life positioned the incarnation as theological justification and the out working of this becomes a pattern for ministry. This finds resonance in the work of Ward,[93] Pimlott and Pimlott,[94] and Griffiths.[95] The idea of like Jesus as model reverberates through the narratives of practice and Dean[96] sees that imitating Christ has long been a staple of youth ministry. There is an interrelation of ideas here that link into relationships as communicative act and as Dean argues, imitating Christ has been adapted by adults who work within youth ministry and value its potential for moral formation and influence. Furthermore, the idea of imitating Christ has a long history within the wider Christian tradition and is still held up as an idea that has relevance with contemporary practice.[97]

This is an important theological and Biblical point, in the classical practice of the church this can be seen as *marturia*, witnessing to the love of God in Jesus Christ, but this is only part of the theological picture. The problem is that in enacting practice like Jesus as model, the person of Jesus operates at the level of an idea, it becomes a model for how to minister. There is a separation between like Jesus and participating within the risen reality of Christ's presence as the power of mission. Enacting practice like Jesus removes us from who he is cosmically and distances us from his risen person and the "Jesus of History."[98] Therefore, what is missing in the articulation of enacted mission amongst young people is the language of collaboration and participation. The practitioners did not verbalize that they took part in this mission with God;[99] they did not join in with or participate in or partner with God in their

---

91. Root, *Revisiting Relational Youth Ministry*, 53.
92. Tanis, *Making Jesus Attractive*.
93. Ward, *Youthwork*, 45.
94. Pimlott and Pimlott, *Youth Work after Christendom*, 75.
95. Griffiths, *Models for Youth Ministry*, 11.
96. Dean, *Practicing Passion*, 46.
97. See Holmes, *The Holy Trinity*.
98. See Yoder, *The Politics of Jesus*, 103, and also Vanhoozer, *Remythologizing Theology*, 280–94.
99. Ward, *Youthwork*, 25.

enacted mission amongst young people. Furthermore, Root[100] sees that we participate in the living active presence of Christ. Following this, the question of "Where is Jesus?" in the understanding of enacted mission amongst young people can be raised. Moreover, as Dean[101] sees, in relation to youth ministry practice, what is at stake in imitating Christ is not about mimicry, but identification, becoming one with Christ through the Cross, as he engrafts our lives onto and in his. Therefore, in practice, we are in Christ and the practice is performed and indwelt by the power of the Spirit, it is participation in God.[102] Furthermore, the language of like Jesus indicates the way the youth ministry practitioners drew on the Gospel stories to inform their practice, this is the process of plastic hermeneutics articulated above. The activity of Jesus that they draw upon is focused amongst the people Jesus served and met. There is no Jerusalem, no event of the Cross, no Soteriology and no Resurrection. Apart from a fleeting mention of the Cross in Rachel's interview, the transformative power of the Cross is not spoken about or articulated in any sense, shape or form. At least in part, proclaiming the passionate love of God, the *kerygma* was absent. Therefore, there are tensions within the theological expression of like Jesus.

As youth ministry practitioners think of themselves as being like Jesus, problems can be seen, that are highlighted by Dean,[103] but are missed by our practitioners. When we reduce the imitation of Christ to its "Xerox" potential we choose selectively what parts of Jesus life to imitate, either through lack of Biblical and theological knowledge or through self-selection. We see this echoed in the narratives of the practitioners as they only model certain aspects of Jesus' life. Furthermore, we can assume that being like Jesus is self-evident and forces a one-to-one correspondence between first century ethics and our own. There are many aspects to being like Jesus, political, angry, prophetic, healer, rabbi, but, within the practice of the youth ministers, like Jesus acts as theological shorthand for model and moral example, with the youth ministers seemingly wanting to distance themselves from more overt evangelism. This

---

100. Root, *Revisiting Relational Youth Ministry*.
101. Dean, *Practicing Passion*, 47.
102. Vanhoozer, *Remythologizing Theology*, 280–96.
103. Dean, *Practicing Passion*, 47 sees that the Greek term "*mimesis*," which we translate as "imitation." "*Mimesis*" means identification with the original and involves "*methexis*" or participation.

resonates with Pimlott and Pimlott[104] as they see youth workers following the work of God's grace as they sought to be like Jesus to young people through practical help. Again, there are reverberations here of Savage et al.[105] work on prior mission.

Furthermore, if the classical church practice of *kerygma* is limited, then *diakonia*, serving and helping others is collapsed with *marturia*, into modelling and being like Jesus. Therefore, at the heart of this practice is a limited Christology because of the emphasis on model. In addition, this focus on Jesus as model loses sight of the whole of the Biblical narrative; opportunities may be missed to adopt wider elements of the richness of the Biblical story to engage young people or to see God's wider communicative activity in the world.

There is then a paradox and a tension here between the theological shorthand expression and the depth of sacrificial action and practice. Therefore, within practice, it would be possible to explore a deep theology that is embodied, lived and enacted. The theological expression of this within the narratives of the youth ministers, why they did what they do, is partial, yet it evokes a richer and deeper theology from within the Christian tradition. Moreover, like the idea of relationships as communicative acts, sometimes the theology is implied and is implicit rather than explicit. Again, like Jesus as model becomes theological shorthand for the complexities of mission amongst young people. Perhaps this is not surprising, for as noted, the idea of model as a pattern is infused within relational youth ministry due, at least in part, to the influence of the Young Life model, and the articulation of this within some of the youth ministry literature: *Youth A Part*,[106] Ward,[107] Borgman,[108] Sudworth et al.,[109] Pimlott and Pimlott,[110] and Griffiths.[111] That said, there is also a paradox here, for within the literature a deeper source of theology

---

104. Pimlott and Pimlott, *Youth Work after Christendom*, 66–67, 75.
105. Savage et al., *Making Sense of Generation Y*, 121, 162.
106. Church of England Board of Education, *Youth A Part*.
107. Ward, *Youthwork*.
108. Borgman, *When Kumbaya Is Not Enough*.
109. Sudworth et al., *Mission Shaped Youth*.
110. Pimlott and Pimlott, *Youth Work after Christendom*.
111. Griffiths, *Models for Youth Ministry*.

is articulated[112] through the work of Dean,[113] Savage et al.,[114] Root,[115] and Griffiths.[116] However, this is not articulated within the practice of the practitioners.

Relationships as Communicative Acts: Being There

The third theme of being there is the enacted presence of the second, like Jesus, and becomes an enacted theological moment in time and space through which the youth ministers act as symbols. As noted above, this idea of symbol is found within the work of Tillich.[117] The youth ministers as symbols embody the qualities of that which they point towards and participate in, but through the narratives this is not articulated—only the language of model, being like Jesus is used. As symbols, youth ministers, through being there, are meaningful on account of their relationship to Christ. Therefore, it is an act of embodied faith that points towards Christ and seeks to be like Jesus, it can be seen as theological shorthand for the complexities of practice.

The expression of the theme of being there is seen in the interrelatedness of this and the others explored so far. Being there, as symbol, is an expression of pastoral care and the coming alongside young people who are suffering and in very difficult situations. Being there is carried and is an expression of relationships as communicative acts. Being there is the way youth ministry practitioners build relationships in their connections with young people and it is how their faith is transmitted. Therefore, as the relationship carries being there this is both the medium, and at least in part, the message. The classical practices of the church through *marturia*, *diakonia* and *kerygma* are collapsed at this point into a network of relationships as communicative acts that enact being there as a practice. Relationships become a contemporary practice. This has an acute focus on orthopraxis. Furthermore, this being there, like Jesus, is modelled over time and through the narrative structure of journey. As the theme of being there is explored, this again will be brought into conversation with

112. Ward, *Youthwork*.
113. Dean, *Practicing Passion*.
114. Savage et al., *Making Sense of Generation Y*.
115. Root, *Revisiting Relational Youth Ministry*.
116. Griffiths, *Models for Youth Ministry*.
117. Tillich, *Dynamics of Faith*.

the youth ministry literature. This theme reverberates through Ward,[118] Borgman,[119] Green and Christian,[120] Dean,[121] Sudworth et al.,[122] Root,[123] Pimlott and Pimlott,[124] and is seen as a transformational practice.[125]

As explored in chapter 5, being there is expressed through the stories of Sam, Jill, Tom, Martin, Dan, David, Kim, Rachel and Mark told. Within these, the care that these youth ministers demonstrate through being there, reflect and point towards God and how He cares for people. Here can be seen the resonance of Ward's,[126] Pimlott's and Pimlott's,[127] and Savage et al.'s[128] thinking about how the care that young people experience can be seen as an activity of God and as a sign of grace. Moreover, we can also see echoes of Dean's[129] insight that when we talk about relational ministry, what we really mean is that young people need the ability to give and receive fidelity. For Dean, this fidelity is glimpsed in human relationships, but is ultimately found in God. As the practice of the youth ministers is investigated, this is what they are hoping for, that their compelling witness of being there for young people will lead the young people they work amongst to discover God, an idea that also finds resonance in Green's and Christian's[130] model of Accompanying, and in Savage et al.[131] concept of patient sowing. In Ward's[132] thinking, the idea of being there is a sign that points to God's grace and in Dean's[133] thinking our being there for young people acts as an icon through which they may glimpse God's fidelity.[134]

118. Ward, *Youthwork*, 59.
119. Borgman, *When Kumbaya Is Not Enough*, 28.
120. Green and Christian, *Accompanying*, 21.
121. Dean, *Practicing Passion*, 90–91, 176–95.
122. Sudworth et al., *Mission Shaped Youth*, 11.
123. Root, *Revisiting Relational Youth Ministry*, 124.
124. Pimlott and Pimlott, *Youth Work after Christendom*, 141–45.
125. Shepherd, *Faith Generation*, 42–47.
126. Ward, *Youthwork*, 59.
127. Pimlott and Pimlott, *Youth Work after Christendom*, 75.
128. Savage et al., *Making Sense of Generation Y*, 164.
129. Dean, *Practicing Passion*, 90.
130 Green and Christian, *Accompanying*.
131. Savage et al., *Making Sense of Generation Y*, 157–59.
132. Ward, *Youthwork*, 53.
133. Dean, *Practicing Passion*, 91.
134. It is worth noting the distinction between a "sign," an "icon" and a "symbol."

What is missing in both the idea of a sign and in the use of the word icon, is that they are static. They point to something rather than dynamically participate and embody the qualities of the item they point towards. As the narratives of practice are considered this is an important distinction. This is because through the youth ministers' relationship with Christ, they participate in Christ. Therefore, it is possible to develop an inferred theme of symbol. The practice of being there as symbol is a powerful idea. That said, there are two interrelated issues. The first centers on the notion of participation but this is not articulated. The symbolic act of being there, within the enacted mission of the practitioners, has value because of the youth minister's relationship with Christ, but this is articulated through the language of model and like Jesus; it is articulated at the level of a sign.

This is because, as explored above, youth ministry has been infused with the idea of model, pattern and imitation, inherited from the Young Life framework. There is then, a disconnection between the theological reality of participation of being in Christ and the articulation of lived practice like Jesus. Secondly, and interrelated to the first, for a young person to understand this being there as a symbolic act needs a certain amount of theological capital. Unless a young person understands wider aspects of the Christian story, being there as symbol and being like Jesus, acts that are and become attributed to God by the youth ministers, may not be interpreted symbolically. They may misleadingly seem to imply ordinary examples of care and concern. Of course, these ordinary examples of care and concern are very important, but the point is, this is not what the youth ministers sees themselves doing as they enact mission amongst young people. They are seeking to build intentional relationships that are to bring about change.[135]

The lived expression of youth ministers as symbol shines through the narratives of practice that were explored in the previous chapter. Through being there, Tom acts as a symbol that points towards a God who cares and this is demonstrated and lived out in the actual practice of care and concern of being there amidst the suffering for this young girl. For Rachel, Kim, and Sam their being there, their care and concern for young people also points toward a God who cares. This resonates with

---

In Tillich's, *Dynamics of Faith* thinking a "sign" is consciously invented and can be removed, whilst a "symbol" embodies the qualities of that which it points towards.

135. Shepherd, *Faith Generation*, 41.

both Ward,[136] Dean,[137] and Shepherd.[138] For David and Martin, being there is very real and has a very practical outworking as an expression of their enacted mission amongst young people. For both David and Martin, being there finds direct correlation with the person of Jesus. What is seen in the youth ministers' practice, is that being there acts as theological shorthand, a way of summing up the complexities of embodied care and concern for young people that is lived out like Jesus and is seen to point towards God. In addition, in the narratives of practice of the youth ministers, being there is seen primarily as an individual's responsibility. This is not surprising, when we consider the direction of travel that is expressed within some of the literature, as is evident within Ward,[139] Borgman,[140] Green and Christian[141] and Senter III.[142] It is evident in this new paradigm that is articulated by Passmore,[143] Sudworth et al.,[144] Pimlott and Pimlott,[145] and Savage et al.,[146] where the missional drive is provided by adults working incarnationaly amongst young people because of their cultural distance from the church. Within the narratives of practice explored, Mark, Rachel and Jill primarily work beyond the boundaries of church. This has echoes with Ward's[147] framework of outside in. Whilst David, Andrew and Tom, primarily work within a church context and echo Ward's[148] framework of inside out. What is not articulated and is not made explicit in *all* the narratives of practice of the youth minister practitioners is the role of the Church and its connection with mission amongst young people. Being there in the expression of the youth ministry practitioners has a focus on the individual's pursuit and not on a congregation.

136. Ward, *Youthwork*, 53.
137. Dean, *Practicing Passion*, 91.
138 Shepherd, *Faith Generation*, 42–47.
139. Ward, *Youthwork*, 43–63.
140. Borgman, *When Kumbaya Is Not Enough*, 28–30.
141. Green and Christian, *Accompanying*.
142. Senter et al., *Four Views of Youth Ministry*, 80.
143. Passmore, *Meet Them Where They're At*.
144. Sudworth et al., *Mission Shaped Youth*, 10.
145. Pimlott and Pimlott, *Youth Work after Christendom*, 66–67, 75.
146. Savage et al., *Making Sense of Generation Y*, 157.
147. Ward, *Youthwork*, 11.
148. Ibid., 7.

That said, there is a corrective to this within the literature, as Ward[149] sees that church is "not an optional extra," and Green and Christian[150] note that young people are to learn the art of stewardship of the church; Sudworth et al.[151] say that young people need to be part of a worshiping community; *Youth A Part*[152] sees the church as the aim of the Gospel; and Senter et al.[153] have a focus on an inclusive congregational approach. Moreover, both Dean,[154] and Root,[155] seek to locate the practice of being there to a congregation and a Christian community. Furthermore, Shepherd[156] argues how groups for young people can become places that shape Christian identity and help young people make sense of faith. This is missing and is not expressed within the narratives of the youth ministry practitioners. The non-articulation of the role of the church community or even the youth group is telling and demonstrates a level of disconnect in the enacted ministry of the practitioners and the richness of the Christian tradition. This is more than mere oversight, the untethering from the tradition isolates our practices and removes us, as Dean[157] sees, from the intergenerational witness of a congregation and isolates us from the broader interpretive lens of the Christian community. Furthermore, through the theological shorthand expression of being there, there is a level of distance from the richness of theology and understanding of those pilgrims and saints[158] who have gone before, that is carried in the tradition, that has carried the story and that may illuminate, critique and serve practice and act as fresh and re-imagined points of connection for young people.[159]

As this theme of being there has been explored, it is possible to see this as the enacted presence of the second theme like Jesus. The articulation of how the youth minister practitioners act as symbol has been investigated, exploring how the enacted mission amongst young people

149. Ibid., 65.
150. Green and Christian, *Accompanying*, 13.
151. Sudworth et al., *Mission Shaped Youth*, 12–13, 102–14.
152. Church of England Board of Education, *Youth A Part*, 37.
153. Senter et al., *Four Views of Youth Ministry*, 1–35.
154. Dean, *Practicing Passion*, 91.
155. Root, *Revisiting Relational Youth Ministry*, 17, 197–217.
156. Shepherd, *Faith Generation*, 56–99.
157. Dean, *Practicing Passion*, 186.
158. Holmes, *The Holy Trinity*.
159. Savage et al., *Making Sense of Generation Y*, 59.

is seen primarily as an individual pursuit with a focus on orthopraxis. In chapter 3, being there was seen as being carried through time and evokes the narrative structure of journey held within relationships as communicative acts. This is either explicit or it is implied by the stories told by the youth ministers. It is this theme that is investigated next, again bringing it into conversation with the youth ministry literature.

Relationships as Communicative Acts: Time and Journey as Liminal Space

The theme of time and journey expresses the commitment of being there. Being there is an enacted theological moment in time and space through which the youth ministers symbolize and embody a greater reality, it is an act of faith. This is seen as being like Jesus as model; therefore, as seen above, both being there and like Jesus act as theological shorthand. Faith is mediated and is given direction and shape through the connections established in the web of relationships that function as communicative acts, but this takes time and is the creation of a liminal space. In this liminal space the youth minister practitioners seek to be like Jesus. This is a place of transition, threshold, of waiting and not knowing, a place of movement and life. Yet, this possibility of a liminal space, a place for encountering God is summed up again as theological shorthand through the notion of time and journey. Within this liminal space, there is an interdependence between the themes, relationship as communicative acts, being like Jesus and being there; these all take time and this is either explicit or it is implied through the idea of journey and is an embodied act of faith in a series of liminal encounters and moments. Following the analysis of being like Jesus, the question can be asked of where our youth ministry practitioners think Jesus is in the embodied moments of faith in this liminal space.

Again, as explored in chapter 5, being there, as an embodied act of faith, is given expression through the words time and journey and is articulated within the thoughts of Andrew, Kim, Dan, Rachel, Terry, Mark, David, Jill, Martin, Sam, Kerry and Tom as they told stories and articulated how they enacted mission amongst young people. The idea of relationships that function as communicative acts through the notion of time finds acute resonance in Ward's[160] work. He sees that the five-stage

---

160. Ward, *Youthwork*, 43–60.

framework which is adopted from Young Life takes a long time and is a long-term process in building and establishing the relationships. Ward[161] sees that "contact work is first and foremost about spending time with a particular group of young people and that it is about long-term relationship building." Furthermore, Ward,[162] argues there is "no substitute" and no "short cut" in this, it is "long term." This framework of time echoes clearly through the narratives of youth ministry practice which we have been exploring. For example, as Andrew, sees, *"it is all about time to share your life"* and again as Tom, notes *"over time obviously you build relationships"* and in Mark's thoughts, *"I suppose over the years, it's me spending time with those individuals."* The notion of sharing your life, as expressed by Mark, resonates with the notion of nurture and the implied time this takes in the work of Pimlott and Pimlott.[163] Furthermore, as articulated in the last chapter, through the ministry of Tom the idea of time is given expression and weight and is seen as a commodity and as a gift. As this idea of the creation of a liminal space is explored, the idea of time as a gift finds resonance in the work of Green and Christian[164] who see in the notion of Accompanying the greatest gift we can give is in the coming alongside or being there for a young person. Within this notion of time as gift is the creation of a liminal space through which the youth ministers seek to enact faith by being like Jesus, through being there as symbol, in relationships as communicative acts. However, Griffiths[165] challenges this notion of *chronos* time and the underlying assumptions that work with young people requires large amounts of time. He continues, too often youth ministry has been expounded from a Christology based on *chronos* time. Griffith's arguments against this are reflected and articulated by Terry who talked about *kairos* time—the possibilities of moments that can be filled with the eternal,[166] single words and actions that hold the possibility of change and encounter with Christ.

Within the narratives of practice, this idea of time is also linked with the narrative structure of journey. For Andrew, it means that you can *"journey with young people"* and for Tom this sense of journey is also

161. Ibid., 49.
162. Ibid., 52–60.
163. Pimlott and Pimlott, *Youth Work after Christendom*, 141–45.
164. Green and Christian, *Accompanying*, 21.
165. Griffiths, *Models for Youth Ministry*, 10.
166. Ibid.

important. The idea of journey again finds resonance within the literature; Green and Christian[167] articulate this sense of journey by accompanying young people on their spiritual quest. In Shepherd's[168] arguments about faith generation, the idea of journey can be seen through exploring plausible faith, forming Christian identity and young people being Christian. Ward[169] sees that "entering the social world of young people is a spiritual journey." This also echoes in the work of Sudworth et al.[170] that youth ministers should lead young people to have "encounters with God" rather than just "belief" in God; and additionally, in the work of Pimlott and Pimlott[171] and Savage et al.[172] the word encounter and the idea of journey is expressed. The word encounter echoes with the idea of journey and the creation of a liminal space. *Youth A Part*[173] sees that faith can be "nurtured through relationship." This idea of nurture resonates with the idea of journey found within the narratives of the youth ministry practitioners. Again, the interplay between relationships as communicative acts, being there and time and journey is played out. A relationship is established and, through being there, a connection and a transmission of ideas is made through circuits of influence—relationships as communicative acts. This becomes a liminal space in which God is pointed towards, through being there as seen in the embodiment of symbol.

Therefore, in the narratives of practice and in the enacting of mission amongst young people for Andrew, Tom, Kim, Sam and Jill, the journey is a process, the creation of a liminal space, a time and place where faith can be enacted and performed, but it comes with no guarantees, it is ambiguous. Enacting mission through time and journey and the creation of liminal spaces is a positive act of faith to be like Jesus and a positive act of waiting amongst the unknown as the youth minister practitioners wait for God to act. The idea of a liminal space is not named as such in the literature, but echoes in the words encounter, spiritual quest, spiritual journey, faith generation, and nurture. What is named in the literature by Dean and Foster,[174] but is not articulated within the narratives of practice is

---

167. Green and Christian, *Accompanying*.
168. Shepherd, *Faith Generation*, 56–99.
169. Ward, *Youthwork*, 51.
170. Sudworth et al., *Mission Shaped Youth*, 13.
171. Pimlott and Pimlott, *Youth Work after Christendom*, 145, 153.
172. Savage et al., *Making Sense of Generation Y*, 168.
173. Church of England Board of Education, *Youth A Part*, 85.
174. Through the story of the Annunciation, Dean and Foster, *The Godbearing Life*,

the idea of the youth minister as "Godbearer." Although not expressed by the practitioners, traces of this idea in the ministry of Andrew, Tom and Jill can be observed. For example, through the sense of journey that Jill articulates, we see this liminal space as representative of a young person on the threshold, as Jill waits for God to act, but Jill is also a crucial link in the process. It is also expressed within the thoughts of Andrew, as he begins to articulate the work of the Holy Spirit.

Therefore, the idea of a "Godbearer" resonates with what is implied, but this is not made explicit within the practice of the youth ministry practitioners amongst young people. The narratives of practice echo with the creation of a liminal space that could be seen to act as a womb and place of incubation for young people as they ponder and struggle with how God knows them and calls them into relationship with him.[175] This finds further resonance in the work of Savage et al.[176] with the Holy Spirit as the "prior missioner par excellence," and again in Green and Christian[177] through their motif of accompanying and their notion of this as a spiritual quest. Through these phrases of prior mission, accompanying and journey as a womb and a place of incubation, the creation of a liminal space within our narratives of practice acts as the opportunity and space for mystery to be explored and embodied.

This liminal space occupies a particular place within the thinking of the youth ministers and here, our four themes collide. If relationships as communicative acts as connection and transmission are the threads that run through the narratives of practice and being like Jesus, through the embodied practice of being there, is what the practice pivots around, then the creation of liminal spaces through time and journey is what the youth ministry practitioners are aiming for. This time of wrestling, this time of threshold, this time of waiting for God to act, becomes a focus for the work. It carries the essence of how the youth ministry practitioners seek to enact mission amongst young people. The creation of a liminal space that is carried by relationships as communicative acts, allows a space where young people can experience the mystery of God, a place where "mystical unions" are made possible. Through the work of

---

49, argue that God employs a third party (an Angel) to bear the good news to Mary. From this they say that youth ministers can re-imagine themselves as God bearers, people who name the activity of God in the lives of young people.

175. Dean and Foster, *The Godbearing Life*, 52.
176. Savage et al., *Making Sense of Generation Y*, 168.
177. Green and Christian, *Accompanying*.

the youth ministers, the mystery[178] of God has the opportunity to be explored and connections made and, if we follow the work of Dean,[179] can be named within their lives. However, within the narratives of practice we have been exploring, it is possible to see these opportunities as being limited by the theological shorthand that is expressed.

The theological shorthand of being like Jesus as model and the theological shorthand of being there as symbol, raises three potential issues. The first is that with being like Jesus as model, the living active presence of Christ by the power of the Spirit is not given enough consideration or even scope, leaving answers to the question, "Where is Jesus?" open and non-conclusive. The second is related to this through the notion of being there as symbol; this contains opportunities to participate in God, an idea that we explore further in chapters 8 and 9. Here we can move towards answering the question, "Where is Jesus?" The third is that because the classical church practices of *marturia*, *diakonia* and *kerygma* are collapsed into this overarching theme of relationships, there is a loss of focus, a blurring of these interrelated but also distinct practices. If this was intentional or named within the youth ministers' practice, we would be on a firmer foundation, but this collapse into relationships seems unintentional and to be no more than a historical accident inherited from the work of Young Life that infuses the narratives of practice and the enacting of mission amongst young people. Therefore, relationships form a distinctly new, enacted and lived practice, but this has not been theologically thought through.

As relationships have continued to be explored through the voices of the practitioners and the voice of the youth ministry literature, this chapter has investigated the correlation between these voices. In the next chapter, how youth ministers live amongst theological fragments and theological shorthand is explored.

---

178. Vanhoozer, *Remythologizing Theology*, 472. "Mysterion," points to God's plan for salvation that was previously hidden but is now made known in Christ.

179. Dean, *Practicing Passion*, 199.

Chapter 7

Youth Ministry, Living Amongst the Fragments?

Rublev's icon invites us to take time and space to reflect, it acts as a window between two worlds, a liminal space. Accepting the invite creates time to dwell with and to discover more about God, to participate and join a journey of encounter.[1] Yet, Rublev's icon is also partial and fragile; it is a fragment of the reality and story it represents. Just as the icon is a fragment, a small part of a much bigger picture and story then it is possible to explore some of the theological fragments that youth ministers live amongst. Like oil paint on a canvas, the worship songs and resources from *Youthwork* magazine paint a picture of the fragmented world of theology that the youth ministers inhabit. These two explorations provide further snap shots (but not the full picture) of youth ministry today and its fragmented theology. They are explorative rather than conclusive, yet demonstrate how the use of theological shorthand and fragments in youth ministry is maintained. Even if this conclusivity was possible, this is an explorative/descriptive study not a hypothesis testing one. Furthermore, when the worship songs and articles are viewed alongside the narratives of practice and the youth ministry literature already explored, then a richer picture emerges of how these fragments inform and rotate around one another in a complex space of theological shorthand.

Youthwork magazine has dealt with difficult subjects and key cultural changes that youth ministers have faced and seeks to introduce and use the Bible to help youth ministers connect with God, the ongoing Recharge

---

1. Persson, *The Circle of Love*, 55–57.

series is a demonstration of this. However, it is also a picture that is drawn from evangelical history. The evangelical world of mediation forms the frame, the resources and articles from *Youthwork* magazine paint the picture. As the resources are analyzed key themes can be seen. Firstly, *Youthwork* magazine mediates ideas from the top down. There is overlap between the writers of the youth ministry literature as they contribute to the magazine;[2] highlighting the transfer of ideas between contexts and across continents. Secondly, the relationships between youth ministers and young people is seen as important via the work of Root.[3] Thirdly, and most problematic, is the playing down of particular contexts and traditions. The Resource Guides offer a one size fits all, demonstrating Rogers[4] notion of plastic hermeneutics in practice. Alongside this, individual church traditions are played down or not mentioned, almost airbrushed out, as moves are made from the Biblical material to application without the identification of, or to a particular tradition. On the one hand, this is understandable, the magazine is an ecumenical project and it resonates with how the literature functions as the normative voice for practice, over and above the tradition of which the youth ministers are a part. Furthermore, the magazine demonstrates an espoused and operative theology[5] in the context of evangelical youth ministry. On the other hand, through this process, theology is abstracted and fragment from the traditions that provides the animation and mediation.[6] A clear example of this is explored below and shows how *Youthwork* magazine seeks to re-imagine Church with young people, but the moves made are abstracted from the Bible without reference to any particular tradition, the move from the Biblical text to contemporary context is clunky and at best naïve. This is weak ecclesiology.

The second half of the chapter will examine the notion of theological shorthand within five contemporary worship songs used within a specific youth ministry context in the UK. The songs were chosen because they were repeated during an evangelical event[7] over two years, they

---

2. Root, "Dietrich Bonhoeffer"; Shepherd, "What's Distinctive about Christian Youthwork?"; Dean, "The Dean of Youth Work."
3. Root, "Relational Youth Ministry."
4. Rogers, "Reading Scripture," 95.
5. Cameron et al., *Talking about God in Practice*, 54.
6. Ward, *Participation and Mediation*, 111.
7. The event is anonymous, other songs and hymns were employed, but the songs chosen demonstrated the emphasis and balance of worship at this particular event.

highlight the significance of theological shorthand within contemporary worship and because they feature heavily on the Christian Copyright International List. The songs act like a lens and are used widely within the charismatic/evangelical worship scene within the UK. This style of worship often plugs-in and plays alongside more established Christian traditions, Anglican, Baptist, and Pentecostal.[8] Through discourse analysis, the texts of the worship songs are examined. A number of differing theological motifs are observed and the words of the songs are classified as espoused and operant theology.[9] The central argument is that key words within this espoused and operative theology function as theological shorthand and are identified as fragments of a coherent theology, a grand narrative.[10] Therefore, the pivotal words used within the songs are full of theological meaning but operate as simplified motifs, metaphors, symbols and fragments of a deeper and richer theological story, but this richer theology, this wider narrative is not expressed and requires a depth of theological capital and Biblical literacy to discern. This is thin theology and within the songs, the worshipper has to fill in the theological gaps.[11]

Youthwork Magazine: Resource Guides—Using the Fragments

Youthwork magazine was chosen because it forms part of the regular reading and use of the youth ministers interviewed. The magazine has formed part of the evangelical youth ministry world for the last 25 years and follows the rise of professional youth ministry in the UK.[12] The magazine also augments the event from which the songs were chosen and staff from Oasis[13] and CYM[14] are regular contributors. Therefore, there is an interrelation between the regular reading of the youth min-

---

The songs chosen could be brought into conversation with other genres of worship e.g., traditional hymns, however this lies outside the scope of this particular project.

8. Cartledge, *Encountering the Spirit*. An example of this would be Holy Trinity Brompton in London. In addition, a number of the students I teach inhabit this evangelical/charismatic world and know the songs well.

9. Cameron et al., *Talking about God in Practice*.

10. Walker, *Telling the Story*.

11. Ward, *Selling Worship*.

12. Thompson, "25 Years," 7–12.

13. Chalke, "The Real Youth Service," 25.

14. Shepherd, "Talk the Walk," 38–40.

isters, the training providers of the youth ministers through Oasis and CYM, and the attendance of these events by the youth ministers that the songs were chosen from. The overlapping of these differing elements helps illuminate how theological shorthand is in play. Furthermore, how theology is fragmented and how theological shorthand functions within *Youthwork* magazine is investigated. To enable this, three years of magazines were examined (2014, 2015, and 2016) and discourse analysis is employed to look at the text. In seeking to provide validity across this process the Resource Guides were chosen. These are ongoing sections within most issues (apart from August of each year) and offer the most consistent way through which to view the fragmented theology and theological shorthand within this context. This section of the magazine is the most regularly used part by six of the youth ministers interviewed (Kim, Sam, Kerry, Martin, Scot and Terry) as they worked amongst young people. Importantly, the analysis demonstrates how theological shorthand is passed on through the informal methods adopted in youth ministry practice and highlights the top down approach.[15] Again, the central argument is that key words within this espoused and operative theology[16] function as theological shorthand and can be identified as fragments of a coherent theology. Therefore, there are pivotal words and phrases used within the articles that are full of theological meaning but operate as simplified motifs, symbols and fragments of a deeper and richer theological story.

Yet, like in the worship songs, this richer theology, this wider narrative is not always expressed. In addition to this, the way the Bible is utilized resonates with a number of Perrin's[17] insights. As discussed above, Perrin[18] argues, that evangelicals read the Bible by seeking to relate the world in the text and then how this is worked out within the readers world and horizons. This is clear in how *Youthwork* magazine uses the Resource Guides and their relationship to the Bible. Further to this, there is often (although not always) a disregard of context and a proof text approach to scripture that pays little or no relation to the

---

15. It needs to be recognized that the magazine also runs the Recharge section—this does seek to explore subjects in a little more depth—however, theological shorthand can still be seen in action. The magazine also includes one off articles on particular subjects that does offer a more in depth look at particular issues.

16. Cameron et al., *Talking about God in Practice*.

17. Perrin, *The Bible Reading of Young Evangelicals*.

18. Ibid., 107.

wider Biblical narrative, to other texts or the text's context/genre. The text is fragmented and disconnected from its wider story and function, and *Youthwork* magazine (within these Resource Guides) can be guilty of selective reading.[19] Furthermore, because the Resources are written for a wide audience a "one size fits all approach" is adopted by the magazine. This enables youth ministers to interpret the differing subjects and texts to their own context and situations, but this produces a polyvalence of interpretation.[20] At its heart *Youthwork* magazine follows the common sense reading approach and youth ministers behave as compliant readers and operate on a hermeneutic of trust.[21] Therefore, this is a largely socialized view of reading scripture,[22] but this is pushed further due to the idiosyncratic environment of youth ministry.[23]

To explore the ideas of theological shorthand and fragmented theology within *Youthwork* magazine three different series of Resource Guides were chosen. They were selected because of their relevance to the issues discussed in this book. This includes a series of eight sessions on reimagining the Church with young people, this set of Resources is important because it highlights how different church traditions are played down, church becomes an abstracted concept. The second four Resources seek to tell the overall story of the Bible, this is key, because one of the arguments of this book is that the context of the Christian story and tradition needs to be given. However, within seeking to tell the whole Biblical story theological shorthand and thin theology are played out as the story becomes fragmented. The final set of Resources seeks to introduce youth ministers and young people to the people Jesus met. This set of four meeting guides highlights and resonates with the idea of being like Jesus. The idea of Jesus as a model for practice is clearly seen and theological shorthand is in animation.

The Resources Guides are designed for youth ministers to help young people explore key concepts within Christian theology. The articles chosen operate as a lens through which to view the theological shorthand within this particular section of the magazine. The pedagogy is located

---

19. Ibid., 87.
20. Ibid., 101.
21. Ibid., 77.
22. Ibid., 80.
23. Dean, *Practicing Passion*, 186.

within informal education and resonates with Brierley's[24] thoughts about how education is best facilitated in small groups as young people consider the Christian faith. As Shepherd[25] sees, this falls into a wider movement within youth ministry and how distinctive approaches to Christian education have become popular in the UK and North America since the 1950s. With this in mind, the Resource Guides sandwich together games, videos, Bible verses and discussion, prayer and reflection into rigorously timed out sections, with the longest being around 20 minutes. Therefore, although located within an overall informal typology the Resources resonate with notions of a non–formal[26] approach and articulate some sort of curriculum.[27] It is important to see that the youth ministers interviewed were very familiar with this format in their work amongst young people and had been brought up on a diet of interaction and interplay. Furthermore, this is reinforced as the training of youth ministers follows a discussion/interactive approach. The sessions selected are about an hour long and are fast moving, designed to keep the attention of young people. Amongst the theological shorthand three key points emerge, weak ecclesiology, the Gospel in code and seeing the Christian story from the outside. Viewing the story from the outside, resonates with the theme of being like Jesus. Therefore, this is about observation and not about participation. In the next chapter theodramatic participation is explored via Vanhoozer.[28]

Reimagining the Church

The subject of the church is explored in *Youthwork*,[29] through eight individual sessions. The overall aim was to reimagine church and introduce young people to the theological concept that the *"church isn't a building, church is people."*[30] This is an important theological point and in the first session is explored through Mark 3:14. The second session explores other

24. Brierley, *Joined Up*.

25. Shepherd, *Faith Generation*, 34–38.

26. For more on this see: http://infed.org/mobi/informal-non-formal-and-formal-education-programmes/.

27. For more on this see: http://infed.org/mobi/curriculum-theory-and-practice/.

28. Vanhoozer, *Remythologizing Theology*.

29. Crowsley, "Reimagining the Church," 34–38; Cook and Henley, "Reimagining the Church," 34–38.

30. Crowsley, "Reimagining the Church," 34.

key theological principles, "*community as a key part of church*" and "*a living community*" via 1 Peter 2:2–10.[31] The third session further investigates the "*move away from the idea of church as building or institution and to focus on some of the key elements taught to us by Jesus, particularly mission and passing on our faith to others*" through looking at John 1:29–42 and Matthew 28:19–20.[32] The final session, in the June addition, looked at Acts 2:42–47 as a "*set of guidelines for building church communities*" and "*can we use these foundations to help reimagine what church could look like today?.*"[33] There was a follow up to this series in the next issue of *Youthwork*[34] that sought to build on "*the theory behind what the church is . . . this month we're going to shake it up a bit and give them the chance to dream about what church could be. Strap yourself in . . . .*"[35]

The next set of sessions sought to reimagine the church amongst young people and is summed up through one of the meeting aims "*How could we change what we do, or do something new to connect with our friends and other young people?*" and was explored through Luke 8:16–17 and Mathew 18:18–20.[36] The other two sessions explored "*How can we make this happen?*" via John 11:1–44 and then explored doubts and questions young people may have about doing church differently. The final session of the July issue was labelled "*Into action!*" and investigated through Ezra 3 and John 20:21–22 how to "*plan to be a new way of being church in a new place, with new people.*"[37] The material is well presented, is very accessible to both youth ministers and the young people they seek to work amongst, and raises important questions of what the church might look like amongst a new generation of young people. It is also augmented with a Bible study[38] (Strickland 2015, p.p.48–49) and an article on reimaging church.[39] As noted above, there is a not seen, or at least, not acknowledged disconnect with the traditions of the established church. Through the Resources, Bible study and article, the concept of church is abstracted from any traditional expression, be that Baptist, Anglican, or

31. Ibid., 36.
32. Ibid., 37.
33. Ibid., 38.
34. Cook and Henley, "Reimagining the Church," 34–38.
35. Ibid., 34.
36. Ibid., 36.
37. Ibid., 37–38.
38. Strickland, "Think Bigger," 48–49.
39. Leach, "Reimagining the Church," 22–23.

United Reformed Church that have carried the story across generations. This is ironic given the subject under discussion. Furthermore, this set of Resources begins to disconnect and untether youth ministry from the lived experience and reality of the Church in everyday life—although the aim of the articles is the opposite. There is no real recognition of the traditional church practices of *diakonia* and *kerygma* or of Baptism or Communion (apart from the reference to Acts 2:42–47). *Koinonia* is mentioned and seized upon as young people are asked to reimagine a new community.[40]

This is the fragmentation of theology, the church is described through a variety of "buzz" words and phrases that function as theological shorthand—"*Church isn't a building, church is people,*" "*A community of living stones*"[41] and "*being and doing church.*"[42] Importantly, each of these key phrases and words have a richness of theology within and behind them. Like the key words of the youth ministers interviewed (relationships, like Jesus, being there, time and journey) and a number of words within the songs they are a straight forward and simplistic way of describing a set of complex practices and the theology embedded within them. The richness of the Christian story from either Anglican, Baptist, The United Reform Church or other perspectives is not drawn upon or articulated. The problem here, is that this sort of process can leave young people and youth ministers disenchanted—the abstraction of the church held up and offered by this particular set of Resources is not achievable in real life. This is weak ecclesiology, lacking the lived experience of church, but at the same time leads to a set of ideas that are held up to be observed and copied, to be imitated. In this sense, it resonates with Ward's[43] thinking on the gravitational pull of the church, but this is articulated from the abstracted blueprint ecclesiology of the New Testament. Not enough attention is given to the original text, either through its political message,[44] the ethical ramifications[45] or how the Gospels narrate the Kingdom of God.[46]

---

40. Cook and Henley, "Reimagining the Church," 38.
41. Crowsley, "Reimagining the Church," 34–36.
42. Cook and Henley, "Reimagining the Church," 36.
43. Ward, "Blueprint Ecclesiology."
44. Yoder, *The Politics of Jesus*.
45. Hauerwas, *The Peaceable Kingdom*.
46. Wright, *How God Became King*.

Therefore, key passages and texts are used to justify the theological moves made, yet these are fragmented from the wider Biblical story. There is no context given or any in depth articulation to the meaning of particular passages chosen. They operate at the level of proof texting for reimaging what the church could look like, this is plastic hermeneutics[47] in action and opens up the text to a polyvalence of interpretation.[48] Youth ministers and young people are left to fill in the theological gaps and just like in the songs below, it requires a relatively high level of Biblical understanding and the animation of theological capital.

The Bible's Big Story

To explore theological shorthand further, the next set of four Resources has a focus on the whole story of the Bible.[49] The format follows a similar one to the Resources used to begin to reimagine church; it is a mix of games, discussions, Bible readings, and prayer. A core argument of this book is that theology is fragmented from the wider Christian story, if this analysis is correct then it is crucial to pay attention to when people are seeking to communicate the Biblical story. However, although it is important to seek to communicate the whole message of salvation, and introduce a young person to the narrative of the Bible, within this process is the fragmentation of theological thought. Again, elements of the story are abstracted and theological shorthand is in play. Allen[50] divides the Biblical story into four sections (one for each hour-long Resource), these are: From Eden to Egypt, From Egypt to Babylon, From Babylon to Bethlehem and From Bethlehem to Heaven. In the first session, Allen introduces the Creation, the Fall, the calling of Abraham, and the Exodus. The Resources are well written, interactive, accessible and at one level, the key parts of the story are communicated, but it is a very thin description of the story—this is the story in fragments and theological shorthand. The key motifs are highlighted but the complex theology within and behind them are not articulated. For example, in the retelling of the Creation story it is recognized that this Creation story is one of many—but there is no reference to genre or the tensions between contemporary scien-

---

47. Rogers, "Reading Scripture," 95.
48. Perrin, *The Bible Reading of Young Evangelicals*, 101.
49. Allen, "The Bible's Big Story," 33–36.
50. Ibid., 33.

tific accounts and the narration of a six-day creation. Allen[51] highlights through "key point 1" a theological reference to the fall, that *"God made everything possible, but we spoiled it by disobedience, yet God hasn't given up on the human race."* Questions circulate here by what Allen means by disobedience—this is theological shorthand for the complex story of the Fall that has been interpreted over the centuries in differing ways, either through the predominant western theology of Augustine or an alternative view developed from Irenaeus. Within Allen's[52] section on Egypt to Babylon, he begins to cover the story from Moses leading the people out of Egypt to the divided Kingdom. To do this he creates the titles of *"The pioneers"* (Moses and Joshua), *"The Part Timers"* (Judges), and *"The Princes"* (Israel's choice to have a King). He makes two key points *"The leaders God uses aren't perfect models of virtue; they can be depressed, frightened and occasionally disobedient, but ultimately their lives are committed to following God in faith, and that's why he uses them."* The second is this *"When God's people lose touch with what he wants and trust their own judgment; they get into a mess pretty quickly. The period of the Judges demonstrates this repeatedly."* This again is theological shorthand, short key sentences and punchy titles are used to cover vast sections of the story. The complex theology of a people wrestling with who YHWH is over many generations and cultures is swept over and the theology becomes abstract, fragmented and thin, with not enough attention paid to the original context. For example, the context of Judges is complex and paradoxical. Within Israel's story, the Judges are to orientate people back towards God, helping them to be faithful, yet here is Jael who breaks and ignores the sacred laws of hospitality; Ehud, who stoops to murder and assassination; Samson who leads a life of sexual promiscuity and whose life ends in an act of horrific violence. This is a complex history of God partnering with people, despite their dubious moral action.

Allen's[53] next two sections focus on the story from Babylon to Bethlehem and then Bethlehem to Heaven. Again, the aim is to communicate the *"Bible better by grasping the overarching narrative of scripture."* To continue the story, Allen[54] highlights the splitting of the Kingdom into North and South and the looking forward to a prophet and leader from Bethle-

---

51. Ibid., 33.
52. Ibid., 34.
53. Ibid., 35–36.
54. Ibid., 35.

hem. To make these points, Allen draws on Lamentations 2:11–13, Psalm 137:1–6, 2 Kings 25: 4–7 and 2 Chronicles 36:15–17. Allen also appeals to Jeremiah 25:11–14; Isaiah 9:1–3,6–7; Micah 5:2–4, Ezekiel 36:25–27 and Jeremiah 31:33–34. A key point he makes and wants young people to take away is that *"God doesn't renege on his promises. When we give up on him, he's still committed to us and his purposes will be accomplished in the end."* Again, this is theological shorthand in animation, life's complicated faith journey of doubt, anguish, fear, faith's twists and turns are simplified and summarized through the term *"give up on him."* Furthermore, what does Allen[55] mean by God's purposes? Again, like the set of Resources on reimaging the church, the moves made are backed up by the proof texts used that draw on scripture, but with no attention paid to actual interpretation, context, and genre. To bring the story to its finale, Allen[56] takes on the entire New Testament. His point is that *"Everything in the big story before Jesus is pointing forward to his death and resurrection. Everything afterwards is altered completely by what he achieved."* It has to be asked if "everything" here is true? Is this really the case? What "everything" does begin to point to is a typological approach to the Old Testament.

This emphasis can miss the importance of individual Old Testament stories and what they might say about YHWH and the Hebraic people. Although Allen is seeking to give context to Jesus' life death and resurrection this is summed up through the words *"Jesus was the crunch moment of the big story! When he died and rose again, our victory over our ancient enemies, sin and death was suddenly complete."* Allen's[57] approach needs to be recognized for what it is, seeking to tell the overall narrative of the Bible, it is positive that the key aspects of the story are in chronological order and in some sort of context. Yet, in doing so, this process functions as theological shorthand—key phrases and pithy sentences are used to sum up very complex and theologically rich parts of the narrative. The story is compressed, squashed and filtered out by the summing up of vast aspects of the narrative. Elements are atomized and fragmented, conceptualized in ways that was never intended—the story is held at the level of an idea. Through this, the Biblical story is viewed from the outside, it becomes a narrative to imitate, a story that runs parallel to our lives rather than a theodrama we participate and act in. Furthermore, the move from whole story to the individual world of the reader, their horizons and contexts,

55. Ibid.
56. Ibid., 36.
57. Ibid., 33–36.

involves, like in the Resources on Reimagining the Church, the process of plastic hermeneutics.[58] The Resources are written as a one size fits all and Perrins[59] insights into the creation of a polyvalence of interpretation, yet again, come into sharp focus.

Jesus Meets

Through the next set of four Resource Guides within *Youthwork*,[60] the moves made begin to take us a little deeper into the lives of the people Jesus met. As this approach is examined theological shorthand is still in play, but the foundations of what is explored are a little stronger. However, as the magazine leads youth ministers and young people to explore the people Jesus met, questions of Christology arise and there is real resonance between these stories and how the youth ministers interviewed articulated their work amongst young people. The phrase like Jesus is used in these meeting guides, the idea of model lies behind this particular series and, as above, through the Resources on the Big Picture, we look at the stories from the outside, they encourage imitation and not Christological participation.

In the sessions under investigation, Jesus meets the Canaanite women (Matt 15:21–28); Nicodemus (John 3:1–21); the women at the well (John 4:1–44) and the woman caught in adultery (John 8:1–12). Again, the Resources are divided into short sections of between 5–20 minutes of discussion, Bible reading and prayer. The first session deals with when Jesus meets a Canaanite woman. A strength is that Long[61] does not ignore the difficulties of interpreting this passage and also provides different understandings of interpretation for the youth ministers and young people to wrestle with. She encourages the questioning of the passage, but no real context to the book of Mathew or the passage is given. As she moves to apply the passage, a one size fits all approach is adopted. Long[62] argues, Jesus had the habit of making people feel uncomfortable in order to grow their faith. *"In this instance he challenged the Canaanite woman*

---

58. Rogers, "Reading Scripture," 95.
59. Perrin, *The Bible Reading of Young Evangelicals*, 101.
60. Long, "Jesus Meets"; Walley, "Jesus Meets"; Whitmarsh, "Jesus Meets"; Boyle, "Jesus Meets."
61. Long, "Jesus Meets," 34.
62. Ibid.

to reveal her faith and unmasked the darkness of the disciple's prejudices." As highlighted above, the move from the world of the Biblical text to the world of the readers is carried out simplistically. At the end of the session, the readers are encouraged to *"grow to look more like Jesus"*[63] as the idea of model comes to the fore. *"Look"* and *"like Jesus"* operates in a similar way as it does amongst the practitioners interviewed—it is a simplified, shorthand way of describing a complex theology of the lived.

The following session looks at how Jesus meets Nicodemus. The story of Nicodemus is referenced by Tom, above, as he wrestled with what it meant to be like Jesus. As Walley[64] explores this story, he gives some context by looking at Numbers 21:4–9, the story Jesus references in John 3:14. Walley makes two key points that he wants youth ministers to take away. It is here that theological shorthand is in action and thin theology is in play. The first key point is: *"God's love for the world looks like Jesus coming to die to bring people eternal life, to rescue people out of their darkness and bring them into light, and to save people from condemnation."* The second: *"You must be born again to see the Kingdom of God. To be born again is to see Jesus and believe in him."* There is rich theology held within these terms, but it is explained straight forwardly with evangelical assumptions that need unpacking. For example, where in John 3 does it say that Jesus came to die? The reference to the serpent in the wilderness could refer to lifting up on the cross, but that is not explicit. God's giving of his only son echoes the Abraham and Isaac story, but this back-story is needed. I would argue that this "giving" refers to the whole of Jesus' career, not simply to his death. That said, the idea of rescue resonates with the atonement[65] and bringing people out of darkness into light is a powerful metaphor for the Gospel, but it needs much more explanation than is given here. This is the Gospel written in code. To understand these metaphors and words requires a high degree of theological capital and Biblical literacy. Walley's[66] description of the Kingdom is particularly thin with no reference to what this actually looks like, and again, the embodiment of the political[67] and ethical implications[68] of this are missed.

63. Ibid.
64. Walley, "Jesus Meets," 35.
65. MacIntyre, *The Shape of Soteriology*.
66. Walley, "Jesus Meets," 35.
67. Yoder, *The Politics of Jesus*.
68. Hauerwas, *The Peaceable Kingdom*.

Whitmarsh,[69] looks at the woman at the well (John 4:1–44) and provides some context to the story as she seeks to demonstrate the inclusive nature of Jesus' ministry. Tom had highlighted this *"as a go to passage in youth ministry"* because of the boundary crossing nature of this story. Whitmarsh,[70] introduces an Ignatius approach to reading the passage, helping youth ministers and young people explore the layers of meaning within this story. Coupled with the context this begins to move away from "proof text" approach seen in some of the other Resources and explores the deeper theology within the passage. There are still tensions with the interchanges made between the context of the story and the world of the readers horizons as she asks, *"As the Samaritan women recognized who Jesus was and went and told others how they too could be liberated and known, so we can do the same, wherever we are and whatever we are doing."* Here youth ministers require theological capital and Biblical literacy to understand the liberation that Jesus offers and how this might take place.

Finally, Boyle,[71] looks at the story of the woman caught in adultery and the ideas of being like Jesus and Jesus as model are demonstrated again. In the meeting aim, she says *"To learn from how Jesus handled being challenged by the Pharisees when presented with a woman caught in adultery—how can we respond more like him?"* Again, this is theological shorthand in action through the phrase *"like him."* To think more about this for a moment, not many of us have had to deal with a woman caught in adultery(!)—let alone the appropriateness of this for young people. That said, it is possible to understand the point she is making, but this occurs as the exchanges made from the Biblical context to now happen through the abstracting of ideas. This is facilitated through the process of theological capital, wider theological ideas are needed to see how we can help and demonstrate compassion to others, the idea about compassion is squeezed out and the essence drawn and fragmented from the story. Furthermore, theological shorthand is animated throughout this session. Boyle's[72] first key point highlights this well: *"Jesus brings conviction and forgiveness—not judgement."* Each of these words is a piece of fragmented theology—it can be questioned what does conviction, forgiveness and

---

69. Whitmarsh, "Jesus Meets," 36.
70. Ibid.
71. Boyle, "Jesus Meets," 37.
72. Ibid.

judgement mean here? Although Boyle[73] gives some indication of this, the youth ministers again require other aspects of the Christian story to illuminate this beyond what is given in the Resource Guide. What is apparent is that more attention needs to be paid to how we discuss and talk about Jesus, it requires a richer vocabulary.

Following the discussions about the Resources Guides, the investigations continue as it is possible to trace the use of theological shorthand in contemporary worship songs.

Worship Songs: Singing the Fragments

The worship was performed within an ecumenical evangelical youth ministry event in the UK. The current conference aims to equip and train youth workers/ministers (both employed and volunteers) who come together to hear from God and find fresh vision for their ministry (stated event aims). The worship was led by a well-known professional worship leader, with approximately 700 people in attendance. The structure of the event included gathered times of worship and teaching (with keynote "big name" speakers from the UK/international context) and then optional seminars on differing topics to do with youth ministry.

Ward[74] traces the changing story of sung worship within the evangelical/charismatic tradition in the UK, highlighting a network of religious entrepreneurs, evangelical business and spiritual marketing. The event and the songs sung enact and embody the outworking of "Selling Worship." Within this story, Ward[75] sees that for the contemporary charismatic, worship[76] equals singing and that charismatic worship has become the default setting within many evangelical churches today.[77] Ward[78] argues that through worship intimacy between the worshipper and God is expressed, intimacy that is both expressive and experimental. Furthermore, the songs of the charismatic movement have not been written to simply express or speak about an encounter with God through worship.

---

73. Ibid.
74. Ibid.
75. Ibid., 198.
76. Peterson, *Engaging with God*, sees that in Biblical theology, worship goes beyond the singing of songs and is a life lived in orientation to God.
77. Ward, *Selling Worship*, 1.
78. Ibid., 199.

As Ward[79] notes, the songs themselves are narratives of encounter, the various metaphors and images within the songs connect us to the idea of coming before God, singing songs to God, sharing in God's blessing and presence. They are places of divine encounter. There are a number of key points here that Ward[80] develops. Firstly, there is an emphasis on the relational encounter between God and the worshiper. Secondly, charismatic worship songs are very explicit; the images often come from the edge or limits of emotional and spiritual experience. Thirdly, theological content, represented through metaphors, requires the worshiper to fill in the theological gaps.[81] It is possible to trace the interrelation of these three key points into the songs investigated. Moreover, it is Ward's[82] third insight that frames our forthcoming discussion. Therefore, this section builds on and takes Ward's[83] initial insights further, seeing that these songs are full of theological fragments and motifs, full of theological shorthand and thin theology, but importantly, these fragments still form part of the Christian story.

The Songs

Before the songs are examined it is vital to remember that these are songs that bring people into a space where God is worshiped, as worship happens we stand on Holy Ground—God meets us and we are changed. These songs are written by faithful servants and in choosing to investigate them I do so through the lens of critical faithfulness outlined above. Turning to the five songs chosen,[84] the framework from Adey[85] will be adopted to

---

79. Ibid., 202.
80. Ibid., 203–5.
81. Ibid., 208.
82. Ibid.
83. Ibid.
84. Ward and Fiddes, "Affirming Faith," see how testimonies and these types of songs operate within a particular baptismal service.
85. Adey, *Hymns and the Christian Myth*.

help analyze the songs.[86] The songs are *Our God*,[87] *Spirit Break Out*,[88] *One Thing Remains*,[89] *You're Beautiful*,[90] and *10,000 Reasons*.[91]

The song *Our God*[92] is largely subjective.[93] The song gives some account of theological and Biblical content, and it includes some reference to the implication of this for the worshipper. The chorus goes: *"Our God is greater, our God is stronger, God you are higher than any other."* In verse one, God is described through the motifs of Jesus' ministry and how Jesus turned water into wine, opened the eyes of the blind and healed. Moreover, a reference is made to Jesus as the light that shines in the darkness, and as our resurrection hope through the metaphor of rising from the ashes. The song continues in the chorus with *"Our God is Healer, Awesome in power, Our God! Our God!"* The bridge section includes the implications for the worshipper: *"And if our God is for us, then who could ever stop us. What could stand against?"* Yet there is an ironic twist at the heart of this song. The phrase: *"there is no one like you, none like you"* taken from Jeremiah 10:6 is repeated, but it is actually very hard to say who this God is because God is described through the fragments of the Biblical narrative - miracle worker, healer, light, our hope, but no theological foundation is given and Jesus is not explicitly mentioned. Moreover, it is these fragments that then frame the uncomfortable description (via binary opposition) that *"Our God is greater, Our God is stronger, God you are higher than any other."* The song raises a number of questions about power, dominance, and triumphalism in an environment that can emphasize the Kingdom of God,[94] these are not answered or described—

---

86. Adapted from Ward, *Selling Worship*.

87. Extracts taken from the song: "Our God" by C. Tomlin, J. Reeves, M. Redman/J. Myrin, Copyright ©2010. Thankyou Music

88. Extracts taken from the song: "Spirit Break Out" by L. Hellebronth, M. Dhillon, T. Hughes, B. Bryant Copyright ©2010. Thankyou Music.

89. Extracts taken from the song: "One Thing Remains" by B. Johnson, C. Black, J. Riddle Copyright ©2010. Cristajoy Music/Bethel Music Publishing & Mercy Vineyard Publishing.

90. Extracts taken from the song "You're Beautiful" Copyright © 2006 Seems Like Music & Phil Wickham, Music/Simpleville Music (adm Music Services/ Song Solutions).

91. Extracts taken from the song "10,000 Reasons (Bless the Lord)" by M. Redman/J. Myrin, Copyright ©2011. Thankyou Music.

92. "Our God," 2010.

93. Adey, *Hymns and the Christian Myth*.

94. For more on issues of power within the Pentecostal and Charismatic movement

the worshiper is left having to piece these fragments together. That said, it might be argued that since Jeremiah used this language, what is wrong with us doing so? Here Jeremiah ridicules the gods, and goes on to exalt YHWH as creator (10:12–16), but this preface is his proclamation of impending judgement on Judah (10:17–22). The final prayer that God will pour out his wrath on the nations is the cry of the devastated (10:25), preceded by significant self-reflection (10:23).

Spirit Break Out,[95] is largely a reflexive song. Within Adey's[96] framework, it concentrates on the act of worship itself. The song has an emphasis that focuses on the worshiper and what is happening within the present moment: *"let this place erupt with praise."* As Ward[97] sees, the "now" of the worship song indicates the extent and influence of the song on the present intimacy between the worshiper and God. There is a focus on *"Our Father,"* on *"revival,"* on the *"Spirit moving,"* on *"all of heaven roars"* and *"heaven touching earth."* The reference about God as *"Our Father"* and the phrase *"heaven touching earth"* resonate with the LORD's Prayer (Matthew 6:10–14). The reflexive content of verse one is clarified by the important naming of *"King Jesus"* (verse two). This provides the theological content as does the reference to God's glory and inference (meant or otherwise) to the Old Testament theme of *Shekinah* and God's presence. The theology of *"King Jesus,"* seeing the *"Kingdom here"* and the reference to glory (*Shekinah*) are rich in meaning. However, without any wider frameworks of interpretation, for example, Wright[98] and Moltmann,[99] they operate as theological shorthand and fragments that may or may not point to a much deeper reality depending on the interpretation made by the worshiper.

In *One Thing Remains*[100] and *You're Beautiful*,[101] the songs are largely lacking in any explicit theological content, they are again principally

---

see Bretherton, "Beyond the Emerging Church," 36–44. Bretherton highlights how the power and Kingdom of God is often emphasized over and against more established churches or denominations, establishing a false dichotomy between the Kingdom of God and the established church that can legitimize a Docetic ecclesiology.

95. "Spirit Break Out," 2010.
96. Adey, *Hymns and the Christian Myth*.
97. Ward, *Selling Worship*, 207.
98. Wright, *How God Became King*.
99. Moltmann, *Spirit of Life*, 47–50.
100. "One Thing Remains," 2010.
101. "You're Beautiful," 2007.

reflexive[102] and use metaphors to explore and describe the Christian life. As Ward[103] sees, these metaphors are powerful because they can connect significant elements of Christian experience with the intimacy within sung worship. In *One thing remains*,[104] the resurrection is alluded to and this is linked to the power of the Cross; the forgiveness of sins is implied, but not specifically mentioned. The chorus "*Your love never fails, never gives up, never runs out on me*" seeks to name the love through—"Your"—but like the song *Our God*,[105] Jesus is not explicitly named—the song requires the context in which it is sung to give meaning to this love. Moreover, without the context or theological capital this song may not be Christian, it could be a song about human rather than divine love. Metaphors are also used in the song *You're Beautiful*,[106] as it switches between subjective and reflexive frameworks[107] the power of creation is used to speak about the beauty of God. The song addresses some of the concerns seen in *One Thing Remains*,[108] there are more explicit references to the Cross and Resurrection. However, Christ is not mentioned and is only inferred—Jesus is seen to be sitting on the heavenly throne. Furthermore, verse four speaks powerfully about eschatology, the Biblical imagery of the church as the Bride of Christ is evoked, here hope is, and we are to sing "*You're beautiful, you're beautiful.*" This is an adjective, perhaps even an anthropomorphist metaphor replacing the Biblical imagery of "Holy, Holy, Holy" (Isaiah 6v3). The Biblical understanding of the suffering of the servant (pre-resurrection) is that he had no beauty or majesty to attract us to him (Isaiah 53v2b). The song is ambiguous (at best) at it changes between the suffering servant and the glorified one in verse three. The song could echo with pantheistic content, especially in verse one and this resonates in verse 2, stretching, and pushing the hermeneutical and exegetical understanding of Psalm 19 and Psalm 27:4 to their limits. Moreover, to understand the imagery within the song means sifting through the metaphors and fragments, constantly relating them

---

102. Adey, *Hymns and the Christian Myth*.
103. Ward, *Selling Worship*, 208.
104. "One Thing Remains," 2010.
105. "Our God," 2010.
106. "You're Beautiful," 2007.
107. Adey, *Hymns and the Christian Myth*.
108. "One Thing Remains," 2010.

back to the Biblical narrative requiring a high degree of theological and Biblical literacy to make the links.

10,000 reasons,[109] is essentially a reflexive song,[110] but verse two is more subjective. The song, is again, full of metaphors. The chorus names the object of the song—"the LORD" as we are to *"Bless the Lord oh my Soul"* taken from Psalm 103 and *"Worship his Holy name."* Verse two seeks to give some theological content to who the LORD is and this resonates with the description of *YHWH* in Psalm 145.v8. The song explores a number of the characteristics of God, the LORD is: *"rich in love," "slow to anger," "your name is great," "your heart is kind."* Yet, these motifs and fragments are problematic, *how* is the LORD rich in love, kind or good? *"Your name is great,"* makes reference to the description in Jeremiah 10:6 and also resonates with *YHWH's* declaration of "I am who I am" (Exodus 3:14).

The tension within all these songs is that theology is removed and dislocated from the Biblical narrative that is needed to give context and meaning to these words. The songs, fueled by theological shorthand and thin theology, use phrases connected to deeper theological constructs, but operate as fragments of a deeper story, fragments that are open to a variety of interpretations and plastic hermeneutics,[111] resonating acutely with the discussion above about the Resources Guides. In the espoused theology[112] of the songs, the Biblical texts are shattered and fragmented out of context, placed alongside one another in fluid or plastic ways that go well beyond their meaning within the original contexts. The meaning, through theological shorthand, is molded by the words of the song and the context in which the song is performed. Importantly, the voice of tradition is quiet and like the Resource Guides the songs operate across particular traditions.

Longing for a Coherent Theology

Taken at first glance, the theological shorthand and fragmentation is not necessarily significant. The songs are given meaning within the context

---

109. "10,000 Reasons," 2010.
110. Adey, *Hymns and the Christian Myth*.
111. Rogers, "Reading Scripture," 95.
112. Cameron et al., *Talking about God in Practice*.

in which they are performed,[113] and all theology be it formal, espoused, operant or normative[114] is both selective, perspectival and therefore limited: it cannot be otherwise.[115] The theological fragments and the songs form part of a larger hermeneutical jigsaw. The theological shorthand displayed within the narratives of practice, the theological shorthand demonstrated in some aspects of the youth ministry literature, the theological shorthand at play within the Resource Guides and the fragments within the songs begin to paint a far bigger and more complex theological picture that resonates beyond the nature of this book. For as Christie[116] sees by asking ordinary churchgoers who they thought Jesus is, they responded with a selected and fragmented view of Christology, disconnected from an orthodox and doctrinal understanding of the Incarnation and Jesus' death as an expiatory sacrifice. This fragmented world may not be present for those who navigate the world of formal theology.[117] Yet, for those with less awareness of the Christian Tradition, with less academic training, who embody this operant and espoused theology,[118] who are shaped more by Jesus' stories than doctrines[119] then perhaps it is significant? It is here that formal theology can shed light on the espoused and operant theology within the songs. To investigate each aspect of the particular songs would require a much longer chapter, but one of the most pertinent can be examined. Christ is only mentioned in *Spirit Break Out*[120] as King Jesus and in the last chorus of *10,000 Reasons*.[121] The other

---

113. I recognize that there is an inherent tension with the CDA approach, due to the cognitive and the rational, when in the complex construction of meaning our emotions and senses are engaged. Furthermore, the context and environment of the event communicates meaning—what people are wearing, where they sit, how the leaders speak, the layout of the building etc. Hughes, *Worship as Meaning*, 13–14, sees that in the context of worship that perhaps it is the music, its choice and execution, that becomes the most powerful conduit of meaning, or importantly for this section, perhaps ciphers without meaning. He sees the complex notion of meaning as involving the process of "sign reception" and construction. To illuminate this, he draws on Peirce's theory of signs. For more on this see: http://plato.stanford.edu/entries/peirce-semiotics/.

114. Cameron et al., *Talking about God in Practice*.

115. Christie, *Ordinary Christology*, 191.

116. Ibid.

117. Cameron et al., *Talking about God in Practice*.

118. Ibid.

119. Christie, *Ordinary Christology*, 191.

120. Smith, "Spirit Break Out," 2013.

121. Redman, "10,000 Reasons," 2011.

songs hint at Christ or his ministry. Nevertheless, King Jesus can be used as an icon to explore the theological significance. Here the words become an icon of epistemology, this is explored in more detail below. However, for now, Wright[122] reminds us that the four Gospels tell the story of how God became King, in and through Jesus, both in his public career and in his death. The cross is first and foremost the culmination of Israel's covenantal history, not a metaphysical transaction. It is the capstone of an entire history of God's steadfast covenant love and, in particular, of the Son's entire life of obedience to the father.[123] The cross is the Kingdom come and has far reaching political significance.[124]

Therefore, the dynamics of the Gospel rests on the life, death and resurrection of the historical Christ, the theology of God revealed in Christ is not just some higher form of theology[125] which only those operating within the realms of academic or formal theology[126] need to know. The theological fragments and shorthand within the songs risk untethering us from the historical Christ,[127] the songs lack an explicit Christology, resonating with how youth ministry practitioners see their practice as being like Jesus. This is more than mere oversight, for to participate in worship as a believer is to be in Christ, to benefit from his words and acts in history, especially the history of Christ. Yet, this is not explicit within the songs. For as Vanhoozer[128] argues, the Father communicates new life in and through the Son, by the Spirit: it is in Christ that there is a new creation. Youth ministers within worship and beyond participate in God's being–in–communicative activity, by being in Christ.[129] Communion with God through union with Christ is at the heart of the Gospel, the substance of faith and humanity's ultimate hope in life.

The songs, of course, do not seek to be doctrinal statements of orthodoxy; or deep theological treatises on Christology, however, neither are they examples of orthopraxis. As described above, they operate as narratives of encounter.[130] The songs are also part of a diet of preaching,

---

122. Wright, *How God Became King*.
123. Vanhoozer, *Remythologizing Theology*.
124. Yoder, *The Politics of Jesus*.
125. Ward, *Selling Worship*, 209.
126. Cameron et al., *Talking about God in Practice*.
127. Vanhoozer, *Remythologizing Theology*, 297–302.
128. Vanhoozer, *Remythologizing Theology*, 283.
129. Ibid., 284.
130. Ward, *Selling Worship*, 202.

liturgy (explicit or implicit), hymns, and other songs sung. Within this, the Christian community can of course express itself internally, through poetry, art, dance, and other creative expressions. Yet, in the event under question, the songs formed the main emphasis and diet of the worship and, as Parry[131] sees, a diluted theology (perhaps thin and shorthand) within worship forms spiritually impoverished worshippers. This raises two wider issues: firstly, of formation (the event is primarily a training and resourcing one), because for Parry[132] Christian worship is the primary place where Christians internalize Christian theology, where they learn the language of faith and find the articulation of this in song, prayer and the sacraments.

Both Parry[133] and Brown[134] see the formational power of worship and hymns, where theology is learnt by osmosis[135] to form a tacit understanding of the Christian faith. This notion of formation is crucial not only in the learning of faith but also in being able to theologically reflect on that faith experience. Not all people are called to navigate the world of formal theology, but all Christians are to think and reflect theologically on the lived experience of faith. The tension is that the historical Christ and the depth of theology articulated by Vanhoozer[136] is hidden and distorted in a world of metaphors, motifs, fragments, and theological shorthand. These point to a much deeper theology and narrative, but this theology needs a (relatively) advanced understanding of theological capital and Biblical literacy for it to be interpreted. This is crucial, Parry[137] argues, because when people are deprived of the rich and subtle language for God, then it may deprive them of the richness of theology, spiritual inheritance and depth of the Christian story and tradition. Secondly, the notion of narrative becomes important, for as MacIntyre[138] sees in talking about virtues, we are what we inherit; there is a specific past that is, to some degree in our present (social practices). We are part of a history and

---

131. Parry, *Worshipping Trinity*, 5.
132. Ibid., 6.
133. Ibid.
134. Brown, *How Hymns Shape our Lives*.
135. Parry, *Worshipping Trinity*, 6.
136. Vanhoozer, *Remythologizing Theology*.
137. Parry, *Worshipping Trinity*, 6.
138. MacIntyre, *After Virtue*, 217–21.

whether we recognize it or not, we are bearers of a tradition[139] that inherits certain practices.[140] It is our Christian history, tradition and practices that are in danger of becoming disconnected from our experience of faith within this contemporary diet of songs.

Now the fragments of theological shorthand have been investigated it is time to turn to construction. The next chapter explores how the fragments and theological shorthand can act as icons of epistemology, the chapter explores how the Trinity can add depth and richness to our vocabulary. It seeks to move us towards theodramatic participation, where we are part of the action and not just observers of it.

---

139. Hauerwas sees that the church as a community that is shaped by a narrative tradition that develops certain characteristics among those who live according to its story (e.g., nonviolence, perseverance, hospitality to strangers). For more on hospitality as holiness and what it means to be part of a tradition, see Bretherton, *Hospitality as Holiness*.

140. Dykstra and Bass, *A Theological Understanding*, 13–32.

PART THREE
Towards a Coherent Theology

Chapter 8

Expanding the Fragments as Icons of Epistemology: Relationships and Trinitarian Theology

The figure in the right of Rublev's icon can be seen to represent the Spirit. The figure is clothed in blue and green, the blue expresses divinity and the green signifies new life. Green is the liturgical color of Pentecost and in the Orthodox Church the symbolic color of the Spirit. The figure touches the table, breaths life, earthing the divine in the ordinariness of reality—all living things owe their freshness to his touch.[1] Rublev's icon acts as a metaphor for participation, we are welcomed at the table, we are to participate within the theodrama.[2] This is the subject explored in the next two chapters. Here a disclaimer needs to be added, taking Ward's[3] point about perilous normativity it should be recognized that the Trinitarian framework used within this chapter as a normative voice for youth ministry practice is offered as a partial ecclesiological blueprint. There are others that could have been used, but Vanhoozer's[4] emphasizes on communicative action and how this builds on his previous work of speech-act-theory fits well with the subject of theological shorthand, in doing so adds depth to the conversations had so far and helps to develop theological literacy. Furthermore, as it has been an evangelical expression of faith that has been under investigation, a scholar from within the

---

1. Persson, *The Circle of Love*, 50–51.
2. Vanhoozer, *Remythologizing Theology*.
3. Ward, "Blueprint Ecclesiology."
4. Vanhoozer, *Remythologizing Theology*.

evangelical tradition creates a symbiotic theological turn. Vanhoozer's[5] work seeks to chart a course of sympathetic disagreement between those who would deny the Biblical witness and who would demythologize God (Bultmann) and those who would mythologize God (Feuerbach, Moltmann,) and the 'voluntary–kenotic–perichorectic–relational–panentheism' which forms much of the contemporary Trinitarian debate. It is in this sense that the next two chapters are offered and through theological reflection it facilitates faith seeking understanding and reflection on divine action and encounter. I call this theodramatic dialogical reflection. This builds on the critical reflective work of Swinton and Mowat[6] in chapter 2, but adds a specific theological category of drama via Vanhoozer.[7] It is worth exploring this in more detail.

Theodramatic Dialogical Reflection

Theodramatic dialogical reflection is the process of faith seeking understanding *(fides quaerens intellectum)*. This is a classical definition of theology and with numerous variations has a long and rich tradition.[8] Augustine sees that it takes the form of "I believe in order that I may understand." According to Augustine, knowledge of God not only presupposes faith, but faith also restlessly seeks a deeper understanding, Christians want to understand what they believe, what they hope for and what they love.[9] It is Anselm who is credited for coining the phrase "faith seeking understanding" and for Anselm, faith not only brings understanding, but Joy as well "I pray, O God, to know thee, to love thee that I may rejoice in thee." Karl Barth stands in this tradition, as theology through faith has the task of reconsidering the faith and practice of the community. Ward[10] argues, that Barth reads Anselm's theological quest as the search for faith, faith seeking understanding is an intellectual knowledge that facilitates positive meditation. For Ward,[11] Anselm seeks a place of rest to contemplate his concerns and this wrestling is the pursuit of God. Ward,

---

5. Ibid., 1–32
6. Swinton and Mowat, *Practical Theology and Qualitative Research*.
7. Vanhoozer, *Remythologizing Theology*.
8. Migliore, *Faith Seeking Understanding*, 2.
9. Ibid.
10. Ward, *Participation and Mediation*, 99.
11. Ibid., 100.

suggests, that the place of rest articulated by Anselm should be seen as a spiritual discipline and the place of meditation and reflection on the tensions and contradictions in practice. This takes the form of participation within the divine life and theological reflection on lived practice becomes a place of divine encounter. Therefore, reflection is concerned with rationality, but it is also a place of prayer that is indwelt by God. When practical theology is reframed as a spiritual practice and a place of divine encounter it becomes recognizable to the everyday practice of the minister. Here the problems of practice co-exist with the questions about doctrine as practitioners wrestle with who God is in the lived experience of faith. It is faith seeking understanding, which participates in the mission of God through reflection. Ward[12] primarily draws his Trinitarian theology of participation from Zizioulas[13] and Fiddes,[14] which is different from the approach adopted here.

In the approach to theodramatic dialogical reflection that is being developed, Ward's thoughts are helpful, especially the insight that theological reflection is a spiritual discipline in which practice and doctrine co-exist. This is important because it can augment the somewhat formulaic methodology of Swinton and Mowat,[15] that was noted in chapter 2. Ward's thinking can, at least in part, be reframed for this project.

In developing a theodramatic approach to reflection Vanhoozer's[16] thinking gives shape to this. Vanhoozer[17] seeks to outline a method of theology that he sees as being a key part of what theology actually is, Christianity is fundamentally neither a philosophy nor a system of morality, but a theodrama, a doing in which God gets the most important speaking and acting parts. As Vanhoozer[18] sees from Niebuhr "The Bible conceives life as a drama in which human and divine action create a dramatic whole." For Vanhoozer,[19] doctrine gives direction for right participation in the theodrama. There are two things here. Firstly, our reflection on practice takes place within this theodrama, we are part of the communicative ac-

---

12. Ibid., 96–97.
13. Zizioulas, *Being as Communion*.
14. Fiddes, *Participating in God*.
15. Swinton and Mowat, *Practical Theology and Qualitative Research*.
16. Vanhoozer, *First Theology*.
17. Ibid.
18. Vanhoozer, *Remythologizing Theology*, xiv.
19. Ibid.

tion. Secondly, it requires a dialogical conversation as one wrestles with what it means to participate with God. As explored below, there are different notions of what it means to participate in God. To define doctrine in terms of fitting participation in the drama of redemption is to locate theology on the borderlands of ontology.[20] Therefore, to explore these ontological questions requires conversation between differing theologies and concepts, it is through the process of sympathetic dialogical discussions and reflection that one can wrestle with what participation in God means. Of course, through this process, one might end up in a completely different place to the argument being constructed, but that is the creative process of faith seeking understanding, the art of developing theological literacy.

Therefore, as theological shorthand is explored through theodramatic dialogical reflection—it is deeply theological because it is faith seeking understanding that takes place (I argue), within God's communicative action and it is dialogically reflective because it weighs up the differing theological arguments under discussion.

As the theological shorthand and fragments act as icons of epistemology there are three interconnected moves made. These are: identification, interpretation and dialogical reflection. Firstly, the process of identification. Chapters 4, 5, 6 and 7 identified the theological shorthand and fragments within the narratives of practice, the youth ministry literature, the Resource Guides and the worship songs. These sketch out how theological shorthand is operating within the world of youth ministry. This is the first stage to identify the theological shorthand and fragments. For example, the language used by the youth ministry participants (relationships, like Jesus, being there and time and journey) has been explored and identified. Secondly is interpretation, how is this language being used and employed? This has been investigated above. The final part of the process is to dialogically reflect upon the language via differing theological views. This deepens the interpretation and offers a new way of seeing. So far so good, but this sounds very similar to the pastoral cycle that Swinton and Mowat[21] employ, the key difference is seen by adopting elements of Ward's[22] and Vanhoozer's[23] thinking. Therefore,

---

20. Ibid.
21. Swinton and Mowat, *Practical Theology and Qualitative Research*.
22. Ward, *Participation and Mediation*.
23. Vanhoozer, *Remythologizing Theology*.

this is primary a spiritual discipline as through prayer, faith is seeking understanding, but this whole process is a means by which God communicates, it takes place within theodramatic participation indwelt by the Spirit. For as Vanhoozer[24] sees, we cannot love God without knowing God and we cannot know God without understanding what he has done in Jesus Christ.

Living and Reimaging the Fragments—Icons of Epistemology

The argument of this book has been the exploration of theological shorthand within youth ministry. However, if this is part of the problem, then, as is beginning to become clear, it may well be part of the solution. Theological shorthand may provide an opportunity for guiding, educating and illuminating. What comes through the narratives of the youth ministers, the Resource Guides, the songs, and the wider investigations on how the youth ministry literature guides practice, is the risk of practice and theological knowledge, at least in part, being untethered from the depth of the Christian story.[25] The problem is that it is not only Christ who is being obscured, but that youth ministry is in danger of being untethered not only from certain aspects of the Christian narrative (e.g. Christology), but core practices (*diakonia, kerygma, marturia*) as well. However, the fragments, via theodramatic dialogical reflection, can act as icons of epistemology that have the potential to lead to a much richer and deeper understanding of the Christian story, they help develop theological literacy. As MacIntyre[26] sees, it is a narrative framework that provides the strongest way in which to understand the world and our identity within it. Both Vanhoozer[27] and Hauerwas[28] build on this idea of narrative as being foundational. Hauerwas[29] argues there is no other fundamental way to talk about God than story, narrative is the primary grammar. This way of theological thinking regards the Christian faith as God's self-narrated

---

24. Vanhoozer, *Faith Speaking Understanding*, xii.
25. Walker, *Telling the Story*.
26. MacIntyre, *After Virtue*, 217.
27. Vanhoozer, *Remythologizing Theology*.
28. Hauerwas, *The Peaceable Kingdom*.
29. Ibid., 25–26.

story.[30] Narrative theology is widely seen as being shaped by Barth's approach to scripture and revelation in that the whole of Christian teaching rests on the unbelievable story of Jesus. It is faith seeking understanding. Therefore, dogmatics is much less a system, than the narrative of an event.[31] Vanhoozer, sees Barth as a fellow remythologizer, and Vanhoozer's work can be seen as having Thomistic ambitions tempered by Barthian anxieties.[32] Canonical narrative theology finds supporters in Hans Frei and Lindbeck, both share the narrative assumption of Barth, that, as Lindbeck[33] sees, to become a Christian involves learning the story of Israel and Jesus well enough to interpret oneself and one's world in its terms.

Hauerwas[34] continues, surely we can talk about God in a more fundamental manner other than story, perhaps through doctrine? It is obvious that the Resource Guides and songs lack a clear and articulate doctrinal base, (like the lack of Christology already mentioned). Moreover, such emphasis ignores the fact that such doctrines are themselves a story, or perhaps better, the outline of a story.[35] Claims such as "Jesus is LORD," or "God is creator" are simply shorthand ways to remind us that we are participants in a much more elaborate story, of which God is the author.[36] At least some fragments of this story are espoused and operate within the language of the youth ministers, the Resource Guides, and songs, and they can be employed as icons, as windows of epistemology. To help youth ministers and young people explore the richness and depth of this larger narrative, the theological shorthand within the language of the youth ministers, the fragmented theological expression within the Resource Guides and the songs can be seen as points of divine encounter. Perhaps facilitating and enabling those of us who work within the world of formal theology[37] to be able to act as dialogical guides and storytellers.

---

30. Graham et al., *Theological Reflection*, 78–79.
31. Hardy, *Theology*, 165–66.
32. Vanhoozer, *Remythologizing Theology*, 222.
33. Lindbeck, *The Nature of Doctrine*, 34.
34. Hauerwas, *The Peaceable Kingdom*, 25.
35. In contrast, Jones, *Graced Practices*, would argue that doctrines are the deep grammar of the story.
36. Hauerwas, *The Peaceable Kingdom*, 26. Vanhoozer, *Remythologizing Theology*, 297–302.
37. Cameron et al., *Talking about God in Practice*.

EXPANDING THE FRAGMENTS AS ICONS OF EPISTEMOLOGY 179

The community as the church[38] becomes the place where this happens. The language of the youth ministers, the words within the Resource Guides and the theological expression within the songs are employed in very particular situations. When theological shorthand is seen to be in play, then it allows these words to operate as a window, as an icon, to see and deepen the theology within them. It gives a richer grammar and literacy to articulate practice. This is the process of theodramatic dialogical reflection. The words and phrases can be highlighted and used to tell the richer story behind them, but as fellow participants in this theological drama, we remind ourselves that we stand on Holy ground.

Therefore, through Trinitarian theology, this chapter seeks to show how the phrases that the youth ministers used: relationships, like Jesus, being there, time and journey, this theological shorthand, can be used as icons of epistemology. These phrases are deepened and re-connected into the Christian story. This provides a rich resource and acts as a normative voice that helps to serve, illuminate and offer a sympathetic critique of youth ministry practice. Through Trinitarian theology, practice can be understood in more authentic and faithful ways. It moves from observing the story to participating in the theological drama.

As the Trinitarian conversation is explored and critiqued, this chapter will again follow, investigate, and develop the themes found in the data. Through this final move of theodramatic dialogical reflection an exciting turn of theological reimagination is employed. A more authentic and faithful understanding of relationships, like Jesus, being there and time and journey is advanced. This requires some theological thought and wrestling as exploring the icons of epistemology means weighing up different and contrasting theological frameworks. It is a process of discussion, it is faith seeking understanding. Moreover, in the analysis of the Resource Guides and in the songs investigated, the theological shorthand reveals an embedded theology that evokes the wider theological picture of the Christian story, yet, this broader narrative is not overtly expressed. Therefore, in the next two chapters, the wider theological picture of the Christian tradition is nuanced and explored through the Trinitarian discussions.

With this in mind, a more explicit description of relationships is advanced, locating them in God's divine communicative action, moving beyond the limited description of relationships within some of the youth ministry literature and the theological shorthand description

38. Hauerwas, *The Peaceable Kingdom*, 96–111.

found within the data. The theme of like Jesus, has been seen as a model, leading to sense of observing the story from the outside. In this chapter, practice can move from being a model of like Jesus to be reimagined as being in Christ, that is held within God's divine communicative action. Importantly, the operant mode of participation is seen as fellowship.[39] Therefore, through the Trinitarian discussions practice is reconnected to being in Christ, thus answering the question of, "where is Jesus?" in relation to practice. The investigation of the third theme of being there is the enacted presence of the second, like Jesus. This becomes a performed theological moment in time and space through which the youth ministers act as a symbol.[40] As a symbol they embody qualities of that which they participate in, what they point towards. This is not articulated, only the language of model is used and is seen as being like Jesus. Through Trinitarian theology a richer definition of being there as symbol can be seen, demonstrating how its participative nature can be located in God's communicative action.[41] With this, we can move from being there to being there in Christ. Furthermore, through moving from being there to being there in Christ, the *diakonia*, the service amongst suffering young people and the locating of this within the practice of the church becomes a litmus test for the normative voice of Trinitarian theology and youth ministry practice. Within the Trinitarian theology adopted from Vanhoozer,[42] practice is reimagined as mission, no longer being focused on the individual youth minister, but located in the ecclesial relationships of the *koinonia*. Adding theological depth and articulation to the weak ecclesiology found within the discussions on the church from the Resource Guides. Additionally, the narratives of practice, demonstrated that in their enacted mission amongst young people, the practitioners are aiming for a liminal space. In the data, this is a place of wrestling, a place of waiting, a threshold where God can move and act. The creation of a liminal space opens the possibilities for mystery, a space where young people can encounter God. However, this is articulated through the theological shorthand of time and journey. Therefore, this becomes a space, not of waiting for God to act, but a place of God's communicative

---

39. Vanhoozer, *Remythologizing Theology*.
40. Tillich, *Dynamics of Faith*.
41. Vanhoozer, *Remythologizing Theology*.
42. Ibid.

action, as Vanhoozer[43] sees. Furthermore, this liminal space is also at work within the worships songs as narratives of encounter. The words within the songs can be explored in more depth and detail as these words become icons of epistemology and connect people through worship into God's communicative action.

Perichoresis and the Trinity

For Trinitarian theology to provide a rich resource which is authentic and faithful for practice, to enable key words to act as icons of epistemology, the Trinitarian discussion requires critique and evaluation for it to provide a normative voice for understanding practice. This is especially pertinent around the term *perichoresis*. The dialogue around this, through the work of Moltmann,[44] Fiddes,[45] Kilby,[46] and Vanhoozer,[47] will help frame the debate as Trinitarian theology is brought into discussion with the themes found in the data. The debate echoes with tensions between classical theology and its reinterpretation in contemporary thought. The concept of relationships and the outworking of this through the *perichoresis* could be held up as an idea that would provide a normative move for the enacting of youth ministry practice. It is possible to see a cozy and symbiotic relationship which is attractive for the lived experience of youth ministry. The question is at what theological cost? For the notion of *perichoresis* has flourished into a theological paradigm and there are some deep-seated problems associated with the moves made within this "new orthodoxy." The relational turn that has taken place in the recovery of doctrine of the Trinity needs to be unpacked.

As Vanhoozer[48] sees, this has sent theologians back to the ontological drawing board. Here, the universe looks less like a conglomeration of separate substances and more like an interactive community. This is particularly the case in Moltmann's[49] Trinitarian theology that is advanced through his idea of "persons in relationship" and located in his notion of

43. Ibid.
44. Moltmann, *The Trinity and the Kingdom of God*.
45. Fiddes, *Participating in God*.
46. Kilby, "Perichoresis and Projection."
47. Vanhoozer, *Remythologizing Theology*.
48. Ibid., 113.
49. Moltmann, *The Trinity and the Kingdom of God*.

perichoresis. Moltmann develops his ideas from the Eastern tradition[50] drawing on the Cappadocians. His ideas are important because, through his theology, the Trinity echoes and resonates with the language of participation and imitation. The idea of imitation chimes with the thoughts of like and model and observe found in the narratives of practice. Moltmann's[51] ideas have also been deeply influential in the out working of providing a model for social relations[52] and our ecclesiological frameworks.[53] Moreover, Moltmann's[54] thinking has been important within youth ministry circles as Dean,[55] Root,[56] and White[57] draw on Moltmann in relation to practice. Through Fiddes'[58] thinking, we will look at a contrasting concept of Trinitarian relationships, of "persons as relationships." This follows the operant mode of participation. Fiddes,[59] constructs his argument on the idea of "subsistent relations."[60] These ideas find their origin in Augustine, who made a move in this direction, but are "named" by Aquinas who gave formality to the notion by creating the term. Fiddes' thoughts are important because he develops a pastoral doctrine of the Trinity that has a strong connection to the lived experience of practice. But these counterintuitive thoughts also require sympathetic evaluation and critique. Through the discussion, a more convincing argument for Trinitarian relations and human participation is set out by Vanhoozer.[61] He again builds on this idea of "subsistent relations," particularly through the work of Aquinas, however, Vanhoozer's[62] idea of "subsistent relations"

---

50. According to Holmes, *The Holy Trinity*, the distinction between the Western and Eastern tradition is false one.

51. Moltmann, *The Trinity and the Kingdom of God*.

52. Boff, *Trinity and Society*.

53. Volf, *After Our Likeness*.

54. Moltmann, *The Trinity and the Kingdom of God*.

55. Dean, *Practicing Passion*.

56. Root, "Youth Ministry."

57. White, *Jürgen Moltmann's Pneumatology*.

58. Fiddes, *Participating in God*.

59. Ibid.

60. Gunton, *The One, The Three and The Many*, is critical of this idea, that following Augustine, through the tradition of "subsistent relations," there has been a loss in the sense of particularity in God.

61. Vanhoozer, *Remythologizing Theology*.

62. Ibid.

differs to that found in the work of Fiddes.[63] The difference is that Fiddes[64] develops his ideas of "subsistent relations" through the notion of "persons as relationships," whilst Vanhoozer[65] develops the idea of "persons as communicative agents" that share a common "communicative agency." Vanhoozer wants to hold onto the traditional division between the immanent and economic Trinity that becomes blurred within the work of Moltmann[66] and Fiddes.[67] Therefore, questions need to be asked about what is meant by this operant mode of participation due to the differing interpretations between Moltmann, Fiddes and Vanhoozer,[68] resonating with Ward's[69] insights into ecclesiological blueprints and perilous normativity.

That said, Vanhoozer[70] is critical of how the doctrine of *perichoresis* has become central in the revival of Trinitarian thought, calling this a "new kenotic–perichorectic relational ontotheology." His insights are important as he seeks to speak about God through God's interpersonal dialogue with the world. He frames this as God's communicative action, a relationship based on divine authorship[71] and dialogical interaction between God and humanity. We come to know God's communicative being, through his communicative acts in the Biblical accounts as God speaks and acts in relation to his revelation, the world and human agency. This moves beyond the idea of theological shorthand as expressed in the data, to a richer, we could say a remythologized,[72] description of the idea

---

63. Fiddes, *Participating in God*.
64. Ibid.
65. Vanhoozer, *Remythologizing Theology*, 244–47.
66. Moltmann, *The Trinity and the Kingdom of God*.
67. Fiddes, *Participating in God*.
68. Moltmann and Fiddes Trinitarian theology can be seen as panentheistic. Fiddes' theology can also be located within process theology. These are points of difference with Vanhoozer.
69. Ward, "Blueprint Ecclesiology."
70. Vanhoozer, *Remythologizing Theology*, 139.
71. For Vanhoozer, *Remythologizing Theology*, xiii, "authorship" acts as a convenient shorthand for the notion of verbal communicative action. He argues that the interpersonal dialogue between God and humanity that the Bible depicts and instantiates is the privileged starting point for Christian theology. Western theologians as diverse as Thomas Aquinas, John Owen, Karl Rahner and Karl Barth employ the notions of communication and self-communication in the context of divine revelation and redemption.
72. As Vanhoozer, *Remythologizing Theology*, argues, this is seen in contrast to

of relationships as communicative acts that is located in God's communicative action and the Biblical *theodrama*.[73] This locates youth ministry practice within the communicative acts and work of God, re-tethering the practice into the richness of the Christian story. Before relationships as communicative acts through connection and transmission are explored, the interrelated ideas of projection and "persons" in relation to the Trinitarian conversation need to be noted.

The Trinity: Projection and Persons

Within the discussion on Trinitarian relationships, Vanhoozer's[74] thinking finds resonance with Kilby's[75] argument. Kilby sees that contemporary Trinitarian theology has developed a "new orthodoxy," especially around concepts of *perichoresis* and the social doctrine of the Trinity, that involves theologians projecting ideas of human relations and relatedness back onto God. Holmes[76] is also critical of the explosion of theological work on this topic within the twentieth century. He sees that this has been misunderstood and distorted the doctrine of the Trinity so badly that it is unrecognizable from what was set out in the fourth century. Kilby[77] argues that over the last three decades there has been resurgence in Trinitarian theology amongst Roman Catholic and Protestant writers. Furthermore, within these writings, there is a lament about how the doctrine of the Trinity has been neglected and needs to be recovered. Kilby[78] sees that this has followed Rahner's diagnosis that Christians were almost monotheists paying lip service to the Trinity, but ignoring the Trinity in practice. However, if there is a consensus about the problem, then for Kilby,[79] there is also something of a consensus as regarding the solution. The solution has been to advance a social understanding of the Trinity. It

---

Bultmann's demythologizing. Remythologizing moves in another direction, taking seriously the Biblical accounts of God speaking and establishes divine communicative action as the formal and material principle of theology.

73. For more on this see Vanhoozer, *Remythologizing Theology*.
74. Ibid.
75. Kilby, "Perichoresis and Projection."
76. Holmes, *The Holy Trinity*.
77. Kilby, "Perichoresis and Projection."
78. Ibid., 1.
79. Ibid.

is within this social understanding of the Trinity that Tanner[80] argues that theologians are enlisting support for particular kinds of community. For example: following Moltmann's[81] social doctrine of the Trinity, of "divine persons in relationships," we see the social models put forward by Boff[82] and Volf.[83] Within these social models, the ideas of imitation and mirror are discovered that, as noted, resonate with the ideas of model and observation found within the data. Furthermore, Kilby[84] is critical of the way the social doctrine of the Trinity has been used and the claims made as the chief strategy of reviving the discussion of the Trinity in recent times. For Kilby, this has gathered pace since Moltmann's *The Trinity and the Kingdom of God*, and although her argument is not directed at the analogies themselves, the authoritarian claims made for the promotion of this social doctrine of the Trinity and the cascading of this into social, political[85] and ecclesiological models and patterns[86] is deeply problematic, especially when worked out through the notion of *perichoresis*.

For Kilby,[87] this is because when the social doctrine of the Trinity is applied as a resource for Christian theology, it draws on *perichoresis* to name what is not understood about the inner reality of God. Kilby[88] sees that the interrelatedness of the Trinity, as played out in the divine *perichoresis*, makes God intrinsically attractive. Here God's "inner life" is presented as having positive implications for that which is not God. For Kilby,[89] this becomes a three-stage process. Firstly, the term *perichoresis* is used to name what is not understood, to name whatever it is that makes the three persons one. Secondly, the term *perichoresis* is filled out rather suggestively with notions taken from experience of relatedness and relationship; and thirdly, it is presented as an exciting resource that Christian theology has to offer the wider world in its reflections on relatedness and

---

80. Tanner, "Trinity," 320.
81. Moltmann, *The Trinity and the Kingdom of God*.
82. Boff, *Trinity and Society*.
83. Volf, *After Our Likeness*.
84. Kilby, "Perichoresis and Projection."
85. Boff, *Trinity and Society*.
86. Volf, *After Our Likeness*.
87. Kilby, "Perichoresis and Projection."
88. Ibid.
89. Ibid., 3–5.

relationships. Although not named by Kilby,[90] these criticisms on relatedness and relationships can also be levelled at Fiddes.[91]

Vanhoozer[92] follows Kilby,[93] at least in part, and, by drawing on Feuerbach, is also critical of how relations and relatedness have been "projected" on to God. For Vanhoozer,[94] Feuerbach sees the Trinity as a projection of the human ideal of a "participated life." He sees Christian doctrine mirroring lived human relations and that humanity as social beings need a God in whom there is society—a "union of beings" fervently loving one another. Kilby[95] and Vanhoozer[96] differ, because Vanhoozer argues that we can participate in the communicative acts of God. This Vanhoozer[97] calls *"theodrama,"* this is a *"doing"* in which God gets the most important speaking and acting parts. Moreover, Kilby[98] argues that the Trinity should become a doctrine that acts like a grammatical framework, due to theologians being unable to "name" the personal attributes of God's being.

As the idea of relationships and Trinitarian Theology is explored, we need to note the discussions around the term "person." This is a complex and well-rehearsed debate and lies outside the scope of this book, but it is Zizioulas[99] who gives the fullest account of the relational nature of "personhood" to date. As Vanhoozer[100] sees, this radically reshapes the nature of "persons" by drawing on the doctrine of the Trinity. God's being is a consequence of his "personhood," this "personhood" is a matter of relationships and not of a self-enclosed "substance." As Holmes[101] sees, Zizioulas, through the Cappadocians, took the classical language of Greek ontology—*ousia* and *hypostasis* and redefined it in personal and relational terms. The basis of reality was no longer "substance," but "rela-

90. Ibid.
91. Fiddes, *Participating in God*.
92. Vanhoozer, *Remythologizing Theology*, 157–59.
93. Kilby, "Perichoresis and Projection."
94. Vanhoozer, *Remythologizing Theology*, 159.
95. Kilby, "Perichoresis and Projection."
96. Vanhoozer, *Remythologizing Theology*, 245.
97. Ibid., xiv.
98. Kilby, "Perichoresis and Projection," 14.
99. Zizioulas, *Being as Communion*, 16–27. Historically, the concept of the "person" is inextricably linked with theology.
100. Vanhoozer, *Remythologizing Theology*, 115.
101. Holmes, *The Holy Trinity*, 13.

tionship," "cause" was fundamentally now not a physical category, but a "personal" one.[102]

Therefore, for Zizioulas,[103] "to be is to be in relation" and the differing interpretations of this through Moltmann,[104] Boff,[105] Volf,[106] and Fiddes[107] has become a foundational thought in the recovery of Trinitarian theology and has brought relationships and relatedness to center stage.

Reimagining Relationships as Communicative Acts: Connection

The interviews with the youth ministers showed how relationships as communicative acts as connection, are important in the enacting of mission amongst young people. As connection is explored as an icon of epistemology it was seen earlier that the notion of connection could be traced back into Ward's[108] work on contact, and beyond into the work of Young Life.

Moltmann's thinking has been influential and important in developing a theology that serves youth ministry practice as Dean,[109] Root,[110] and White[111] argue. Therefore, just as these academic thinkers have linked Moltmann to contemporary practice, it would be possible to find resonance between relationships as communicative acts as connection and Moltmann's[112] thinking. This move could be made in two ways: firstly, how he views the Trinitarian relationships as human participation and, secondly, how this becomes a model for our social relationships. Both of these thoughts could be expanded and interwoven into how we connect and participate with God and how this models our connections with oth-

---

102. Zizioulas, *Being as Communion*, 38, notes that the history of the terms "substance" and "hypostasis" is extremely complicated. For a full account of this dispute see footnote 30. [x-ref]
103. Ibid.
104. Moltmann, *The Trinity and the Kingdom of God*.
105. Boff, *Trinity and Society*.
106. Volf, *After Our Likeness*.
107. Fiddes, *Participating in God*.
108. Ward, *Youthwork*, 46–59.
109. Dean, *Practicing Passion*.
110. Root, "Youth Ministry."
111. White, *Jürgen Moltmann's Pneumatology*.
112. Moltmann, *The Trinity and the Kingdom of God*.

ers in community as an example of youth ministry practice. Yet, on closer inspection, this is worked out in ways that are not entirely successful and convincing, we are invited to participate in these relationships and at the same time these Triune relations are to be used as a model for our own social relationships.[113] How does this work?

In Moltmann's[114] theology, the Trinitarian persons are in relationship through his idea of *perichoresis*. Here, he sets forth a social doctrine of the Trinity, God's being is an open fellowship of love, God's unity is community, a community of relationships, this becomes relational metaphysics. Moltmann[115] describes the *perichoresis* in the following way:

> The Father exists in the Son, the Son in the Father, and both of them in the Spirit, just as the Spirit exists in both the Father and the Son. By virtue of their eternal love they live in one another, and dwell in one another, to such an extent that they are one. In the perichoresis the very thing that divides them becomes that which binds them.

For Moltmann,[116] the circulation of the eternal divine life becomes perfect through the fellowship and unity of the Father, Son and Spirit in their eternal love for one another. Yet, the major problem within Moltmann's,[117] and subsequently, Boff's[118] and Volf's[119] Trinitarian theologies, as Tanner[120] argues, is how do we move from a discussion about God, to a discussion of human relations? It is here that these ideas become limiting. In the work of Moltmann,[121] Tanner,[122] argues that the problem revolves around the acute focus on the so-called immanent Trinity. In the description of *perichoretic* relationships found within Moltmann what the Trinity says about human relations is not exactly clear. Other questions circulate as well, "divine persons" are "equal" to one another, but in what sense? The divine persons are "in" one another, but what

---

113. Bauckham, *Theology of Jürgen Moltmann*, 160.
114. Moltmann, *The Trinity and the Kingdom of God*.
115. Ibid., 174–75.
116. Ibid., 175.
117. Ibid.
118. Boff, *Trinity and Society*.
119. Volf, *After Our Likeness*.
120. Tanner, "Trinity," 324.
121. Moltmann, *The Trinity and the Kingdom of God*.
122. Tanner, "Trinity," 324–25.

does "in" mean here? For Moltmann[123] humanity comes to participate in God's nature and being, we could say—connected to the divine life. But this has radical implication for the relationship between God and the world. For Moltmann, the Gospel becomes about the history of the divine persons in the world and for the sake of the world. Following Rahner's thesis, Moltmann[124] *almost* collapses the immanent Trinity into the economic. This move creates a tension between the created and the creator, between love and freedom. Vanhoozer[125] argues that this move is deeply problematic. This is because God's history is "open" to the world and it leads Moltmann[126] to see that the unity of the three persons is inclusive not exclusive, creatures can participate in the divine relational matrix. Furthermore, there is real tension here between participation within the Trinity and the Trinity as a model for our human relations that, as seen below, causes numerous theological dominos to fall.

In Moltmann's[127] thinking, these two ideas are held in paradoxical tension. Bauckham[128] sees that, firstly, the life of the Trinity is an interpersonal fellowship in which we participate, through Moltmann's[129] use of the *perichoresis*. Secondly, the life of the Trinity provides the prototype on which human life should be *modelled* and imitated. Furthermore, Bauckham[130] is critical of this, seeing that this view of relationships in regard to the Trinity goes beyond the canon of Scripture and that the combination of these thoughts is particularly problematic. According to the first idea (participation), we are to experience the Trinitarian relationships from the "inside," from the stand point of differentiated relationships to each of the three persons: we know Jesus as God who became human; we know God the Father as his and our Father; and we know the Holy Spirit as the indwelling of life and power. With the second idea (model), we are invited to stand outside this participation in the Trinity, and our specific

---

123. Moltmann, *The Trinity and the Kingdom of God*.
124. Ibid., 158–60.
125. Vanhoozer, *Remythologizing Theology*, 152.
126. Moltmann, *The Trinity and the Kingdom of God*.
127. Ibid.
128. Bauckham, *Theology of Jürgen Moltmann*, 160.
129. Moltmann, *The Trinity and the Kingdom of God*.
130. Bauckham, *Theology of Jürgen Moltmann*, 160.

relationships with each of the three persons, and view the Trinity as an external model which human relationships are to imitate and reflect.[131]

As the theme of relationships as communicative acts, as connection in conversation with *perichorectic* ideas is explored, Fiddes also develops the idea of *perichoresis*. Fiddes,[132] sees that the term *perichoresis* expresses the permeation of each divine person by the other, their co–inherence without confusion, taking up and developing the words of Jesus in John 17:21–22.[133] Fiddes,[134] differs to Moltmann[135] because his ideas on the *perichoresis* are developed through the notion of "subsistent relations." Fiddes[136] argues that this notion is often misunderstood. It does not just mean the divine *hypostases* which can only be distinguished by their relations with one another, nor does "subsistent relations" just mean that the relations between the divine "persons" entirely make them what they are. Fiddes[137] continues that, properly understood, "subsistent relations" mean that the *relations* in God are as real and "beingful" as anything which is created or uncreated and their ground or existence is themselves. Here he differs from Moltmann,[138] yet his ideas resonate with Vanhoozer.[139] Fiddes[140] argues that, if we use the term *hypostasis* as the early theologians did for a "distinct" reality which has "being," then the relations are

---

131. Bauckham, *Theology of Jürgen Moltmann*, 166, are Moltmann and Boff really suggesting that, as we step beyond the differentiated relationships of the Trinity, we then come into contemplation of the three persons in their perichoresis, we then come "face to face" or "observe" God's eternal being? And are we then to reflect this in our human relations and community? If this is the case, then, how does this work?

132. Fiddes, *Participating in God*.

133. Two Latin terms were used which together bring out well the sense of the Greek term. First *circuminsessio*, which means that one person is contained in the "another"—literally "seated" in the "another," filling the space of the other, present in the other—this was preferred by Aquinas. Secondly, *circumincessio* is a more active word, evoking a state of doing, the interpenetrating of one person in another; it captures the sense of moving in and through the other.

134. Fiddes, *Participating in God*.

135. Moltmann, *The Trinity and the Kingdom of God*.

136. Fiddes, *Participating in God*.

137. Ibid., 34.

138. Moltmann, *The Trinity and the Kingdom of God*.

139. Vanhoozer, *Remythologizing Theology*. Fiddes also differs from Cunningham, *These Three Are One*. Cunningham calls "subsistent relations," relationships without remainder.

140. Fiddes, *Participating in God*, 34.

hypostases. Therefore, there are no "persons" at the end of relations, as in Moltmann's[141] thought, the "persons" are simply the "relations."

These ideas find their origin in Augustine, who made a move in this direction, but are "named" by Aquinas who gave formality to the notion by creating the term. For Aquinas, "subsistent relations" meant stating that "divine person" signifies something subsisting; "person" signifies relation directly and nature indirectly, yet relation is signified, not as relation but as *hypostasis*. Fiddes[142] notes that Aquinas arrived at this point through the influence of the Aristotelian view that the divine essence must be simple, or radically unified. If this is so, both the properties and the relations of the essence must be identical with it, so the relations in God will have the same reality as the one essence. This leads Fiddes,[143] to talk about God as "an event of relationships." Thus, as Fiddes[144] sees, taking a cue from Karl Barth's insistence that with regard to the being of God, the word "event" or "act" is final, we may speak of God as an "event of relationships." From here Fiddes[145] develops his idea of *perichoresis* as "three movements of relationship subsisting in one event." For Fiddes, this is not the language of a spectator, but the language of a participant. Furthermore, it only makes sense when we see our participation, our connection and involvement in the network of relationships in which God "happens."

We could, then, hold up the *perichoresis* in the work of both Moltmann[146] and Fiddes[147] as a normative move that could give a richer description to relationships as communicative acts, as connection in terms of youth ministry practice. However, as we have seen through Kilby[148] and Vanhoozer,[149] there are problems associated with *perichoresis*. This notion within contemporary theological thought has gone far beyond anything the Cappadocians could have considered. Vanhoozer[150] continues that rather than performing a technical function in the Trinitarian discussion about how the three are one, the concept of *perichoresis* has

141. Moltmann, *The Trinity and the Kingdom of God*.
142. Fiddes, *Participating in God*, 35.
143. Ibid., 37.
144. Ibid., 36.
145. Ibid.
146. Moltmann, *The Trinity and the Kingdom of God*.
147. Fiddes, *Participating in God*.
148. Kilby, "Perichoresis and Projection."
149. Vanhoozer, *Remythologizing Theology*, 157.
150. Ibid.

flourished into a problematic full blown theological paradigm. Firstly, this is due to the collapse of the relationships between humanity, God and the world, and the tensions between participation and model in the work of Moltmann.[151] Secondly, as Vanhoozer[152] argues, through God's "being in relational communion" that is seen in the work of Moltmann[153] and Fiddes,[154] interpersonal relationality has become an all-inclusive idea.

What's more, Moltmann's[155] and Fiddes'[156] thinking on Trinitarian ideas about "persons in relationship" and "persons as relationship," are different enough to cause us to pause and ask questions as to how they can be derived from the same doctrine?[157] These contrasting ideas are, at least in part, due to the problems associated with projection which we have noted in the work of Kilby[158] and partly because of the received understanding of the Trinitarian tradition. As noted, Fiddes[159] develops his ideas from a so called Western tradition through Augustine, although he also draws on Eastern ideas as he develops his idea of the divine dance. Whereas, Moltmann[160] seeks to root the main thrust of his ideas in the so called Eastern tradition. For Holmes,[161] this is a false division.[162] It follows, therefore, that, for all the promise of connection through the inclusivity and openness of *perichoresis* in the work of Moltmann[163] and Fiddes,[164] this falls short of being able to offer a normative voice for youth ministry practice. It would just replace the construct of relationships as

---

151. Moltmann, *The Trinity and the Kingdom of God*.
152. Vanhoozer, *Remythologizing Theology*, 157.
153. Moltmann, *The Trinity and the Kingdom of God*.
154. Fiddes, *Participating in God*.
155. Moltmann, *The Trinity and the Kingdom of God*.
156. Fiddes, *Participating in God*.
157. Holmes, *The Holy Trinity*, 26, makes a similar point about how Zizioulas and Boff come up with differing theologies from the doctrine of the Trinity, again, resonating with the insight of Ward, "Blueprint Ecclesiology."
158. Kilby, "Perichoresis and Projection."
159. Fiddes, *Participating in God*.
160. Moltmann, *The Trinity and the Kingdom of God*.
161. Holmes, *The Holy Trinity*, 146.
162. Ibid., 26, sees that Augustine is the most capable interpreter of Cappadocian Trinitarianism and that by the end of the fourth century there is no fundamental difference between East and West.
163. Moltmann, *The Trinity and the Kingdom of God*.
164. Fiddes, *Participating in God*.

seen within the data and in the youth ministry literature, with another, a construct of projected and theological ideas. Furthermore, this is a poor analogy of the relationship between God and the world, of relationships as communicative acts as connection because our human relationships are fundamentally *not* like the intraTrinitarian communion. Therefore, a move can be made to talk about and locate relationships as communicative acts as connection in the idea of covenant and fellowship that is held in Christ as Vanhoozer[165] argues. Vanhoozer locates this in the idea of God's divine authorship and dialogical communicative action. To do this Vanhoozer has to take a number of theological turns. This subject is explored now.

Reimagining Relationships as Communicative Acts: Transmission

The theme of transmission is held in the idea of relationships as communicative acts and again acts as an icon of epistemology. The data showed how the youth ministry practitioners used relationships as circuits of influence and mediation, a communicative act. Above, it was explored how this resonates in the literature through the incarnation, as worked out in *Youth A Part*,[166] Ward,[167] Borgman,[168] Sudworth et al.,[169] Savage et al.,[170] Pimlott and Pimlott[171] and how Root[172] is critical of this. To explore this as an icon of epistemology through Trinitarian theology, Vanhoozer's[173] argument is convincing. He sees that God's being is in communicating. This resonates acutely with the idea of relationships as communicative acts, as transmission inferred within the data. For Vanhoozer,[174] the Triune life of God is made known through God's communicative presence and activity in history and through the Biblical *mythos*. This *mythos* of

165. Vanhoozer, *Remythologizing Theology*.
166. Church of England Board of Education, *Youth A Part*.
167. Ward, *Participation and Mediation*.
168. Borgman, *When Kumbaya Is Not Enough*.
169. Sudworth et al., *Mission Shaped Youth*.
170. Savage et al., *Making Sense of Generation Y*.
171. Pimlott and Pimlott, *Youth Work after Christendom*.
172. Root, *Revisiting Relational Youth Ministry*.
173. Vanhoozer, *Remythologizing Theology*, 245.
174. Ibid.

redemption consists not only in a series of events but through the work of human agents. Drawing on the work of Aquinas, the relationships in God are distinguished from one another because they are "founded on action."

Indeed, the three persons are not only the *dramatis personae* but the activity of God's being in communication: the *personae* are the drama.[175] Therefore, God's being is an eternal communicative act and is the basis for his self-presentation to creatures, his "historical speaking out." As Vanhoozer[176] sees, "the life of the incarnate Christ expresses the very action or movement of his eternal procession. Each of the three persons is a 'subsistent relation' in what is essentially a communicative act. The one God who exists as self-communicative activity does so in three 'subsistent relations.'" This involves the life of the Father, Son and Spirit not only in a generative act but communicative relations. God's being is in conversing. Thus, the divine persons' are not only in dialogue, they are dialogue.

Therefore, God is the Father addressing the Son, the Son responds to the Father, and the Spirit overhearing. Moreover, the Spirit has a distinct personal identity of witness and participation in the communication that exists between the Father and the Son. At this point, we could begin to level the accusations of projection drawn from Kilby[177] and see this reflected in Vanhoozer's[178] thinking. However, Vanhoozer,[179] through the Biblical narrative, sees these actions in the economy (e.g. creation, revelation and redemption) as being attributed to each person and contributing to the same action in distinct ways. Therefore, everything God does through communicative action is ultimately Triune, a unified action with three dimensions. As Gregory of Nyssa sees, "every operation which extends from God to the creation has its origin from the Father, proceeds through the Son and is perfected in the Holy Spirit."[180] This leads Vanhoozer to see Father, Son and Spirit as distinct communicative actions, but that they share a common communicative agency. This communicative agency is

---

175. This resonates with Fiddes, thoughts on "persons as relations."
176. Vanhoozer, *Remythologizing Theology*, 245–46.
177. Kilby, *Perichoresis and Projection*.
178. Vanhoozer, *Remythologizing Theology*, 246.
179. Ibid., 247.
180. Ibid.

depicted through Scripture as interpersonal dialogue and it is through this that the *theodramatic* action unfolds.[181]

Yet, it is in the incarnation that God communicates all that he is in Jesus Christ. This is God's definitive self-communicative act. This is the form of the Son's self-presentation, the humanity of Jesus and this becomes the norm for thinking and knowing about God's being. This is the ultimate pattern for God's being in communicative act—embodied in the incarnate Word. This is nothing less than the divine content (i.e. nature) in human form: the ways of God made flesh. Therefore, as Vanhoozer[182] sees, "what Jesus says and does, God says and does for in Jesus is the plentitude of grace and truth (Jn. 1:14)." The human life of Jesus is a self-communicative act, rooted in a particular human history, the enacting of the incarnate Son's words, acts and suffering. The *mythos* of Jesus Christ, the historical drama of his birth, life, death, resurrection and ascension is the divine communicative action of which the church becomes its living effect and theology the response. God is the unauthored author of his incarnation. For Vanhoozer,[183] the *kenosis* that Paul speaks about (Phil 2:7) is not a matter of divine self-destruction (i.e. the abandoning of the divine nature and attributes) but of authorial "self emplotment." The *kenosis* involves a change, not in the content of God's being in communicative act but only its form.[184] God continues to be all that he is under the veil of humanity. The subject of this human hero, Jesus, is the divine Author, the Son of God. This is love: that the Author, while remaining all that he is, pours his uncreated self into created human form in time and space—made flesh, human blood and bone in order to communicate his love, light and life to others.

As the theme of relationships as communicative acts as transmission is considered this is an exciting move. The idea of communicative action through divine agency reverberates not only with the theme of transmission but with also connection. For in the narratives of practice and within the worship songs, although not expressed, the youth ministers participate in this communicative action. This locates relationships

181. Ibid., 355–57.
182. Ibid., 357.
183. Ibid., 358.
184. This is a Chalcedonian position. Vanhoozer, *Remythologizing Theology*, 423–24, follows Cyril, who sees that the incarnation is about the person of the divine son becoming the subject of a fully human life. Jesus is the person of the Son, enfleshed as a man.

as communicative acts in a deeper and more profound theological framework. It moves beyond the limited description of the incarnation in the youth ministry literature. It locates the practice of youth ministry in the economy of salvation, held within the communicative revelation and act of God in his work within the world. It moves the enacted, lived and performed practice of youth ministry away from theological shorthand and sets it into a rigorous, theological framework located in the canonical Biblical *theodrama* of creation, revelation and redemption, re–tethering relationships as communicative acts into the Christian tradition—this is how these words act as icons of epistemology. Moreover, it gives the youth ministers a more extensive theological expression that enables them to articulate their practice in deeper and richer terms. Furthermore, it means however limited the Resources Guides are theologically, or however, thin the language within the worships songs is, as people use them or sing the songs as acts of worship they are part of God's communicative action. Additionally, the collapsing of the traditional church practices of *marturia*, *diakonia* and *kerygma* into the relational that is observed in the data can begin to be untangled, made more distinct through a richer theological description held in God's divine authorship and communicative action. The question becomes how?

Vanhoozer[185] suggests that to participate in God's being that consists of communicative action and activity is to be caught up in the *theodrama*. But here, the traditional distinction between the immanent and the economic, that is blurred in Moltmann's[186] and Fiddes'[187] thinking is preserved. Therefore, in Vanhoozer's[188] thinking, the creator and created distinction is held, and acknowledges the distinction between God as uniquely the source of his own divine communicative agency, and the communicative activity of his created creatures.[189] As this is explored, what this means for relationships as communicative acts, and as Trinitarian theology as a normative voice for youth ministry practice is considered, the distinction between the created and creature relationship needs to be persevered,

---

185. Ibid., 242.

186. Moltmann, *The Trinity and the Kingdom of God*.

187. Fiddes, *Participating in God*.

188. Vanhoozer, *Remythologizing Theology*, 242.

189. Vanhoozer, *Remythologizing Theology*, 167–69, is critical of the idea put forward by Fiddes that God "self-limits" himself, as he sees that if this is the case, then as Pannenberg observes, the creature is no longer dependent on God alone but on other powers.

rather than collapsed into a fusion of relationships between humanity and the divine. These ideas pivot around the operant mode of participation and it is this concept that is investigated in the next chapter.

Chapter 9

Expanding the Fragments as Icons of Epistemology: Participation, Relationships, and Trinitarian Theology

This chapter builds on the last chapter as the explorations continue, using participation as a key motif. Within the narratives of practice, the practitioners sought to be like Jesus. It has been argued how this has become modelled on the incarnational framework adopted from Young Life. The weakness of this approach was established as being based on like and model, invoking observation rather than participation. In chapter 7, the theological shorthand found in the Resources Guides also pivoted around the idea of observation. Furthermore, in the Resource Guides and the worship songs it has been seen that there is a lack of ecclesiology and Christology, requiring the worshiper and reader to fill in the theological gaps and to do this requires a depth of theological capital. Therefore, to construct a more faithful and authentic view of practice, a move from seeing practice as being like Jesus to being in Christ, to participate in the communicative activity of God[1] needs to be made. To do this, and to explore like Jesus as an icon of epistemology, further considerations of both Moltmann's[2] and Fiddes'[3] ideas on participation need to be explored. Then a more convincing argument as articulated by Vanhoozer[4] is advanced as theological literacy is developed.

1. Vanhoozer, *Remythologizing Theology*.
2. Moltmann, *The Trinity and the Kingdom of God*.
3. Fiddes, *Participating in God*.
4. Vanhoozer, *Remythologizing Theology*.

In the description of *perichorectic* relationships found within Moltmann,[5] what the Trinity says about human relations is not exactly clear.[6] Vanhoozer[7] sees there are inherent problems with his idea of participation because of the near collapse of the immanent into economic. For Bauckham,[8] this collapsing of the immanent Trinity into the economic, found with Moltmann,[9] is forced because he interprets the Trinity through the cross.[10] Here, as Bauckham[11] sees, Moltmann's interpretation of the cross is seen as the event of God suffering solidarity with the world.[12] This theme of suffering runs like a thread through the data and the youth ministry literature and becomes important as a normative Trinitarian move for youth ministry practice is sought, but to locate suffering within God, as Moltmann does, is deeply problematic. To make this theological move of God suffering solidarity with the world, Moltmann has to take three decisive turns in developing his Trinitarian doctrine of God. As Bauckham[13] argues, firstly, as an event between the Father and the Son, God suffers the god–forsakenness that separates the Son from the Father and this required a Trinitarian language that emphasized the inter–subjective relationship between the divine persons as worked out through Moltmann's[14] concept of *perichoresis*. Secondly, he developed the idea that God can suffer pain and be affected by his creation.

Vanhoozer[15] is critical of this, seeing within *perichorectic* relational theism, as conceived in Moltmann[16] and that echoes through Fiddes's[17]

5. Moltmann, *The Trinity and the Kingdom of God*.

6. Tanner, "Trinity," 324–25, argues that, for Moltmann the problem, here, revolves around too greater focus on the so-called immanent Trinity.

7. Vanhoozer, *Remythologizing Theology*, 151–54.

8. Bauckham, *Theology of Jürgen Moltmann*, 5

9. Moltmann, *The Trinity and the Kingdom of God*.

10. Gunton, *The One, The Three and The Many*, 178–86, argues against Moltmann's (and also Jungel, von Balthasar and Barth) idea of the cross as the key to Trinitarian theology.

11. Bauckham, *Theology of Jürgen Moltmann*, 304.

12. Written in the long dark shadows of Auschwitz, Moltmann wants nothing to do with the all-powerful God of Christian theism, here God is not sovereign, but becomes a fellow sufferer.

13. Bauckham, *Theology of Jürgen Moltmann*, 304.

14. Moltmann, *The Trinity and the Kingdom of God*.

15. Vanhoozer, *Remythologizing Theology*, 163.

16. Moltmann, *The Trinity and the Kingdom of God*.

17. Fiddes, *Participating in God*.

thinking, in which creatures can affect God[18] as they themselves are influenced, then it is impossible to escape the conclusion that God's being and existence is constituted by his relations *ad extra*. This vulnerability raises classical concerns, for, if within this view, God can voluntary relinquish his aseity, how does this preserve divine sovereignty and prevent God from becoming a victim whose goal for creation is at the risk of failure? For Vanhoozer,[19] this has implications for the Gospel, for the Gospel is only good news if it contains an assurance that all will indeed end well. The problem from a classical view is that within the doctrine of God, as presented by Moltmann,[20] God is less of a divine agent who can be at work, but is an empath who is voluntarily susceptible to others.

This is because Moltmann's[21] understanding of God's love is bound up with his creation. Yet, Aquinas sees that God's love is his willing the good (*ben + volere*) for others and salvation is "the plan of God to communicate his own goodness." The response of these "others" is the goal of God's love and not an intrinsic element within it. Therefore, the cross becomes primarily about the love of God in the giving of Christ rather than receiving, as Vanhoozer[22] argues. The Third problem in Moltmann's[23] thinking, as noted, is that he abandons the traditional distinction between the immanent and the economic Trinity. For Moltmann, the cross becomes a Trinitarian "event" between the Father, Son and Spirit, this gives us a Trinitarian history of God, in which the mutual involvement of God and the world is increasingly stressed. Moreover, God experiences a history with the world in which he both affects and is affected by the world and this becomes the history of God's own Trinitarian relationships. These relationships are bound up in *perichoretic* love with the world and this leaves Moltmann,[24] to *nearly* surrender the traditional distinction between the immanent and the economic Trinity. This is because for Moltmann, the difference between the immanent and economic is only

---

18. This raises questions about the "Open Theism" debate. This lies outside the scope of this chapter but the debate finds an opponent in John Piper and an advocate in Gregory Boyd.

19. Vanhoozer, *Remythologizing Theology*, 163–65.

20. Moltmann, *The Trinity and the Kingdom of God*.

21. Ibid.

22. Vanhoozer, *Remythologizing Theology*, 165.

23. Moltmann, *The Trinity and the Kingdom of God*, 6.

24. Ibid., 160.

necessary if we see God as either liberty or necessity. Here, Moltmann[25] argues that God's liberty is his love and God has to love the world as he loves himself.

Therefore, for Moltmann,[26] we discover this God through our love and through our perception, and what we perceive changes us to be like God. In Moltmann's framework, we can only know God through doxological participation.[27] As Torrance argues,[28] this weakness of the near collapse of the immanent into the economic Trinity, is because of Moltmann's struggle as to what takes precedence: God's divine freedom or his divine love. Because of this, he seems to adopt a form of *panentheism*, a point that Vanhoozer,[29] also sees, and therefore, fails to distinguish between God's time and created temporality.[30] Moreover, the result of this is that transcendence which is intrinsic to Moltmann's[31] concept of doxological participation is undermined. As Torrance[32] and Vanhoozer[33] see, this is because God's history is placed or cemented[34] into the process of human life and struggle. This failing to see God's participation in humanity as free *ekstasis* (apart from how God has his being and which is in no sense arbitrary) means that Moltmann[35] does not seem to appreciate that participation in God's intra–divine glory has to be described as humanity's participation in the transcendent Triune life as Torrance[36] argues.

---

25. Ibid., 151.

26. Ibid., 152.

27. This, ibid., 152–53, calls *real* theology, knowledge of God that finds its expression in thanks and praise which is expressed because of our experience of salvation. Doxological theology becomes a responsive theology. Moltmann argues that the immanent Trinity becomes the counter, part of praise and the economic Trinity becomes the embodiment of history and salvation.

28. Torrance *Persons in Communion*, 311.

29. Vanhoozer, *Remythologizing Theology*, 153.

30. For clarification on this Torrance, *Persons in Communion*, 312, as he cites Barth's discussion, "The Eternity and Glory of God" (C.D.2.1) and especially 612–19.

31. Moltmann, *The Trinity and the Kingdom of God*, 152.

32. Torrance, *Persons in Communion*, 311.

33. Vanhoozer, *Remythologizing Theology*, 162–63.

34. Torrance, *Persons in Communion*, 311, notes that it is Rahner who uses this phrase. Rahner sees that this cementing of the human struggle into God does not help him to escape from his mess and despair if God is in the same predicament.

35. Moltmann, *The Trinity and the Kingdom of God*.

36. Torrance, *Persons in Communion*, 313.

Therefore, doxological participation becomes an event of grace,[37] an idea which Moltmann barely mentions, and not about any human response. The implications of this, as Tanner[38] contends, is that Moltmann does not have to explain what Trinitarian relationships would be like with human beings "in" them. The Trinity appears as a dialogical fellowship of love and mutual service, the kind of Trinity that human beings could imitate and model, an idea that, Bauckham,[39] Kilby,[40] and Vanhoozer[41] see is problematic and unconvincing.

As the Trinity is considered as a normative voice for practice in relation to the theme of like Jesus and as this is explored as an icon of epistemology, we can begin to move away from the paradoxical ideas of participation *and* model held within Moltmann's thinking and consider another view of participation. As introduced above, this idea of participating in God finds resonance in Fiddes[42] and Vanhoozer's[43] thinking, but these theologies differ on their interpretation of what this means. For Fiddes,[44] we are drawn into the Trinitarian relationships in which God "happens." But, what does it mean to participate, to be swept up, into this event of relationships in which God "happens"? Fiddes[45] develops these thoughts as he sees Christ as the divine Logos and through the incarnation, we are enabled to participate and, therefore, are drawn into the Triune relationship in God. Theologically this is worked out because, as Fiddes[46] argues, if Christ is deeply immersed in the flow of relationships within God and the incarnation, then he becomes the point of access where humanity can enter and participate in the divine dance of the *perichoresis*. We are in Christ and, therefore, we are summoned to participate in God who, with great humility, participates in our lives. To help

---

37. Moltmann, *The Crucified God*, 236 in arguing for the doctrine of the trinity in the cross, notes that even the doctrine of grace is monotheistic and not Trinitarian in practice.
38. Tanner, "Trinity," 327.
39. Bauckham, *Theology of Jürgen Moltmann*, 160.
40. Kilby, "Perichoresis and Projection."
41. Vanhoozer, *Remythologizing Theology*.
42. Fiddes, *Participating in God*.
43. Vanhoozer, *Remythologizing Theology*.
44. Fiddes, *Participating in God*.
45. Ibid., 279–80.
46. Ibid., 86.

articulate this, Fiddes[47] argues that the New Testament describes prayer as being to the Father through the Son and in the Spirit. This means that, as we pray to God as Father, we are fitting into a movement like that of speech between a son and father. This involves a movement and response of self-giving, like of a father sending forth a son, which the early theologians called eternal generation and which we experience in the mission of God in history, an idea that resonates in Vanhoozer's[48] thinking.

For Fiddes,[49] as we pray in this "event," we find these movements of response and mission are interwoven by a third: Spirit. It is the Spirit, who disturbs, opens, deepens and provokes, and this leads Fiddes to see how people become playgrounds for the Spirit. The traditional formulation that the Spirit proceeds from the Father through the Son points to a movement which renews all relations from and to the other. Through identifying the divine "persons" as relations, Fiddes brings together a way of understanding the nature of *being* (ontology) with a way of *knowing* (epistemology). Therefore, the being of God is understood as an "event" and relationship through an epistemology of participation and each only makes sense with the other. Thus, we cannot observe the Trinitarian God, as in Moltmann,[50] a being which is relationships; we can only know God through the mode of participation. Through the notion of *perichoresis* and "subsistent relations." Fiddes[51] sees that God is wholly constituted by relationality and, as we have seen, Vanhoozer[52] and Kilby[53] are critical of this "new orthodoxy." This notion of participation requires further investigation. Fiddes,[54] develops his idea of *perichorectic* participation through his notion of "subsistent relations" and through the analogy of the *perichoresis* as being like a divine dance. Here, Fiddes,[55] makes a counterintuitive move. This is because of how he develops "persons as relations" through his thinking on the *hypostases*. Fiddes[56] concedes that there are objections to this idea. The participatory rather than observational lan-

---

47. Ibid., 37–38.
48 Vanhoozer, *Remythologizing Theology*, 247.
49 Fiddes, *Participating in God*, 37–38.
50 Moltmann, *The Trinity and the Kingdom of God*.
51. Fiddes, *Participating in God*.
52 Vanhoozer, *Remythologizing Theology*, 139–77.
53. Kilby, "Perichoresis and Projection."
54. Fiddes, *Participating in God*, 34.
55. Ibid., 71–81.
56. Ibid., 81–93.

guage that is used within "subsistent relations" means we have to face the criticism that, unless the divine persons are conceived as subjects and agents, they will lose their distinct identity (*hypostasis*).

There are two core arguments against it; these revolve around identity and activity. Firstly, let us consider this idea of identity. Here there is a danger that the lack of diversity within God means the submerging of the persons into an all "embracing dominance of oneness of substance." This then is the objection that the "relations" in God have no particular identity of their own.[57] Fiddes'[58] counter argument to this is how can there be anything more distinct from each other than a "movement of relationship" like that from a father to a son (Father) and a movement like that from a son to a father (Son) and an opening up of these relationships to new depths and possibilities (Spirit)—but what exactly does "movement of relationship" mean here and how exactly do they remain distinct?

For Fiddes,[59] this is worked out through and spoken about within the medium of participation and this leads us to concrete ways of speaking about the particular. Although this is helpful, it is not altogether convincing. Furthermore, it requires us to think at the level of Spirit. We can only participate—join in, with these "movements of relationship," if we see our spirit connecting with God as Spirit. The second main objection is how can one think of a relationship as doing anything? This revolves around the idea of activity. Here, it could be said that "actions" can only be ascribed to communicative agents involved in communicative activity as in Vanhoozer's[60] thinking. This second idea of activity is tied into the first idea of identity. This is the part of Fiddes'[61] argument that is so counterintuitive. This is partly because it is so hard for us to imagine a "relation" as a "person." However, perhaps this is because of the construct of "persons" that has developed in the received tradition of Plato and Aristotle, where to be a "person" was to have particular attributes.[62]

---

57. Gunton, *The One, the Three, and the Many*, 191 sees this and argues against, through his idea of substantiality.

58. Fiddes, *Participating in God*, 83.

59. Ibid.

60. Vanhoozer, *Remythologizing Theology*, 245.

61. Fiddes, *Participating in God*, 85.

62. Cunningham, *These Three Are One*, 165, also sees how these concepts can be misleading, since we usually assume that relations exist between things and that this tendency is compounded by the modern understanding of human persons as first and foremost individuals.

For both Moltmann[63] and Fiddes,[64] the operative concept is participation, however, within both of these approaches, as they are conceived through the notion of *perichoresis*, they are both filled out with projected ideas about human relationality, as Kilby[65] and Vanhoozer[66] see. Again, the work of Moltmann[67] and Fiddes,[68] remain an unconvincing move in terms of providing a normative voice in how Trinitarian theology can serve youth ministry practice as authentic and faithful in terms of this operant notion of participation. Therefore, a way of moving from being like Jesus, from the ideas of model and imitation, to being in Christ through a more convincing Trinitarian theological framework of participation is needed. It is Vanhoozer[69] who provides a different and more robust argument for a move in this direction.

In the narratives of practice, the data demonstrated how the youth ministers enact mission amongst young people through being like Jesus. In chapter 6, and in the Resource Guides in chapter 7, the limits of Christology were explored, seeing that the imitation of Christ is only part of the theological picture. Vanhoozer's,[70] thinking resonates with this, seeing that being in Christ involves more than just following Christ's example, more than observation. To explore theologically what this participating in Christ is like, a more authentic and faithful expression of what reimagined relationships as communicative acts and youth ministry practice can move to is required. Vanhoozer[71] sees that the challenge for communicative theism is how to specify how God remains God while allowing creatures to participate in his Triune life. Here he argues, that we need to distinguish between God's attributes (God's being *ad intra*) and his redemptive work (God's being *ad extra*). Therefore, to participate in Christ, in the life of God, is to benefit from his words and acts in history, especially the history of Christ. It is seeing, as Vanhoozer[72] argues, how

63. Moltmann, *The Trinity and the Kingdom of God*.
64. Fiddes, *Participating in God*.
65. Kilby, "Perichoresis and Projection."
66. Vanhoozer, *Remythologizing Theology*.
67. Moltmann, *The Trinity and the Kingdom of God*.
68. Fiddes, *Participating in God*.
69. Vanhoozer, *Remythologizing Theology*, 289.
70. Ibid.
71. Ibid., 279.
72. Ibid., 283.

the Father communicates new life in and through the Son, by the Spirit: it is in Christ that there is a *new creation*.

The company of the saints partake in the divine nature—God's being-in-communicative activity, by being in Christ. Communion with God through union with Christ is at the heart of the Gospel, the substance of faith and humanity's ultimate hope in life. Jesus is the *archegos*—the author of our salvation (Heb 2:10) whose main claim is that participating in God means participating in his Triune being-in-communicative-activity. Vanhoozer[73] continues, in Christ, according to the apostle Paul, is used as a virtual shorthand for salvation.

Therefore, being in Christ becomes a central description of salvation as to the effect of the work of Christ. For Vanhoozer[74] union with Christ—being in Christ, is a matter of *theodramatic* participation. Importantly, communicants do not become one with the divine essence, but participate in God's communicative action, in the economy of revelation and redemption, in God's mission in and to the world.[75] Therefore, to be in Christ is to be in the thick of the Trinitarian action; to be in Christ is to be constituted as a willing participant in the *theodrama*. This moves beyond the partial theological description, or theological shorthand found in the songs, and locates worship in the richer theological description of being in Christ. Subsequently, for Vanhoozer,[76] those who enjoy being in Christ are not caught up in his essence or nature, as in the work of Moltmann[77] and Fiddes,[78] but are participants in the effects of his personal history, we come to be remade in his *mythos*, in the plot of his history. To partake in the divine nature is to participate in the *theodrama* that is God's being-in-communicative activity through the Son's fellowship with the Father and the Spirit. Therefore, the economic Trinity communicates the immanent Trinity. The God who is with us, is the God who has perfect light, life and love in himself and it is as communicative agents in eternal relationship that Father, Son and Spirit engage in the economy of communication with the world.

In relation to youth ministry practice, this moves beyond the partial theological description, the theological shorthand of like Jesus, as

73. Ibid., 284.
74. Ibid., 293.
75. Ibid., 261.
76. Ibid., 293.
77 Moltmann, *The Trinity and the Kingdom of God*.
78. Fiddes, *Participating in God*.

expressed through the narratives of practice, and the Resource Guides and locates this in the richer theological description of being in Christ, that has the possibility to be enacted and performed through relationships as communicative acts. It resonates acutely with the expressions of ministry as connection and transmission and it locates these communicative acts not only in the Biblical *theodrama* but, more specifically, in the history of Christ's person. Moreover, the moving from like Jesus to being in Christ, through theological reimagination of relationships as communicative acts becomes an enacted expression of *marturia*, the witnessing of the self-giving love of God in Christ. Therefore, this is not only an inward turn to those within the church but an inclusive invitation and orientation to God's Kingdom and new creation.[79] Therefore, it is possible to begin to unravel this particular church practice from collapsing into the expression of relationships discovered in the narratives of practice. Furthermore, the next theme of being there which in the data was the enacting of like Jesus can be explored.

Relationships as Communicative Acts: Being There to Being There In Christ

As the data demonstrated, the third theme of being there is the enacted presence of the second, like Jesus. As these icons of epistemology are explored they become a performed theological moment in time and space, through which the youth ministers act as a symbol.[80] As a symbol, they embody qualities of that in which they participate, that which they point towards, however, as the data showed, this participation is not articulated—only the language of model is used and is seen as being like Jesus. Through theological reimagination and relationships as communicative acts a richer definition of being there as symbol, can be seen. Building on the insights above the participative nature of this can be held in God's communicative action.[81] Moving from being there as symbol, as demonstrated in the enacted mission of the youth ministry practitioners, to being there—in Christ, thus locating this in the participative nature of symbol.[82]

79. Wright, *How God Became King*.
80. Tillich, *Dynamics of Faith*.
81. Vanhoozer, *Remythologizing Theology*.
82. Tillich, *Dynamics of Faith*.

Furthermore, through moving from being there to being there—in Christ, the *diakonia,* the service amongst suffering young people and the locating of this within the practice of the church becomes a litmus test for the normative voice of Trinitarian theology and youth ministry practice. Therefore, the move from seeing mission as no longer focused on the individual youth minister, to the locating of this in the *ecclesia* and the historic practice of the *koinonia* can be made. This is an important point which we will return to below. It also deepens the theology found with the series on the Church within the Resource Guides. Within this, the historical practices of *diakonia* and *kerygma* can begin to be teased apart; again, helping to unravel the collapsing of practices into the concept of relationships that is expressed within the narratives of practice by the youth ministers.

As the investigations have shown, Fiddes explores how the Trinitarian God is open to us through his doctrine of "subsistent relations." Within this, Fiddes[83] makes an important point that, within the threefold relations of God, Father, Son and Spirit, we need to take bodies as seriously as God does. This means paying particular attention to people as they actually are.[84] Fiddes[85] argues, that we need to value people as images of God. As Fiddes[86] develops his argument, he sees that God commits himself to bodies as a meeting place with us and, through this, his idea of walking sacrament[87] is outworked. What he means by this, is that the minister embodies and enacts the presence of God—becomes a sacrament in the sense that in his or her body is a place of encounter, an interface with the movements of God's life of love. As Fiddes[88] sees, ministers, therefore, do not just exercise a function, or fulfil a task, but there is a fusing between person and function, between doing and being. Here is not the promotion of the ideal Christian, but a walking sacrament who symbolizes an ultimate value, who embodies an ideal without being

---

83. Fiddes, *Participating in God,* 301.

84. This theme of the particular has resonance with Gunton's, *The One, The Three and The Many.*

85. Fiddes, *Participating in God,* 301.

86. Ibid., 296.

87. Ibid., 281. Sacraments can become part of the ecstatic movements of love within God; moreover, they become access points into the "dance" of the perichoresis within God.

88. Ibid., 296.

EXPANDING THE FRAGMENTS AS ICONS OF EPISTEMOLOGY

an ideal, who participates in and throws open the doors to the divine *perichoretic* dance of God.

In this, Fiddes[89] is developing Tillich's[90] concept that as walking sacraments people are symbols in the sense that they participate in the reality to which they point, an idea that finds acute resonance with this book. Therefore, in many ways this is an important move and, Fiddes'[91] thinking, begins to move theology away from the abstract and into the lived. But this relationality as expressed in these terms is problematic. We can again see Kilby's[92] and Vanhoozer's[93] argument of projection being utilized to name what is not understood, especially around Fiddes[94] concept of the divine *perichoretic* dance of God. Furthermore, there are other challenges here due to the creator/creature and the God/world relationship that we have been discussing. For example, what exactly does it mean for our bodies to be a place of encounter and an interface with the movements of God's life of love—how does this work? In addition, there is again a collapsing into all things relational. In Fiddes'[95] thinking, relationships become sacramental, therefore, at least in part, losing the distinctiveness of the traditional understanding of church sacraments and practices.

With this in mind, the data showed how important being there was in the ministry of the youth ministers, as they worked amongst young people in their joys and in their sufferings, and has a focus on orthopraxis. The stories of enacted mission amongst marginalized and suffering young people ring through the narratives of practice. It also echoes in the literature on youth ministry particularly through the work of Dean,[96] Root,[97] and Pimlott and Pimlott.[98] To consider a deeper description of relationships as communicative acts, to explore further the depth of theology held in relationships as an icon of epistemology, moving from being there to being there—in Christ, the issue of suffering highlights a number

---

89. Ibid., 282.
90. Tillich, *Dynamics of Faith*.
91. Fiddes, *Participating in God*.
92. Kilby, "Perichoresis and Projection."
93. Vanhoozer, *Remythologizing Theology*.
94. Fiddes, *Participating in God*, 296.
95. Ibid., 294.
96. Dean, *Practicing Passion*.
97. Root, *Revisiting Relational Youth Ministry*.
98. Pimlott and Pimlott, *Youth Work after Christendom*.

of issues. Although a full discussion of the divine impassibility debate lies outside of the scope of this book, the theme of suffering runs like a thread through Moltmann's[99] thinking. The suffering of Jesus on the cross becomes the foundation of his doctrine of God. Moltmann,[100] interprets the cross as signifying the concept of death within God, here Moltmann views salvation in terms of God voluntarily accepting and absorbing pain, death and suffering in the world into himself. Fiddes[101] develops a similar view that, within the divine *perichoresis*, all three movements within God are involved in suffering. He differs from Moltmann[102] by drawing on Balthasar's concept of distances in God. Through this, Fiddes[103] sees that these are spaces within the dance of *perichoresis*, spaces in the weaving currents of relational love and in these spaces humanity can participate. Here God enters with empathy and identifies with the experience of suffering in the lives of humanity.

This is a powerful idea, and is born out because of Fiddes's[104] concern to locate the Trinity within pastoral practice. Therefore, a theological move could be made through the work of Bonhoeffer[105] to see how it is only the suffering God can help. In the youth ministry literature, Root[106] makes a similar move.

Therefore, it would be possible to see how both Moltmann[107] and Fiddes[108] could provide a normative voice in terms of Trinitarian theology and youth ministry practice that is authentic and faithful for relationships as communicative acts. Fiddes'[109] thinking on walking sacrament could be pushed in terms of the youth minister being there and suffering alongside young people. This could be held up as a very attractive idea for complexities of practice, but at what theological cost? For within this

---

99. Moltmann, *The Crucified God*; Moltmann, *The Trinity and the Kingdom of God*.
100. Moltmann, *The Trinity and the Kingdom of God*, 101.
101. Fiddes, *Participating in God*, 184.
102. Moltmann, *The Trinity and the Kingdom of God*.
103. Fiddes, *Participating in God*, 185.
104. Ibid.
105. Bonhoeffer, *Christ the Centre*.
106. Root, *Revisiting Relational Youth Ministry*.
107. Moltmann, *The Trinity and the Kingdom of God*.
108. Fiddes, *Participating in God*.
109. Ibid.

thinking, held by Moltmann[110] and Fiddes,[111] Vanhoozer[112] argues that by the near collapsing of the immanent into the economic Trinity, passiblities can come to define God only by what he suffers on and after the cross rather than by his free authorial communicative activity outside that history as well.

This raises two issues, the first, as Vanhoozer [113]argues, in a canonical context, the cross, is not a symptom of God's general metaphysical relationship to the world, but the climax of God's particular relationship with Israel that began with a divine promise to Abraham. It is the sign of the Kingdom come[114] and how God became King.[115] Therefore, only a canonical and covenantal *mythos* can hope to make sense of the God/world dynamics. Secondly, for Vanhoozer,[116] God is not the fellow sufferer who understands and suffers with us, as in Moltmann[117] and Fiddes,[118] for in this line of thinking suffering is normalized within God, but the sovereign sufferer who withstands, transforms and redeems suffering. This important point finds resonance in a number of converging themes in Paul's notion of sharing in—*koinonia*, Christ's sufferings. For Vanhoozer,[119] this is a *communion of passio*. The fellowship in Christ's sufferings is Paul's picture of the life of Christ. Therefore, to participate in God is to be caught up into the life of Christ and into the life of the Triune God. As described earlier, this is to participate in Jesus' history, to participate in this history is to participate in the covenantal history that serves as the framework for the meaning of Jesus' life, death and resurrection. The covenant between humanity and God finds its clearest expression in the picture of the church, the church is a community of communicants, the company of those who in Christ share in the Triune God's communicative action to the world.

---

110. Moltmann, *The Trinity and the Kingdom of God*.
111. Fiddes, *Participating in God*.
112. Vanhoozer, *Remythologizing Theology*, 460.
113. Ibid., 461.
114. Yoder, *The Politics of Jesus*.
115. Wright, *How God Became King*.
116. Vanhoozer, *Remythologizing Theology*, 466.
117. Moltmann, *The Trinity and the Kingdom of God*.
118. Fiddes, *Participating in God*.
119. Vanhoozer, *Remythologizing Theology*, 464.

For Vanhoozer,[120] this communicative action is dialogical, this has real resonance with the theme of relationships as communicative acts as connection and transmission.

The faith by which the Spirit unites us to Christ comes through the hearing and experience of the Word. In this, Jesus both speaks and is spoken about by the Father. Jesus engages in communicative action, yet, Jesus is also the Word of the Father. The Father utters the Word, the Son is who gets communicated—the content of the Father's speech, the Spirit is the channel that carries the Word. Dialogical union with Christ ushers communicants (us) into a Triune conversation whereby God shares with us the relationship he has between the "persons" of the Trinity. This resonates with Fiddes'[121] thinking on being part of the speech between Father, Son and Spirit. In Vanhoozer's[122] communicative framework, the Spirit incorporates the faithful communicants into the Son so they receive and respond to the diverse communicative acts that structure their relations to their covenant LORD. However, this relationship is asymmetric, as Jesus remains LORD, but there is also covenantal intimacy and friendship in communicating with God. However, within this dialogical friendship there is not the fusing of horizons, whereby one's individuality and name are absorbed into the Godhead, but a dialogical union in which Christ's voice leads our thinking and feeling.

Therefore, to be in Christ is not to lose one's identity, but find one's true identity through salvation. Here, through Jesus' agency and the Spirit's actions, we are drawn into the sphere of the new covenant and into the fellowship of his Triune life. There is fellowship and not fusion, but this divine communicative action is the source and structuring principle of the new covenantal being in Christ. The outworking of this divine communicative action, which incorporates us, is the body of Christ. The body of Christ corresponds most to God and his communicative action when its members pour out their lives for the sake of others in various kinds of communicative acts—*diakonia*, we could call this being there—in Christ for others especially when they are suffering. This again resonates with Fiddes'[123] thinking, but is reframed through divine communicative action and human agency. For Vanhoozer,[124] what God communicates to suffer-

---

120. Ibid., 291.
121. Fiddes, *Participating in God*.
122. Vanhoozer, *Remythologizing Theology*, 291.
123. Fiddes, *Participating in God*.
124. Vanhoozer, *Remythologizing Theology*, 289.

ing people (in our case young people) is the hope of an imperishable inheritance. Vanhoozer[125] argues that being in Christ has an eschatological movement, it is to participate in his history (the already) and future (the not yet), it is to participate in his death and resurrection, to be a *new creation* is to participate in a new Spirit empowered mode of existence. This *new creation* is the church and the people of God share in God's communicative activity to and for the world.

For Vanhoozer,[126] being in Christ is not something that happens to isolated individuals, but to a company of people, the *ecclesia*. Union with Christ implies union with others and to be in Christ implies a corporate existence and incorporation into Christ that becomes lived out and embodied through the church.[127] This is a deeper and more profound theology than seen in the Resource Guide series on the Church, acting as icon of epistemology and developing a theological literacy for a richer ecclesiology and how the church can be there for suffering young people. It forms a powerful critique of the common practice of youth ministry as carried out by the lonely professional minister and as voiced by the interviewees. It points to a new model of youth ministry as the youth minister acts as a dialogical guide which is spelt out in chapter 10.

Within Vanhoozer's [128] theology of being in Christ, three interconnected moves can be identified. This can advance a more authentic and faithful expression of being there. Firstly, the location of the idea of the youth minister as symbol into the theological expression of participating in Christ, moving beyond the limits of theological shorthand of imitation, like and model and observation that is expressed in the narratives of practice and in the Resource Guides. Secondly, to understand that being there—in Christ also includes the *koinonia*. This includes a turning away from an individualist understanding of youth ministry that echoed through the data and in the narratives of practice and also reverberates through the literature of Borgman,[129] Ward,[130] and Pimlott and Pimlott.[131] Thirdly being there—in Christ, contains two important elements. The

---

125. Ibid.
126. Ibid., 292.
127. Dykstra and Bass, *A Theological Understanding*, 13–32.
128. Vanhoozer, *Remythologizing Theology*, 292.
129. Borgman, *When Kumbaya Is Not Enough*.
130. Ward, *Youthwork*.
131. Pimlott and Pimlott, *Youth Work after Christendom*.

traditional Christian practices of *kerygma* and *diakonia* as communicative acts need to be made more explicit within youth ministry practice if it is to be more authentic and faithful to the Gospel. As the data showed, the youth ministers demonstrated multifaceted examples of *diakonia*, but this presence, this coming alongside young people as they suffer, in acts of serving and prior mission needs to be teased apart from being collapsed into this all-encompassing idea of relationship, and needs to be re-rooted in the traditional practice of *koinonia*. Furthermore, there seemed a real reluctance to *speak* about the Gospel; there is very limited attention and witness paid to *kerygma*. This is a point of challenge for contemporary youth ministry practice, to rediscover what it means to speak about God through relevant contextualized ways and story, ideas explored in the final chapter. Moreover, there is again real interrelation here with the themes of relationships as communicative acts as played out through the ideas of connection and transmission that is explored above and with the theme of time and journey as liminal space that is explored next.

Relationships as Communicative Acts: Time and Journey as Liminal Space

The data showed how this descriptive theme of time and journey is articulated through the practice of the youth ministers. This acts as theological shorthand for the multifaceted aspects of this embodied practice. It shines through the narratives of practice; it is both explicit and implied in the interrelated themes of being there and relationships as communicative acts through connection and transmission. Relationships as communicative acts are carried over time and through this sense of journey. As the data demonstrated the youth ministers are aiming for this place of liminal space, this time of waiting for God to act. In chapter 6, the investigations show how this theme of time and journey resonated through the youth ministry literature, particularly in the work of Ward,[132] Green and Christian,[133] and Pimlott and Pimlott.[134] In chapter 7, this liminal space is seen within the worships songs as narratives of encounter. In this section, it is argued that this is not only a place of waiting for God to act, but also

---

132. Ward, *Youthwork*.
133. Green and Christian, *Accompanying*.
134. Pimlott and Pimlott, *Youth Work after Christendom*.

a liminal space for God's communicative action. The themes of time and journey can be explored as icons of epistemology.

Subsequently, Vanhoozer[135] sees that time is a space for communicative action and there is acute resonance here with the narratives of enacted practice. Vanhoozer argues that to be is to communicate and that eternity is a predicate of God's own life, the communication *ad intra* of God's light and love. God's time (eternity) is a form of God's communicative action, the way God lives, the mode of God's existence. Our understanding of time by contrast is the form and space of God's communicative action *ad extra*. Therefore, as eternity is the form of God's life, so time is the form of the human creature's life. Within this, time is not impersonal causation, but personal communication; this becomes a space for relational existence. As the data is reviewed, relationships as communicative acts and the liminal spaces created by them become the place of action through God's communicative acts to each of us. As Vanhoozer[136] sees, the Biblical authors conceived time not as mere duration, but in terms of events that make a difference—time for deeds to be done (Eccl 3:2–8). Therefore, time provides us with opportunities to align ourselves with the created order as God acts and time opens up the possibility of interacting with others. Therefore, to live is to have time for communicative action, to make a liminal space for God to act, to allow God to communicate through his Spirit. Time becomes the medium and journey for interpersonal speaking and listening. As relationships as communicative acts through the theme of time and journey is considered, it becomes reframed as the out-working of God's communicative action, a liminal space in which the youth ministers participate through being in Christ. God becomes an agent in time but, as its author, is not limited by it. Eternity and sovereignty mark the ontological divide that distinguishes God from the world. Through time, God's communicative being as "eternal" throws the creator/created relationship into sharp relief, rather than becoming blurred as in the work of Moltmann[137] and Fiddes.[138] The question is how?

As this is considered, a move away from standing outside the story, of observation, as seen in the Resource Guides and a return to the

---

135. Vanhoozer, *Remythologizing Theology*, 320.
136. Ibid., 321.
137. Moltmann, *The Trinity and the Kingdom of God*.
138. Fiddes, *Participating in God*.

operant issue of participation needs to be made. Through the analysis, the data showed how the youth ministers, as they enacted mission amongst young people, aimed for a liminal space, a space that allowed God to work, a place of wrestling. As this is investigated, Vanhoozer[139] argues that it is important to distinguish two kinds of being in or participation in Christ. For Vanhoozer, this is advanced through a general cosmological participation in the Son through whom all things hold together and were made (Col. 1:16) and a more Christological abiding in the Son with whom there is reconciliation. Moltmann[140] also sees a similar division between the work in Creation through the Spirit as *Ruach* and in some of the particular occurrences and manifestations of God's Spirit in the Old Testament as *Shekinah*. The latter is the personal character of the Spirit and ties into Moltmann's[141] theme of suffering, as he sees that it is the Spirit who suffers with those who suffer.

However, for Moltmann[142] the Spirit as *Shekinah* is not passive, but leads those who are suffering onward into a more life-giving future but, as observed, this is not worked out in convincing ways. Furthermore, Moltmann,[143] draws together the Spirit of *Ruach* and *Shekinah* and unites them in the person of Christ.[144] For Moltmann,[145] the Spirit is grounded in the resurrection of Christ and it is the Spirit of Christ that awakens us and emboldens us for justification. Fiddes[146] again follows Moltmann's[147] theme in how the Spirit awakens in us a consciousness of Christ and alerts us to the Father, whom his Son is representing. For Moltmann,[148] it is the Spirit that both glorifies the Father and the Son unifying them in glorification; this returns to the outworking of Moltmann's theology of the *perichoresis*. However, the central problem within Moltmann's[149] thinking is that the unifying work of the Spirit in Creation affects the

---

139. Vanhoozer, *Remythologizing Theology*, 281.

140. Moltmann, *Spirit of Life*, 39–42.

141. Moltmann, *The Crucified God*; Moltmann, *The Trinity and the Kingdom of God*.

142. Moltmann, *Spirit of Life*, 39–42.

143. Ibid., 58–65.

144. White, *Jürgen Moltmann's Pneumatology*.

145. Moltmann, *Spirit of Life*, 123–98.

146 Fiddes, *Participating in God*, 259.

147. Moltmann, *Spirit of Life*.

148 Moltmann, *The Trinity and the Kingdom of God*.

149. Ibid.

union of the Father and the Son. This becomes eschatological for the world and for God and problematic too, because the history of the world becomes united with God. Furthermore, Fiddes[150] also adopts this line of thinking as creation is collapsed into the creator.

Yet, this theme of awakening echoes through the literature of youth ministry, particularly in Green and Christian,[151] Dean,[152] Ward,[153] Savage et al.,[154] and Pimlott and Pimlott,[155] it also reverberates through the narratives of practice as relationships as communicative acts are embodied. Vanhoozer[156] develops a similar theme, but seeks to keep the creator/created distinction that is in danger of being lost in the work of Moltmann[157] and Fiddes.[158] To do this he reimagines time as a Trinitarian communicative act. As this notion of time is brought into play it echoes with a sense of journey and reverberates with the idea of a liminal space, acting as an icon of epistemology. Time, as noted above, becomes a particular sphere of communicative action and it is through a process of dialogical communication that God acts not on persons, but within and through them. By acting through the Spirit's agency and grace, God invites people to be as they were always meant to be. Vanhoozer[159] sees this as God speaking and calling to and through people. This calling is communicative and it opens people through their personhood, in a way that respects both God's sovereignty and human freedom.

Vanhoozer[160] sees these openings not only as the work of Grace, but through the activity and power of the Word and the Spirit. Through a communicative act which is not achieved by manipulating but by communicating, God invites us to participate in the light and life of his fellowship. It is a process of Triune dialogics, as God brings about a change in people as they come to understand and come to see who he is. The Spirit is the world's empowering presence, the earthly presence and agent of

150. Fiddes, *Participating in God*, 260.
151 Green and Christian, *Accompanying*.
152. Dean and Foster, *Godbearing Life*.
153. Ward, *Youthwork*.
154. Savage et al., *Making Sense of Generation Y*.
155. Pimlott and Pimlott, *Youth Work after Christendom*.
156. Vanhoozer, *Remythologizing Theology*, 370.
157. Moltmann, *The Trinity and the Kingdom of God*.
158. Fiddes, *Participating in God*.
159. Vanhoozer, *Remythologizing Theology*, 372.
160. Ibid., 372.

the risen Christ (Rom 8:9, Phil 1:19). Here Vanhoozer[161] sees that Christ empowers his disciples (us) to witness by the Spirit. This is a communicative act which liberates and brings understanding. The Spirit liberates and sets people free to respond to the Father's voice, speaking of the beauty of Christ in a way that does not violate, but preserves, sanctions and sanctifies our created natures by the Creator. Vanhoozer[162] argues that salvation, this coming to understand, this seeing, this awakening means relating covenantally to Christ, to be in Christ, means we participate in this Triune communicative act.

As the inferred theme of liminal space is considered, it becomes reimagined not as a place of wrestling and waiting for God to act, but as a place of communicative action. Here, relationships as communicative acts come to the fore but, as noted through the interrelated theme of being there—in Christ, there needs to be a rediscovery of speaking of *kerygma* that, as the data showed within the narratives of practice, had limited scope. For youth ministry, through relationships as communicative acts, to be authentic and faithful to the Gospel within these liminal spaces there needs to be a rethinking of how relationships have collapsed the traditional practices of the church. These can be reimagined within a liminal space as communicative acts, relationships can still be at the center, but reframed not only to the enacted *presence* of being there, in Christ, the *diakonia*, but also to the *kerygma*—to the *witness* of speaking out, to the communicating of God's Word and action through the Spirit. Therefore, there needs to be *both* purposeful presence *and* wise contextual witness. There needs to be a theological reimagining of the use of actions, words and story as divine communicative action.[163] In relation to this book, it is the faithful presence of the youth ministers being there alongside young people in the midst of their stories of marginalization and suffering that resonates with the practice of *diakonia*, this focus on orthopraxis and right action needs to be affirmed.

Yet, to move this practice to be more authentic and faithful to the Gospel, it means youth ministry practice, through the traditional practices of *marturia*, *diakonia* and imaginative theological storytelling through the *kerygma* could, with great care and thought reframe this

---

161. Ibid., 365, 372.

162. Ibid., 281.

163. Cray, *Disciples and Citizens*, God's power was as much in action in the telling of parables as in the healing of the sick and this was subversive engagement with Israel's understanding of its story.

marginalization and suffering, not through God as fellow sufferer, as in the work of Moltmann[164] and Fiddes,[165] however attractive this is, but to see that God withstands suffering and redeems, transforms and unmasks its power, as Vanhoozer[166] argues. This requires *commanding compassion.* Vanhoozer sees that divine passion is *kyriotic;* it is not commiserating but commanding, an *effectual compassion.* This does not only share, but transforms the sufferer's situation, it is *self-moved*. This commanding compassion is *effectual*, because it is less of a passion than a power and it has the capacity to effect change and relieve suffering; divine compassion is an enabling power by which the Triune God shares and communicates his own life. This communicative act of God's covenantal concerns—his saving grace and goodness, provide comfort and transformation by placing suffering in a new perspective (Rom 8:18; 2 Cor 4:17). Through being there in Christ and relationships as communicative acts the person of Jesus Christ can be made known through the *diakonia* and the *kerygma*, through purposeful presence and the wise contextual witness of the *koinonia.* Therefore, from the perspective of salvation, suffering may or may not be removed, but it can be reframed and re-orientated, to see and awaken the hope of an imperishable inheritance, providing the power to resist what can be resisted and the power to consent to that which cannot. Yet, within this, God's apparent inactivity is never a matter of indecision or impotence—but an expression of his constancy. God's patience is a form of his goodness, as he waits for people to respond to his communicative action through his expansive gift of time. It resonates with the theme of time and journey and of liminal space because the gift of time amidst suffering creates room for divine communicative action, a liminal space, a space for bringing about a change of human perspective, a liminal space in which there is time and the journey for repentance and response, a liminal space that allows the communicative act of divine mercy.

A theologically imaginative move, so constructed, would complement some of the practices of enacted mission amongst young people. With this in mind, Vanhoozer,[167] sees that we participate in God as we actively image and dramatize *theos*— it is ultimately the Spirit who rec-

---

164. Moltmann, *The Trinity and the Kingdom of God.*
165. Fiddes, *Participating in God.*
166. Vanhoozer, *Remythologizing Theology*, 446–49.
167. Ibid., 283, 496, 497

reates the image of God in us by efficaciously ministering the Word of God. The prime task of the Spirit is to communicate Christ, the Triune God freely decides to make what is his, his light, life and love, *ours* and then towards *others* who are yet to know him. This divine communicative action is ultimately orientated to communion; this is a divine/human fellowship that effects sanctification and the transformation of human communicants into the image of Jesus Christ. What God is ultimately authoring is a royal priesthood and holy nation, a peaceable kingdom characterized by justice and rightness that goes beyond how the Resource Guides described the church. This is a rich theological relationship as communicative acts which is held within the traditional practice of *marturia* but leads to a life of *doxologia*, praising and giving thanks to God in Christ. The fragments of theology seen within the worship songs, can act as icons of epistemology, and given time, the words sung can be seen as deep liminal spaces of God's communicative action. The words used, with careful thought, can help people see the depth of theology at play and at work within songs as narratives of encounter. Furthermore, it gives a rigorous, theological framework for the enacting of mission amongst young people.

This chapter has explored relationships as communicative acts and Trinitarian theology in conversation with the key words (relationships, like Jesus, being there and time and journey) used by the practitioners within their narratives of practice. These have acted as icons of epistemology, deepening this theological shorthand and fragments of theology and has sought to reconnect this with aspects of the Christian story. The Christological language within the songs and the observational language highlighted with the Resource Guides have been deepened and located within the notion of theodramatic theological participation. This has been facilitated by theodramatic dialogical reflection that has pursued faith seeking understanding. In the final chapter, faith seeking understanding is explored further.

Chapter 10

Towards a Coherent Theology: The Christian Story as Grand Narrative

Rublev's icon has facilitated a way of seeing, as each aspect of the picture has been investigated, there is more going on than meets the eye. The same can be said of theological shorthand. The words used by the practitioners are straightforward and simplified ways of talking about the complexities of practice. This is a redaction of theology. The last chapter facilitated Theodramatic dialogical reflection that sought to unpack the theological shorthand that has been under investigation. Through this process it is possible to see the richness that is held within relationships, that these relationships function as means of God's communicative action. Liminal spaces allow time for God to move and act in the lives of young people who do not yet know him. The discovery that this mission takes place in the divine communicative action of the Triune God of love is crucial for the contemporary practice of youth ministry. Therefore, this chapter begins to move from the more theoretical discussions in the last chapter to the lived experience and performance of faith. As this is explored the importance of the wider Christian story[1] and grand narrative[2] is important. The notion of narrative begins to frame a coherent theology. Furthermore, the theological shorthand and fragments of theology that have been seen as icons of epistemology can move to virtues of epistemology. Intellectual virtue, held within the theological virtues of faith, hope and love facilitates the youth minister as dialogical guide, this sees

---

1. Hauerwas, *The Peaceable Kingdom*.
2. Walker, *Telling the Story*.

the identification of significant words and language acting as keys that unlock the wider story, this continues the process of developing theological literacy. However, before this is explored the important notions of choice, sense and use from the work of Shepherd is examined.

Choice, Sense and Use

Shepherd[3] sees that faith in a secular age has particular characteristics, which if not addressed, will see faith continue in decline. For Shepherd, this will be at the fault lines between generations as faith is not shared. Shepherd's argument revolves around three issues—choice, sense and use. Being Christian is a series of choices and these choices are made in relationship to skepticism and indifference, making a choice to be Christian has implications for a person's identity and opens up people to conflict and challenge. Shepherd[4] continues, being Christian involves learning to detect how we sense God and make sense of God in the midst of life. Being a person of faith connects people to a community and lifestyle, and in times of difficulties that community will be help sustain and create faith. This faith generation takes a different shape in differing contexts—yet, in each one, it is focused on the same outcome—enabling young people to indwell and construct faith identity. This requires a "focus on children, young people and their parents and a challenge to identify how the church can best invest in people, programs and strategies which will encourage young people actively to continue to explore faith."[5]

To help young people make a choice, sense God, and make use of the church community is a very helpful contribution to the ongoing discussions about youth ministry. However, tensions exist with how choices are being made, how God is sensed and how young people become part of a church community. My argument so far, is that the language that youth ministers use and the some of the Resource Guides and songs that begin to sustain the arena of youth ministry operate in fragments and theological shorthand. There is an unspoken tension behind the opportunities for faith generation that Shepherd[6] identifies. For if youth ministry is part of the solution, as Shepherd[7] suggests, then it might also be part of the

---

3. Shepherd, *Faith Generation*, 171.
4. Ibid., 171.
5. *Church Growth Research Project*.
6. Shepherd, *Faith Generation*.
7. Ibid., 172.

problem. By examining how youth ministers talk about their practice, and by identifying that youth ministry is guided by the normative voice of youth ministry literature, it has been demonstrated that some of the thin theology contained here is problematic. This is because the practice of youth ministry is at risk of being untethered from the wider practices of the church. Therefore, the very thing that is required for faith generation—youth ministry and the church—is at risk of operating in a world of fragmented theology and of being expressed as theological shorthand—of being disconnected from the wider Christian story and narrative.

If youth ministry is at risk of being untethered from the wider aspects of the Christian story then a return to the theme of narrative is a helpful move. Above, through the work Hauerwas,[8] the central place of narrative was argued, as were how doctrines are part of a wider story. It is this wider story that is central in providing a broader, more coherent meaning and understanding to the theological shorthand and fragments of theology expressed. The choice, sense and use that Shepherd[9] articulates are part of the theodrama expressed by Vanhoozer,[10] choice, sense and use are participatory practices that generate faith,[11] but this happens in intentional groups and what he calls plausibility shelters. Behind these lie the Christian narrative and tradition. Christian convictions constitute a narrative, a language, it is a story that requires looking *along*. The challenge is to move beyond theological shorthand and fragmented theology, expressed in some aspects of youth ministry, it is the challenge of looking *along*, to see the bigger picture of what it means to learn and grow into the story of Jesus. To be faithful to and be part of this new reality of the Kingdom established by Jesus.[12] To participate in the theodramatic means to take seriously what God is doing in and through Christ as the metadrama in whose light we come to understand everything else.[13] Therefore, the plausibility that Shepherd[14] speaks of, is discovered and found not only by participating in youth groups, but also in the wider theodramatic participation of Christ, to take part in the Trinitarian ac-

---

8. Hauerwas, *The Peaceable Kingdom*.
9. Shepherd, *Faith Generation*, 171.
10. Vanhoozer, *Remythologizing Theology*.
11. Shepherd, *Faith Generation*, 6–117.
12. Wright, *How God Became King*.
13. Vanhoozer, *Remythologizing Theology*, 29.
14. Shepherd, *Faith Generation*, 117.

tion of the communicative activity of God made flesh.[15] This is discovered as young people begin to take part in this story expressed in groups for young people, as Shepherd[16] sees. It is also important to recognize the language and expressions of faith at play, to recognize and see the possibility of theological shorthand in action.

Narrative and Story

For Hauerwas,[17] narrative is not secondary to our knowledge of God, there is no "point"—(no fragment or theological shorthand) that can be dislocated and separated from the story. In fact, the narratives through which we learn about God are the point. It is why the fragmentation of the story into splinters is so challenging. Stories are not substitute descriptions we can someday hope to supersede with more straightforward accounts, no, in contrast, stories are fundamental to our understanding of reality and our existence, they are plausibility structures, resonating with Shepherds[18] language. The very fact that youth ministers told stories about themselves and their work amongst young people, the fact the Resource Guides operated in the observational language of story and the songs functioned as narratives of encounter point to the fact that stories operate on differing levels but have within them similar epistemological status.

Nevertheless, the significant place of narrative has not been without critique. Walker[19] sees that Lyotard has argued that after the eighteenth century it was no longer possible to talk about western culture as being driven by a central narrative. For Lyotard, the rational dominance of modernity made such narrations impossible and for him the enlightenment generated its own "myths" of progress, which he calls "master" or "meta" narratives. Yet, here, Lyotard just replaces one narrative with another. Walker[20] wants to resist the collapse of narratives and he argues for the idea of a master narrative. Walker's language for this is the grand narrative and this is a mythopoeic story that gives meaning and direction to

15. Vanhoozer, *Remythologizing Theology*, 29.
16. Shepherd, *Faith Generation*, 117.
17. Hauerwas, *The Peaceable Kingdom*, 26.
18. Shepherd, *Faith Generation*, 117.
19. Walker, *Telling the Story*, 4.
20. Ibid., 4–5.

life, it is a coherent theology. For Walker,[21] the idea of a grand narrative is important and one that we would wish to recommend to the world as a story to live by, but it is not a story which can be imposed. Ward[22] sees the importance of Walkers grand narrative as he argues that Walker's contribution is that the Gospel is subject to cultural contingency. For Walker does not claim any specific authority for his presentation, what he claims is that across time, cultures and contexts it is possible to see a roughly consistent Christian narrative, or to put this another way the rough shape of a coherent theology. This means that although the story might take on diverse accents and radically altered interpretations it still remains recognizable as the story of Jesus Christ. Therefore, Walkers'[23] grand narrative operates as a map, guiding and keeping the story on course as Christians retell and reimagine the narrative in different contexts and situations. The grand narrative becomes a way of keeping the church faithful to its story[24] it operates as a coherent theology in which we live. Consequently, the fragmentation of the story is problematic, because if the story operates as theological shorthand, it holds the possibility that it may become unrecognizable, the map of the grand narrative could be so torn and shredded that it becomes impossible to follow, impossible to recognize the key landmarks and features echoing deeply with MacIntyre.[25]

Therefore, the Christian story (with all its tensions, problems and baggage), is what has shaped and still shapes our identity and gives us the theological capital to talk about plausibility shelters,[26] but this is the very thing that is under threat due to the fragmentation and thin theology discovered in the narratives of practice, Resource Guides and worship songs. This is why the retethering of youth ministry to this Christian story, this grand narrative, is important as youth ministry seeks to be faithful to the differing expressions of the Gospel. Any retelling of a story with which we identify is an interpretation of history, it means that we do not think of ourselves as individuals, but we are constituted by how one learns to tell their particular story and history in relation to others. Therefore, narrative becomes an important category for the knowledge

21. Ibid., 5.
22. Ward, *Liquid Ecclesiology*, 93.
23. Walker, *Telling the Story*.
24. Ward, *Liquid Ecclesiology*, 91.
25. MacIntyre, *After Virtue*.
26. Shepherd, *Faith Generation*, 76.

of the self, but it is also important for the knowledge of God, the other, and the church in the pursuit of discipleship.[27] For Hauerwas,[28] we come to know who we are only when we can place ourselves, locate our stories, within God's story. Vanhoozer,[29] as noted above, calls this the Biblical mythos, this renders both divine and human reality. Therefore, to speak of Biblical mythos is to indicate the dramatic whole that describes and renders not only human action and participation, but also the reality of God. The Biblical mythos becomes about the one and the many. There is one overall plot and drama, the story of God's history with Israel and Jesus Christ. Yet, this story and drama is spoken by many different voices. The numerous literary forms of the Bible are theologically important, both for what they say (content) and how they say it (discourse). This becomes the written form of God's self-presentation. As such, the Bible becomes the plumb line for right Christian speech about God. To discover the beauty of this narrative is to see the Biblical polyphony and recognize the dialogical nature of participating in the theodrama. What this means is that it takes many voices, points of view, literary forms, and conceptual outlines to fully articulate the reality of God and the truth, depth and beauty of the Gospel. For Hauerwas,[30] the extraordinary claim is that God wants to include us and wants us to participate in this story. To learn to grow into the story of Jesus is to see, to look *along* the story and recognize that at its center is the cross and resurrection.

Virtues of Epistemology

To learn to grow into the story of Jesus requires some work. To discern the different voices and points of view that will lead to a deeper and thicker understanding of the Christian narrative and Gospels requires time and space. Behind the narratives of practice, the creation of the Resource Guides, the writing of the worship songs are people of faith, people who faithfully seek to retell the story, as with any retelling this has flaws and problems. As has been seen, the story is shortened, and fragmented. Yet, this is still a process that participates in the theodrama.[31]

27. Augsburg, *Dissident Discipleship*.
28. Hauerwas, *The Peaceable Kingdom*, 27.
29. Vanhoozer, *Remythologizing Theology*, 7.
30. Hauerwas, *The Peaceable Kingdom*, 27.
31. Vanhoozer, *Remythologizing Theology*.

To carry the story over time requires a certain kind of people. Hauerwas[32] sees that it is the church that sustains and gives voice to the story over time. To bear this story requires people of virtue, not simply any virtue but the virtues required for remembering, telling and retelling the story of a crucified savior. In Walkers'[33] words the telling of the grand narrative. For Hauerwas[34] this requires people of faith, hope and love. The theological virtues of faith, hope and love run like an unspoken thread through narratives of practice, Resource Guides and the worship songs as youth ministers, writers and worship leaders seek to faithfully express the story. This, however fragmented the expression, is to recognize the diversity of theological voices at play in the fluid[35] expression of ecclesiology. To begin to interpret and recognize these diverse, complex and sometimes contradictory theological voices requires the virtue of epistemology. What I mean by this is that if epistemology is the theory of knowledge, then knowledge can be studied and explored, it can be seen as good and useful, as Vanhoozer[36] sees. It is about developing theological literacy as chapters 8 and 9 have begun to show.

Therefore, a move from icons of epistemology to learning a virtue of epistemology can be made. In the last two chapter the words the youth ministers used to speak about their practice—relationships, like Jesus, being there and time and journey functioned as icons of epistemology, this was facilitated by theodramatic dialogical reflection. I have used key words to unlock the richer and deeper story. It is faith seeking understanding and opens up a more profound understanding of what is really going on, it is the process of developing theological literacy. This attempted to flesh out the depth behind the language spoken, by looking *at* it enabled a deeper looking *along*. Following these discussions and seeing how to understand the depth and beauty of the story, it is possible to frame epistemology as a virtue, this is not disconnected from the embodied theological virtues of faith, hope and love, in fact, it is held in these. Furthermore, it requires the virtues of faith, hope and love to be faithful,[37] to provide a dialogical way of discovering and navigating the

---

32. Hauerwas, *The Peaceable Kingdom*, 103.
33. Walker, *Telling the Story*.
34. Hauerwas, *The Peaceable Kingdom*, 103.
35. Ward, *Liquid Ecclesiology*.
36. Vanhoozer, *First Theology*, 351.
37. Hauerwas, *The Peaceable Kingdom*, 103.

richness and beauty of what it means to participate in and articulate the Biblical mythos. This sits well within the evangelical tradition as it has sought to communicate and mediate ideas and the values of faith as seen in chapter 3, and a virtue of epistemology seeks to begin to reframe this in a robust and intentional way. To facilitate this entails a return to the concept of practical wisdom, *phronesis*, as discussed in chapter 2. This is the process of grasping the significance of the Christian story, Biblical narrative and the contemporary situation though practical reason. *Phronesis* is about wisdom and moral action, how one lives and acts. For Vanhoozer,[38] theology must reorient itself to wisdom and not just knowledge, here he argues that modernity and post-modernity have torn asunder metaphysics, theory, practice and morals. This echoes the fragmentation and separation of ethics from an overall narrative that MacIntyre[39] highlights. Wisdom becomes the practice of integrating universals and particulars, and it is the Christian narrative and Biblical story that generates imagination and interpretive frameworks, for giving words to our experience and beliefs. In turn, these become the central means of cultivating *phronesis*. Therefore, wisdom becomes an effective way of integrating seeing, doing, judging and acting, resonating with Hauerwas[40] as a way of understanding and integrating oneself, one's history and God's history.

For Vanhoozer,[41] virtue epistemology can be seen to begin with the insight that we are responsible for what we believe. This has ramifications for how the youth ministers expressed their practice and how the Resource Guides and worship songs communicate who God is. It has been seen in the data that the emphasis of youth ministers was on orthopraxis, right action and this needs to be commended. However, the marginalization of the articulation of the theological is something that should be addressed. The youth ministers interviewed were people of faith, hope and love, this comes across through their profound and sacrificial care of the young people they serve. Yet, in the midst of this is a thin articulation of theology, a thin description of the depth of the Gospel and Christian story. Moreover, if one is responsible for ones' beliefs as Vanhoozer[42] argues, and if believing is something that is done, it is subject to evaluation

---

38. Vanhoozer, *First Theology*, 348.
39. MacIntyre, *After Virtue*.
40. Hauerwas, *The Peaceable Kingdom*, 26.
41. Vanhoozer, *First Theology*, 351.
42. Ibid., 351.

and critique, in some sense it can be right or wrong, done well or done poorly. Zagzebski[43] sees, that a virtue is "a characteristic motivation to produce a desired end and reliable success in bringing about that end."

This is a helpful, but MacIntyre,[44] offers a much deeper explanation for the shifting nature of this notion. MacIntyre sees there are many different and almost incompatible concepts of the virtues for there to be any real unity to the idea. However, it is still possible to navigate this complex arena. For example, Homer's list of virtues differs from Aristotle's,[45] furthermore, the relationship of virtues to the social order has changed. For Homer, the paradigm of human excellence is the Warrior, for Aristotle, it is the Athenian gentleman. Therefore, it is also impossible to deny that the most striking contrast with Aristotle's catalogue is not found in Homer, but in the New Testament. The New Testament importantly prioritizes virtues that Aristotle did not, faith, hope and love. Furthermore, it was Aristotle who first distinguished the intellectual from the moral and the intellectual virtues differ from their moral equivalents in two ways. 1) Intellectual virtues arise from the desire for truth. 2) The intellectual virtues cultivate habits that seek to attain this motive.[46] Yet, this is a false distinction as both should be governed by *phronesis*.[47] Consequently, the meaning of virtue is fluid, but virtue epistemology has a firmer footing. Virtue epistemology seeks to discover the normative element in believing, but as discussed above via Ward,[48] this itself can be perilous! Vanhoozer,[49] however, argues that truth (at least partially) can be discovered and acquired by acts of intellectual virtue. Intellectual virtue is pursued via open mindedness, contentiousness and impartiality. These notions can be pushed further, learning about the richness and diversity of theologies that make up the Christian narrative requires wrestling, critiquing and evaluating—developing theological literacy. At its heart, is the desire to try and discover the richness and depth of the story.

---

43. Zagzebski, *Virtues of the Mind*, 137.
44. MacIntyre, *After Virtue*.
45. Ibid., 182.
46. Vanhoozer, *First Theology*, 351.
47. Zagzebski, *Virtues of the Mind*, 137–58.
48. Ward, "Blueprint Ecclesiology."
49. Vanhoozer, *First Theology*, 352.

Vanhoozer[50] sees that there is a difference between intellectual skill and intellectual virtue, the former is about capacity, the later about excellence. As virtue is a character trait, it can be learnt and developed. People can acquire the deep and enduring excellence of an intellectual virtue by imitation. The focus is on people not just process, but virtue becomes a good lens through which to view the rightness of an act as an embodied belief. Therefore, in the embodied faith of the youth ministers the faithfulness of practice has to be revered, yet it is the articulation of the beliefs behind those practices, as described via theological shorthand that require the lens of intellectual virtue, a virtue of epistemology, to wrestle and grapple with the deeper aspects of the Biblical narrative and Christian story, to grapple with the contextual expression of the grand narrative.[51] It is in the wrestling, in the pursuit of truth that the bigger picture gets discovered, theological literacy is developed. This grows into an affair of the heart, a passion that seeks to discover more of the story through faith, hope and love.[52] This becomes not only about a theological articulation, the art of reasoning well, rationality, that is able to tell and re-tell the story but also about the wisdom of living well.[53]

Dialogical Guides—Developing Intellectual Virtue

Vanhoozer[54] highlights that people learn intellectual virtue by imitation, it is learnt by being an apprentice. It is important to remember that this imitation takes place as one participates in the theodrama of God's communicative action. Becoming a dialogical guide is the process of developing intellectual virtue. As youth ministry is explored, youth ministers can be dialogical guides, bringing experience and context into conversation with the depth and richness of the differing expressions of the Christian story and tradition. It is dialogical because as has been seen in the divergent expressions of Trinitarian theology investigated, this is a process of exploration and negotiation as different aspects of the Christian story are examined in relation to each other and in regard to the youth ministers experience and practice amongst young people. This dialogical process

---

50. Ibid., 352.
51. Walker, *Telling the Story*.
52. Hauerwas, *The Peaceable Kingdom*, 103.
53. Vanhoozer, *First Theology*, 373.
54. Ibid., 253.

creates theological literacy, guides wise contextual story dwellers who are able to navigate, name and express the depth of the Christian story, enacting theology that is shaped by deep exploration and thought. To draw an analogy from music, youth ministers become like jazz musicians improvising and experimenting around the key and beat of the music. For a jazz musician to improvise requires a deep understanding of musical theory, and then the ability to express this creatively and freely in the moment of the song. To explore what it means for youth ministers to be dialogical guides, people who can improvise and creatively bring the story alive, a threefold move is made. The first two moves involve the development of youth ministers and the third is the youth minister being a dialogical guide amongst young people.

Firstly, youth ministers develop as dialogical guides through the process of theodramatic dialogical reflection. The highlighting of theological shorthand and theological fragments present an opportunity to engage, learn, perhaps re-learn, navigate and practice the complex art of continuous theodramatic dialogical reflection. Through this process, as a spiritual discipline and practice,[55] youth ministers can begin to articulate more emphatically why they do what they do from a theological perspective, learning the skills of intellectual virtue. Therefore, key words within worship songs, or Resource Guides or how practice is articulated can be explored, these words hold the potential to become keys that unlock the wider Christian story and facilitate theological literacy. As this is undertaken, the insight that relationships function as communicative acts and how this is expressed as theological shorthand is crucial as it illuminates and critiques current youth ministry practice.

However, the slowing down of the youth ministry process that this book has explored can be acted upon. As these insights are made known youth ministry practitioners will be able to see, name, and begin to articulate the process of youth ministry and the current tensions within this. Therefore, this theological shorthand could be made clear. Once understood that the current practice of the youth ministers operates in this way then the process of working and enlarging the theological fragments that function within youth ministry can be acted upon. This becomes the process of leaning intellectual virtue, opening up a world requiring vision, wider horizons and vistas in the pursuit of the beauty and depth of the Biblical mythos and Christian narrative. This would help explore some of

---

55. Ward, *Participation and Mediation*.

the theological misunderstanding and misrepresentation articulated by the youth ministers interviewed, especially seen in how they articulate being like Jesus and the individualist expression of faith. Questions circulate here about how youth ministers relate to the wider congregation and church. As individuals trying to be like Jesus has an effect on understanding appropriate boundaries, raising questions about how the youth ministers understood their ministry. This in turn leads to overworking and a reliance on themselves that is not healthy. The impact of this on mental health has the potential to be detrimental. Developing intellectual virtue that enables theological literacy and *phronesis* has the potential to re-engage youth ministry with the wider ecclesiological traditions of which the youth ministers are part, locating them beyond individual networks and connections into the broader ecclesiological webs and mutuality of the congregation. Enabling and opening up opportunities to see God's Spirit at work, to participate with God's communicative action, having a language to articulating God's divine presence would help youth minsters see that they don't have to do ministry on their own.[56]

Secondly, this involves the apprenticeship and ongoing training of youth ministers, to mature as dialogical guides requires intentional development alongside wise theologians, more experienced youth ministers and informed clergy who are further down the theological road. People who can act as conversation partners, exploring the depth of the Christian story, people who can sign post and articulate the grand narrative, a wise friend and mentor who can bring critical faithfulness to bear as practice and theology are explored in conversation. As youth ministers develop as dialogical guiders, this discussion with others also has the potential to facilitate greater exploration and understanding of the Biblical narrative. To move beyond the idea of plastic hermeneutics discussed in chapter 3, to wrestle with a deeper exegetical and hermeneutical understanding of the text. To seek to exchange the theological shorthand and fragmentation of theology seen with a deeper and more profound understanding of the story. This brings together the concepts of narrative and intellectual virtue, requiring youth ministers to go beyond the more familiar world of the New Testament story and to grapple with other parts of the Biblical narrative. This is about expanding theological literacy and *phronesis*; youth ministers should be encouraged to engage

---

56. Root, *Revisiting Relational Youth Ministry*; Dean, *Practicing Passion*; and Shepherd, *Faith Generation* all express different aspect of this but it is not expressed by the youth ministers interviewed.

in the wider theological disciplines of Biblical and systematic theology, to excite, evoke and explore the dramatic, imaginative landscapes of the Bible and Christian doctrine. They need to move away from the shorthand descriptions of practice, to a discovery, connection, and dialogue with the rich variety of work within these other important arenas.

The particular traditions of which the youth minister is part of, be it Anglican, Baptist or United Reformed etc. could be explored and investigated, seeing the particular foibles of these. Noticing and reflecting on the distinct practices and idiosyncrasies of a denomination and particular church community would help expand a youth minister's theological literacy. With this in mind, Hauerwas[57] sees that one has to continually check one's particular reading of the story; this is the process of intellectual virtue highlighted by Vanhoozer.[58] Importantly, Hauerwas[59] reasons, that this takes place best in the community of the church. "The church not only is, but must be, a community of moral discourse—that is, a community that sustains a rigorous analysis of the implications of its commitments across generations as it faces new challenges and situations." This is the process of wrestling with the theology behind and within the fragment and theological shorthand. It is the development of theological literacy and how dialogical guides are formed. Yet, as Ward[60] contends, the presence of the Holy Spirit does not offer a guarantee against inerrancy, this is the paradoxical reality of the church that it can somehow be a place of divine presence and encounter, but still be prone to error in the fluidity of the churches' expression. For often, the implications of the larger narrative are not seen in one generation. Hauerwas,[61] continues, that there is no assurance that this working out will be faithful to the kind of discipleship required by Jesus[62] and it is important that this

---

57. Hauerwas, *The Peaceable Kingdom*, 131.

58. Vanhoozer, *First Theology*, 351.

59. Hauerwas, *The Peaceable Kingdom*, 131.

60. Ward, *Liquid Ecclesiology*, 93.

61. Hauerwas, *The Peaceable Kingdom*, 191.

62. Hauerwas cites the development of just war theory as a case of how the church in seeking to be faithful to the Gospel and respond to an increasing responsibility to wider society was a misguided mistake. Some Christians involvement and non-action about slavery in the late eighteenth century is another example of this, of course, was then championed by Christians, but not before considerable resistance. A more contemporary illustration is seen in the struggle by LGBT+ Christians; perhaps, in future generations, the marginalization of this group will be seen in the same light to how abhorrent slavery is now.

process does not only rest with the "experts," this should be an activity participated in by the whole church community. It takes a community to develop youth ministers as dialogical guides. As Hauerwas[63] notes, that often some of a communities' best casuists may be those who do not possess the strongest rational skill set. Those with intuitive gifts may simple know better than they can say as to what the Gospel requires, resonating with Vanhoozer[64] about how an intellectual virtue goes beyond knowledge to wisdom. The church has to facilitate moral discourse and intellectual virtue in a way that honors the voice of the prophet.[65] For the fragments of theology to be expanded, via intellectual virtue, held with the theodramatic, the importance of context comes to the fore.

Therefore, the third and final move is that youth ministers skilled in the art of theodramatic dialogical reflection could practice this at an appropriate level with young people, they themselves become dialogical guides and help develop theological literacy. This is about wise and contextual witness, knowing the grand narrative and helping young people enter this story at different points. The presence of the youth ministry practitioners amongst the suffering of young people needs to be affirmed. Yet, this practice can also be an act of contextual witness that goes beyond what is seen in the data, raising inquisitive questions amongst young people. These questions can lead to creative, contextual story telling[66] that does not impose, but challenges and unmasks the contemporary narratives of the day. Contextual witness means having the language and theological literacy to talk about the story, to practice the art of *kerygma*. This is about the youth minister knowing the culture of the young people they work amongst and then having the ability to make story telling a normal part of their ministry, functioning as dialogical guides.

The key is doing this in a way that does not feel forced or out of touch with the group. This is a well-rehearsed idea within youth ministry,[67] but is missed by the youth ministers under investigation. Wise contextual witness that moves beyond purposeful presence to speaking about the story amongst young people needs to be employed or rediscovered. Youth ministers as dialogical guides are key in exploring and translat-

---

63. Ibid., 134.
64. Vanhoozer, *First Theology*, 351.
65. Hauerwas, *The Peaceable Kingdom*, 134.
66. Walker, *Telling the Story*.
67. Ward, *Youthwork*, 96–101.

ing the story,[68] making the Gospel known amongst young people. The discovery or rediscovery and the ability to theologically reimagine the richness and scope of the Biblical narrative could bring aspects of the Christian story alive in the contemporary culture and context of young people. Acting as contextual points of connection and transmission for relationships as communicative acts that take place in the liminal spaces of God's communicative action. The speaking about God, through the practice of *kerygma* within the midst of purposeful presence needs to be amplified and facilitated through a process of theodramatic dialogical reflection that equips the youth minister as a dialogical guide.

It is the mutuality of purposeful presence and wise contextual witness that are important.

Walker[69] gives an important reminder by drawing on Leslie Newbigin, that a local community, be it Anglican, Pentecostal or Baptist is the hermeneutic of the Gospel. The Gospel is a story lived by people. As Walker[70] and Shepherd[71] see, Christianity cannot survive without plausibility structures, as my argument has demonstrated, it will also not deepen without exploring the language, the fragments and theological shorthand of youth ministry and ecclesial expression. This requires a holy community, a local church who live, enact and embody the story. Walker[72] argues that communities are icons, and the church community become windows into a larger world, telling pictures that represent a different reality. As youth ministers indwell the story and participate in God's theodramatic communicative action, God's love will be mediated.

As story dwellers and not just story tellers, the reminder is that the Christian story with all its depth and beauty is a story to live by, it is the story of Jesus Christ. Walker[73] reasons "if we cannot demonstrate the proof of our story by living it we will never convince people of its truth by talking about it. A story is telling, after all, only if it produces a striking effect on its listener." The purposeful presence of the youth ministers bears testament to this, but again, youth ministry should move beyond the individual expressions to be practiced by congregations. There is the

68. Ibid., 96–101
69. Ibid., 199.
70. Ibid.
71. Shepherd, *Faith Generation*, 71.
72. Walker, *Telling the Story*, 199.
73. Ibid., 201.

potential for *phronesis* to flourish in a symbiotic relationship were youth ministers become dialogical guides, helping to theologically educate churches into work amongst young people, whilst wise critical friends and church communities develop the intellectual virtue and theological literacy of the youth minister.

Conclusion and Implications

As the ideas of theological shorthand and the fragmentation of theology have been explored, we have answered the question: How does theological shorthand operate within youth ministry? To do this, the first part of the book charted the ground and laid out the methodological map behind the investigations. In chapter 1, the limits of language were highlighted and questions of epistemology were raised and the tensions of this briefly examined. Through the work of C.S Lewis it has been possible to grasp the difference of looking *at* and looking *along*. By working with Lewis, it was demonstrated that looking *at* fragments, splinters and separates, whilst looking *along* seeks to take in the whole picture. This resonated with the thoughts of Walker[74] and the bigger picture of fragmentation within morality and larger conceptual schemes as rendered by MacIntyre.[75] The place of mystery was explored as theological shorthand was illuminated in more detail. How the four voices of theology[76] operate and are at play within this particular study were then highlighted and critiqued.

Chapter 2, outlined the methodological journey and youth ministry's relationship to practical theology was investigated. This chapter raised important questions and sought to provide some answers to where theology is relative to practice and the conversation between theology and epistemology was reviewed. The chapter outlined the relevant discussions within practical theology and provided a theological reflective framework through which Trinitarian theology can act as the normative voice for practice (however provisional this is). Importantly, through this, the empirical work was placed within a theological hermeneutic provided by key methodological dialogue partners Swinton and Mowat.[77]

---

74. Ibid.
75. MacIntyre, *After Virtue*.
76. Cameron et al., *Talking about God in Practice*.
77. Swinton and Mowat, *Practical Theology and Qualitative Research*.

In addition to this, the importance of a narrative approach for exploring practice and communicative action was outlined.

Chapter 3 pushed the methodological discussions further, here, the relationship between youth ministry and Christian practices has been examined and the complex connections between doctrine and practice investigated. An argument has been constructed for how theology acts as the normative voice in serving and critiquing practice and differing understandings of Christian practices were outlined. The second part of chapter 3 continued the analysis as the mediation of the evangelical tradition was examined. Here, the pivotal place of relationships and the relational hermeneutic within evangelical thought was explored and articulated. The influence and reach of Young Life on youth ministry in the UK was emphasized and this led to the analysis of plastic hermeneutics and Biblical interpretation within the evangelical tradition. It was argued that the way ideas are passed on through a top down approach leads to an approach in which the youth ministry literature has become the normative voice for practice.

Part two, sought to examine current practice—this has been at the center of the empirical enterprise. In chapter 4, the youth ministers were introduced, this short, but critical chapter was a reminder that the youth ministers are real people, who sought to faithfully embody the Gospel. The youth ministers are people with real histories, in real situations as they work amongst young people. The liminal spaces the youth ministers indwell is Holy Ground and these story dwellers are in the center of the theodramatic action. Chapter 5, recapitulated the key research themes of how the youth ministers embody and communicate their practice. This was principally seen in the way the youth ministers enacted and performed their faith. The whole process can be summed up as an embodied communicative act and the central argument has been that this is a set of complex communicative practices, but is articulated through the simplified terms of relationships, like Jesus, being there, and time and journey. The argument has been that this is theological shorthand in motion and action.

Chapter 6, developed these themes in critical conversation with the selected literature on youth ministry. The relationship between embodied faith and the theological expression of youth ministry within the literature was reflected upon and critiqued. This process identified a tension and problem with the theological expression of youth ministry. Therefore, it was argued that contemporary youth ministry practice is seen to be guided by the normative voice and expression of relationships that is expressed through the literature on youth ministry. Moreover, importantly, it was argued that this normative voice is louder than the ecclesial traditions of which the youth ministers are part—this resonated with the mediation of the evangelical tradition. Additionally, the focus on relationships as theological shorthand facilitates the collapse of the classic elements of the church's practices of *diakonia*, *kerygma* and *marturia* into the relational. As the arguments have been marshalled, this process can be seen to turn relationship that function as communicative acts into a contemporary practice, but this is not deliberate and is not founded or acted upon by robust theological reflection. This can be articulated as theological shorthand, as thin theology and the fragmentation of the wider Christian story and narrative. Enacted mission is centered around the individual youth minister and not amongst the congregation.

In chapter 7, the songs and Resource Guides highlighted the employment of theological shorthand in the diet of worship and Biblical material that youth ministers receive and consume. Through the analysis it has been demonstrated that the Resources Guides function principally through the lens of observation. Here it was argued that readers view the story from the outside and what is offered, and is at play, is a conceptualized understanding of church and the Bible outside of specific contexts and situations, resonating again with the mediation of the evangelical tradition from the top down. Likewise, the Resource Guides demonstrate the fragmentation of theology and the idea of plastic hermeneutics. Additionally, the Resource Guides and the songs require the reader and worshiper to have a confident grasp of both theological and Biblical capital in order to bring the fragments, story and narrative back together.

In part three, the construction began, here, chapter 8 returned to the theme of theological reflection, but importantly this was reframed in the theodramatic. This was an advancement of the reflective conversations and dialogue carried out within chapter 2. Through this process the theological shorthand and fragments of theology already explored are expanded as the crucial words function as icons of epistemology. These words act as keys to unlocking the wider Christian story, developing theological literacy. This was employed through a critical dialogue with

Trinitarian theology via Moltmann,[78] Fiddes,[79] Kilby,[80] and Vanhoozer.[81] Chapter 9, continued the examination and investigation of the fragments and theological shorthand debated. Significantly, participation was upheld as a crucial Trinitarian motif that sought to reframe practice as the icons of epistemology continue to be expanded.

Chapter 10, has drawn the discussions to a conclusion. The importance of the wider Christian story and narrative as a coherent theology for understanding God and ourselves has been articulated. Through this, it is possible to move from icons of epistemology to a virtue of epistemology held within the theological virtues of faith hope and love. This facilitates a critical dialogue on and conversation about the theology that flows between doctrine and practice and enables a range of voices to inform, deepen and enrich the story as youth ministers function as dialogical guides and develop *phronesis* and theological literacy.

Implications

This book has explored snapshots of youth ministry: the practice and voices of the twelve youth ministers interviewed, the Resource Guides and the worships songs. As implications are draw from the investigations care should be taken. It was noted that it was not possible to generalize from the research undertaken, however, the ideas discussed should resonate and chime with youth ministry practitioners. With this in mind, some implications are suggested:

A recognition that the relationships youth ministers establish with young people are seen as communicative acts, they take part in the communicative actions of God.

Acknowledgement that the words used to describe youth ministry practice can be seen as fragments of a wider story and operate as theological shorthand. It is the recognition of the paradoxical tension between theological expression and sacrificial service. Yet, these words can act as keys that have the potential to unlock the grand narrative of the Christian story. When key words are reflected upon they can act as icons of epistemology, windows into a wider world, this presents the opportunity to

---

78. Moltmann, *The Trinity and the Kingdom of God*.
79. Fiddes, *Participating in God*.
80. Kilby, "Perichoresis and Projection."
81. Vanhoozer, *Remythologizing Theology*.

get to know the depth of and richness of the Christian story, developing intellectual virtue and theological literacy.

To recognize that theological shorthand and fragmented theology operate in the arena of youth ministry, as seen in the Resource Guides and worship songs investigated. To be familiar with and challenge this where appropriate. To identify and acknowledge the process of plastic hermeneutics at play.

To understand the tension that exists in how the youth ministry literature can be seen as the normative voice of practice. The recognition that this can be a stronger voice than the Bible and the church traditions of which the youth ministers are a part and that this risks untethering youth ministry from the wider ecclesial frameworks. Therefore, youth ministers should explore the richness and story of their own traditions.

The focus on relationships collapses the classic elements of the church's practices of *diakonia*, *kerygma* and *marturia* into the relational. The fact that relationships function as communicative acts, as a contemporary practice, can be celebrated, but the richness of intertwined practices of *diakonia*, *kerygma* and *marturia* can be revisited and explored expanding the vocabulary and language of theological literacy.

A more explicit and robust theological reimagining of relationships as communicative acts has been advanced, locating this within a Trinitarian frame work of communication. Here, God's divine authorship is held within the divine communicative action and through this theological reimagination the practice of youth ministry is retethered into the richness of the Christian tradition. This gives the youth ministers a more extensive theological expression and grammar that enables them to articulate their practice in deeper and richer terms. It expands the fragments and theological shorthand in play, develops *phronesis* and theological literacy, facilitating practitioners as dialogical guides, helping to deepen and articulate the grand narrative amongst young people.

There is a prerequisite for youth ministers to continually question and be inquisitive about the Christian story and their faith. To theologically reflect and develop an intellectual virtue, to mature as dialogical guides and develop theological literacy. To be intentional about on-going theological training, to seek mentoring or spiritual direction in order to develop this. Supplementary theological education and CPD and supervision by those who are further down the theological journey could open up spaces for deeper theodramatic dialogical reflection.

This study raises questions about the support and supervision of youth ministers and how they relate to the wider congregation and church. Not understanding appropriate boundaries raises further questions about how the youth ministers understood themselves. This has the potential to lead to over working and reliance on themselves that is not healthy and the impact of this on mental health may be detrimental.

The emphasis of mission amongst young people can be seen to be currently driven by individual youth ministers. This should move to being located within congregations, mission amongst young people is a task of the whole church. The church community and youth ministers are not diametrically opposed. It is not only the youth ministry specialist who can reach or disciple young people, the youth minister should function as a facilitator, a dialogical guide in helping churches explore faith with young people, creating plausibility structures resonating with Shepherd's thoughts.[82] Symbiotic relations can be established between youth ministers and congregations where they both can flourish through *phronesis* and theological literacy in their ministry and mission with young people.

As the discussions have unfolded, it can be seen that *both* purposeful presence as demonstrated so faithfully in the lives of the youth ministers and wise contextual witness is needed. This is how young people begin to hear and see the Christian story in action. To do this faithfully, requires a deeper theological grammar and language than is at play in the expression of embodied youth ministry, requiring theological literacy and moving beyond the individual acts of the youth minister to the hermeneutic of the local church. It necessitates a slowing down of practice, to examine practice frame by frame—it is a process of stopping, looking and listening—a method of noticing, the act of noticing forges the depth and rigor required to explore the story in more complexity and detail—to see the beauty. This leads to a rediscovery of wise contextual witness by where the Christian story is not only embodied, but also spoken and articulated in a way that is faithful to participation within the theodramatic communicative action of the Trinitarian God.

---

82. Shepherd, *Faith Generation*.

BIBLIOGRAHPY

Adey, L. *Hymns and the Christian Myth*. Vancouver: University of British Columbia Press, 1986.
Allen, J. "The Bible's Big Story." *Youthwork* (April 2015) 33–36.
Anderson, Ray S. *The Shape of Practical Theology: Empowering Ministry with Theological Praxis*. Downers Grove, IL: InterVarsity, 2001.
Astley, Jeff. *Ordinary Theology: Looking, Listening and Learning in Theology*. Aldershot: Ashgate, 2002.
Bailey, David. "Enacted Faith, Youth Ministry and Theological Shorthand." *Journal of Youth and Theology* 13/2 (2014) 25–39.
———. "Living Amongst the Fragments of a Coherent Theology: Youth Ministry, Worship and Icons of Epistemology." *Journal of Youth and Theology* 15/2 (2016) 173–95.
Baker, D. G. "Evoking Testimony through Holy Listening: The Art of Interview as a Practice in Youth Ministry." *Journal of Youth and Theology* 4/2 (2005) 53–68.
Ballard, Paul. H. "Pastoral and Practical Theology in Britain." In *The Blackwell Reader in Pastoral and Practical Theology*, edited by J. Woodward and S. Pattison, 59–69. Malden, MA: Blackwell, 2000.
Ballard, Paul H., and John Pritchard. *Practical Theology in Action: Christian Thinking in the Service of Church and Society*. 2nd ed. London: SPCK, 2006.
Bass, D. C. *Life Together: Practicing Faith with Adolescents*. Princeton: Princeton Theological Seminary, 2001.
Bauckham, Richard. "Jürgen Moltmann." In *The Modern Theologians: An Introduction to Christian Theology of the Twentieth Century*, edited by David F. Ford, 1:147–62. Oxford: Blackwell, 1989.
———. *The Theology of Jürgen Moltmann*. Edinburgh: T. & T. Clark, 1995.
Blackman, S. "Youth Subcultural Theory: A Critical Engagement with the Concept, Its Origins and Politics, from the Chicago School to Postmodernism." *Journal of Youth Studies* 8 (2005) 1–20.
Boff, Leonardo. *Trinity and Society*. Sao Paulo: Burns and Oates, 1988.
Bonhoeffer, Dietrich. *Christ the Centre*. San Francisco: HarperCollins, 1960.
Borgman, Dean. *When Kumbaya Is Not Enough: A Practical Theology for Youth Ministry*. Peabody, MA: Hendrickson, 1997.
Boyle, A. "Jesus Meets." *Youthwork* (September 2015) 37.
Bretherton, Luke. "Beyond the Emerging Church." In *Remembering Our Future*, edited by Andrew Walker and Luke Bretherton, 30–58. Milton Keynes: Paternoster, 2007.
———. *Hospitality as Holiness*. London, Routledge, 2006.

Brierley, Danny. *Joined Up: An Introduction to Youthwork and Ministry*. Carlisle: Authentic, 2003.

Bright, Graham, and David Bailey. "Youth Work and the Church." In *Youth Work: Histories, Policy and Contexts*, edited by Graham Bright, 145–56. London: Palgrave, Macmillan, 2015.

Brown, Rosalind. *How Hymns Shape Our Lives*. Cambridge: Grove, 2004.

Browning, Don S. *A Fundamental Practical Theology: Descriptive and Strategic Proposals*. Minneapolis: Fortress, 1996.

———, ed. *Practical Theology: The Emerging Field in Theology*. Church and World. San Francisco: Harper and Row, 1983.

Cahlan, Kathleen A. "Introducing Ministry and Fostering Integration: Teaching the Bookends of the Master of Divinity Program." In *The Life Abundant*, edited by Dorothy C. Bass and Craig Dykstra, 91–116. Grand Rapids: Eerdmans, 2008.

Cahlan, Kathleen A., and James R. Nieman. "Mapping the Field of Practical Theology." In *The Life Abundant*, edited by Dorothy C. Bass and Craig Dykstra, 62–90. Grand Rapids: Eerdmans, 2008.

Cameron, H., et al. *Talking about God in Practice*. London: SCM, 2010.

Chalke, S. "The Real Youth Service." *Youthwork* (August 2016) 25.

Christie, Ann. *Ordinary Christology*. Farnham: Ashgate, 2012.

Chung, H. K. *Struggle to be the Sun Again: Introducing Asian Women's Theology*. Maryknoll, NY: Orbis, 1990.

Church of England Board of Education. *Youth A Part: Young People and the Church*. London: Church House, 1996.

Church Growth Research Project Report on Strand 3b: An Analysis of Fresh Expressions of Church and Church Plants Begun in the Period 1992-2012. Sheffield: Church Army Research Unit, 2013.

Coffey, A., and P. Atkinson. *Making Sense of Qualitative Data*. London: Sage, 1996.

Cohen, L., et al. *Research Methods in Education*. 6th ed. London: Routledge, 2007.

Cook, A., and J. Henley. "Reimagining the Church." *Youthwork* (July 2015) 34–38.

Cray, Graham. *Disciples and Citizens*. Nottingham: InterVarsity, 2007.

Crowsley, K. "Reimagining the Church." *Youthwork* (June 2015) 34–38.

Cunningham, David S. *These Three Are One: The Practice of Trinitarian Theology*. Oxford: Blackwell, 1998.

Dean, Kenda C. "The Dean of Youth Work." *Youthwork* (May 2014) 24–26.

———. *Practicing Passion: Youth and the Quest for a Passionate Church*. Grand Rapids: Eerdmans, 2004.

Dean, Kenda C., and Ron Foster. *The Godbearing Life: The Art of Soul Tending for Youth Ministry*. Nashville: Upper Room, 1998.

Dykstra, Craig R., and Dorothy C. Bass. "A Theological Understanding of Christian Practices." In *Practicing Theology: Beliefs and Practices in Christian Life*, edited by Miroslav Volf and Dorothy C. Bass, 13–32. Grand Rapids: Eerdmans, 2002.

Farley, Edward. *Theologia: The Fragmentation and Unity of Theological Education*. Philadelphia: Fortress, 1983.

Fiddes, Paul S. *Participating in God: A Pastoral Doctrine of the Trinity*. London: DLT, 2000.

Gee, Paul P. *An Introduction to Discourse Analysis: Theory and Method*. New York, Routledge, 2010.

Geertz, Clifford. *The Interpretation of Cultures*. New York: Basic Books, 1973.

Graham, Elaine. *Transforming Practice: Pastoral Theology in an Age of Uncertainty.* London: Mowbray, 1996.
Graham, Elaine, et al. *Theological Reflection: Sources.* London: SCM, 2005.
Green, Maxine, and Chandu Christian. *Accompanying Young People on Their Spiritual Quest.* London: Church House, 1998.
Griffiths, Steve. *Models for Youth Ministry.* London: SPCK, 2013.
Gunton, Colin E. *The One, The Three and The Many.* Cambridge: Cambridge University Press, 1993.
Hardy, Daniel W. "T. F. Torrance." In *The Modern Theologians: An Introduction to Christian Theology of the Twentieth Century,* edited by David F. Ford, 1:163–77. Oxford: Blackwell, 1989.
Harris, Harriet A. *Fundamentalism and Evangelicals.* Oxford: Clarendon, 2007.
Hauerwas, Stanley. *The Peaceable Kingdom.* Notre Dame: University of Notre Dame Press, 1986.
Healy, Nicholas M. *Church, World and the Christian Life: Practical Prophetic Ecclesiology.* Cambridge: Cambridge University Press, 2000.
———. *Hauerwas: A (Very) Critical Introduction.* Grand Rapids: Eerdmans, 2014.
Hebdige, D. *Subculture: The Meaning of Style.* London: Routledge, 1988.
Hoey, Brian A. "From Pi to Pie." *Journal of Contemporary Ethnography* 34/5 (2005) 586–624.
Holmes, Steven R. *The Holy Trinity.* Milton Keynes: Paternoster, 2012.
Hughes, Graham. *Worship as Meaning: A Liturgical Theology for Late Modernity.* Cambridge: Cambridge University Press, 2003.
Jones, Serene. "Graced Practices Excellence and Freedom in the Christian Life." In *Practicing Theology: Beliefs and Practices in Christian Life,* edited by Miroslav Volf and Dorothy C. Bass, 51–77. Grand Rapids: Eerdmans, 2002.
Kilby, Karen. "Perichoresis and Projection: Problems with Social Doctrines of the Trinity." *New Blackfriars* 81/957 (2007) 432–45.
Leach, S. "Reimagining the Church." *Youthwork* (June 2015) 20–23.
Lindbeck, George A. *The Nature of Doctrine: Religion and Theology in a Postliberal Age.* London: SPCK, 1984.
Long, S. "Jesus Meets." *Youthwork* (September 2015) 34.
Lovejoy, T. *Making Connections.* Bletchley, UK: Scripture Union, 1999.
MacIntyre, Alasdair. *After Virtue: A Study in Moral Theory.* London: Duckworth, 1996.
MacIntyre, J. *The Shape of Soteriology.* Edinburgh: T. & T. Clark, 1992.
Malley, Brian. *How the Bible Works: An Anthropological Study of Evangelical Biblicism.* Walnut Creek, CA: Altamira, 2004.
Mason, J. *Researching Your Own Practice: The Discipline of Noticing.* London: Routledge, 2002.
McGrath, A. E. *Christian Theology: An Introduction.* Oxford: Blackwell, 1994.
McLuhan, Marshall. *The Medium Is the Message.* London: Gingo, 1964.
Migliore, Daniel L. *Faith Seeking Understanding.* Grand Rapids: Eerdmans, 2004.
Moltmann, Jürgen. *The Crucified God.* Minneapolis: Fortress, 1974.
———. *The Spirit of Life.* Minneapolis: Fortress, 1992.
———. *The Trinity and the Kingdom of God.* Minneapolis: Fortress, 1981.
Moschella, Mary C. *Ethnography as Pastoral Practice.* Cleveland: Pilgrim, 2008.
Osmer, Richard R. *Practical Theology: An Introduction.* Grand Rapids: Eerdmans, 2008.
Parry, Robin. *Worshipping Trinity.* Milton Keynes: Send the Light, 2013.

Passmore, Richard. *Meet Them Where They're At*. Bletchley: Scripture Union, 2003.
Pattison, Steven. "Pastoral Studies: Dust Bin or Discipline?" In *The Challenge of Practical Theology: Selected Essays*, 247–52. London: Jessica Kingsley, 2007.
———. "Practical Theology: Art or Science?" In *The Challenge of Practical Theology: Selected Essays*, 261–89 London: Jessica Kingsley, 2007.
———. "Some Straws for the Bricks: A Basic Introduction to Theological Reflection." *Contact* 99/2 (1989) 29.
———. "The Use of the Behavioural Sciences in Pastoral Studies." In *The Foundations of Pastoral Studies and Practical Theology*, edited by Paul H. Ballard, 79–85. Cardiff: University College, Cardiff, 1986.
Pauw, Amy P. "Attending to the Gaps between Beliefs and Practices." In *Practicing Theology: Beliefs and Practices in Christian Life*, edited by Miroslav Volf and Dorothy C. Bass, 33–51 Grand Rapids: Eerdmans, 2002.
Perrin, Ruth H. *The Bible Reading of Young Evangelicals*. Eugene, OR: Pickwick, 2016.
Persson, Ann. *The Circle of Love*. Abingdon: BRF, 2010.
Peterson, David. *Engaging with God*. Downers Grove, IL: InterVarsity, 1992.
Pimlott, Jo., and Nigel Pimlott. *Youth Work after Christendom*. Milton Keynes: Paternoster, 2008.
Punch, K. F. *Introduction to Social Research*. London: Sage, 2005.
Riessman, C. K. *Narrative Analysis*. London: Sage, 1993.
Rogers, Andrew. "Reading Scripture in Congregations: Towards an Ordinary Hermeneutic." In *Remembering Our Future*, edited by Andrew Walker and Luke Bretherton, 81–107. Milton Keynes: Paternoster, 2007.
Root, Andrew. *Christopraxis: A Practical Theology of the Cross*. Minneapolis, Fortress, 2014.
———. "Dietrich Bonhoeffer." *Youthwork* (October 2014) 16–18.
———. "Relational Youth Ministry." *Youthwork* (May 2015) 16–18.
———. *Revisiting Relational Youth Ministry: From Strategy of Influence to a Theology of Incarnation*. Downers Grove, IL: InterVarsity, 2007.
———. "Youth Ministry as Discerning Christopraxis: A Hermeneutical Model." *Journal of Youth and Theology* 1/1 (2007) 9–30.
Saunders, M. "Culture Shift." *Youthwork* (August 2016) 14–17.
Savage, S., et al. *Making Sense of Generation Y: The World View of 15 to 25 Year Olds*. London: Church House, 2006.
Senter, M., et al. *Four Views of Youth Ministry and the Church: Inclusive Congregational, Preparatory, Missional, Strategic*. Grand Rapids: Zondervan, 2001.
Shepherd, Nick. *Faith Generation*. London: SPCK, 2015.
———. "Talk the Walk." *Youthwork* (May 2014) 38–40.
———. "Trying to Be Christian: A Qualitative Study of Young People's Participation in Two Youth Ministry Projects." PhD diss., Kings College London, 2010.
———. "What's Distinctive about Christian Youthwork?" *Youthwork* (May 2014) 38–40.
Stout, Jeffrey. "Virtue Among the Ruins: An Essay on MacIntyre." *Neue Zeitschrift fur Systematische Theologie und Religionsphilosophie* 26/2-3 (1984) 256–73.
Strauss, A. L., and J. M. Corbin. *Basics of Qualitative Research: Techniques and Procedures for Developing Grounded Theory*. London: Sage, 1998.
Strickland, D. "Think Bigger." *Youthwork* (July 2015) 48–49.

Sudworth, T., et al. *Mission Shaped Youth: Rethinking Young People and Church.* London: Church House, 2007.
Swinton, John, and Harriet Mowat. *Practical Theology and Qualitative Research.* London: SCM, 2006.
Tanis, Gretchen S. *Making Jesus Attractive.* Eugene, OR: Pickwick, 2016.
Tanner, Kathryn. "Theological Reflection and Christian Practices." In *Practicing Theology: Beliefs and Practices in Christian Life,* edited by Miroslav Volf and Dorothy C. Bass, 228–42. Grand Rapids: Eerdmans, 2002.
———. "Trinity." In *The Blackwell Companion to Political Theology,* edited by Peter Scott and William T. Cavanaugh, 317–31 Oxford: Blackwell, 2004.
Thompson, P. "25 Years of (Premier) Youthwork." *Youthwork* (August 2016) 7–12.
Thomson, Jeremy. *Telling the Difference.* Cambridge: YTC, 2007.
Tillich, Paul. *Dynamics of Faith.* New York: Doubleday, 1962.
———. *Systematic Theology.* Vol 1. Chicago: University of Chicago Press, 1951.
Torrance, Alan T. *Persons in Communion.* Edinburgh: T. & T. Clark, 1996.
Tracy, David. *Blessed Rage for Order.* New York: Seabury, 1975.
———. "The Foundations of Practical Theology." In *Practical Theology: The Emerging Field in Theology, Church and World,* edited by Don S. Browning, 62–82. San Francisco: Harper and Row, 1983.
Van Deusen Hunsinger, D. *Theology and Pastoral Counselling: A New Interdisciplinary Approach.* Grand Rapids: Eerdmans, 1995.
Vanhoozer, Keven J. *Faith Speaking Understanding: Performing the Drama of Doctrine.* Louisville: Westminster John Knox, 2014.
———. *First Theology: God, Scripture, and Hermeneutics.* Downers Grove, IL: InterVarsity, 2002.
———. *Remythologizing Theology.* New York: Cambridge University Press, 2010.
Volf, Miroslav. *After Our Likeness: The Church as the Image of the Trinity.* Grand Rapids: Eerdmans, 1998.
———. "Theology as a Way of Life." In *Practicing Theology: Beliefs and Practices in Christian Life,* edited by Miroslav Volf and Dorothy C. Bass, 245–63. Grand Rapids: Eerdmans, 2002.
Volf, Miroslav, and Dorothy C. Bass, eds. *Practicing Theology: Beliefs and Practices in Christian Life.* Grand Rapids: Eerdmans, 2002.
Walker, Andrew. *Telling the Story.* London: SPCK, 1996.
Walley, M. "Jesus Meets." *Youthwork* (September 2015) 35.
Ward, Pete. "Blueprint Ecclesiology and the Lived: Normativity as a Perilous Faithfulness." *Ecclesial Practices* 2/1 (2015) 74–90.
———. *Growing Up Evangelical.* London: SPCK, 1996.
———. *Liquid Ecclesiology.* Boston: Brill, 2017.
———. *Participation and Mediation.* London: SCM, 2008.
———. *Selling Worship.* London: Paternoster, 2005.
———. *Youthwork and the Mission of God.* London: SPCK, 1997.
Ward, Pete, and Fiddes, Paul. "Affirming Faith at a Service of Baptism in St Aldate's Church, Oxford." In *Explorations in Ecclesiology and Ethnography,* edited by Christian Sharen, 51–70. Grand Rapids: Eerdmans, 2012.
Wells, Sam. *A Nazareth Manifesto: Being with God.* Chichester: Blackwell, 2015.
Wetheral, Margaret, et al. *Discourse as Data: A Guide for Analysis.* London, Sage, 2001.

White, David. *Jürgen Moltmann's Pneumatology as Narrative Frame for Youthful Epiphanies of Purpose*. Unpublished paper, IASYM International Conference, January 3rd– 6th, 2013.

———. "The Fire and Light at the Heart of Youth Ministry." *Journal of Youth and Theology* 16/1 (2017) 46–59.

Whitmarsh, L. "Jesus Meets." *Youthwork* (September 2015) 36.

Wright, Andrew. *Christianity and Critical Realism: Ambiguity, Truth and Theological Literacy*. London: Routledge, 2012.

Wright, N. T. *How God Became King*. London: SPCK, 2012.

———. *Surprised by Hope*. London: SPCK, 2014.

Yoder, John. *The Politics of Jesus*. Notre Dame: University of Notre Dame Press, 1972.

Zagzebski, L. T. *Virtues of the Mind*. Cambridge: Cambridge University Press, 1996.

Zizioulas, John. *Being as Communion: Studies in Personhood and the Church*. Crestwood, NY: St. Vladimir's Seminary Press, 1985.